Business Result

SECOND EDITION

Upper-intermediate *Student's Book* with **Online practice**

Michael Duckworth, John Hughes
& Rebecca Turner

Contents

Contents

Introduction

Welcome to *Business Result Second Edition Upper-intermediate*. **In this book you will find:**

- 15 units
- 5 Viewpoint video lessons
- Practice files
- Communication activities
- Audio scripts
- Access to the Online practice

What's in a unit?

Starting point
- an introduction to the theme of the unit
- discussion questions

Working with words
- reading and listening about a work-related topic
- focus on key words and phrases

Business communication
- improve your communication skills for meetings, presentations, socializing, and phone calls
- *Key expressions* list in every unit

Language at work
- grammar presented in authentic work contexts
- *Language point* box focuses on the key grammar points

Practically speaking
- focus on an aspect of everyday communication at work
- helps you to sound more natural when speaking

Talking point
- focus on interesting business topics and concepts
- *Discussion* and *Task* activities improve fluency and allow you to apply the topics to your own area of work

What's in the *Practice files*?

Written exercises to practise the key language in:
- *Working with words*
- *Business communication*
- *Language at work*

Use the *Practice files*:
- in class to check your understanding
- out of class for extra practice or homework

The *Practice files* include a *Grammar reference* section with more detailed explanations of the grammar from each unit.

Follow the links to the *Practice file* in each unit.

What's in the *Communication activities?*

- role cards and information for pair and group activities

What's in the *Viewpoint* lessons?

The *Viewpoints* are video lessons that appear after every third unit. The topic of each *Viewpoint* lesson relates to a theme from the main units.

Each *Viewpoint* is divided into three or four sections, with a number of short video clips in each lesson. A *Viewpoint* lesson includes:
- A focus to introduce the topic.
- Key vocabulary and phrases from the videos.
- Video interviews on interesting business-related topics which develop listening and note-taking skills, and build confidence in listening to authentic language in an authentic context.
- Activities which provide speaking practice about the topic of the lesson.

All of the videos in the *Viewpoint* lessons can be streamed or downloaded from the *Online practice*.

The *Viewpoint* video lessons include authentic interviews with leading academics, business experts, and course participants from **Saïd Business School**, University of Oxford.

About Saïd Business School

Saïd Business School is part of the University of Oxford. It blends the best of new and old – it is a vibrant and innovative business school, yet deeply embedded in an 800-year-old world-class university. Saïd Business School creates programmes and ideas that have global impact – it educates people for successful business careers and, as a community, seeks to tackle world-scale problems. The school delivers cutting-edge programmes and ground-breaking research that transform individuals, organizations, business practice and society.
Find out more at www.sbs.ox.ac.uk

What's in the *Online practice?*

- practice exercises for each *Working with words, Language at work,* and *Business communication* section
- unit tests
- email exercises for each unit
- automatic marking for instant answers
- gradebook to check your scores and progress

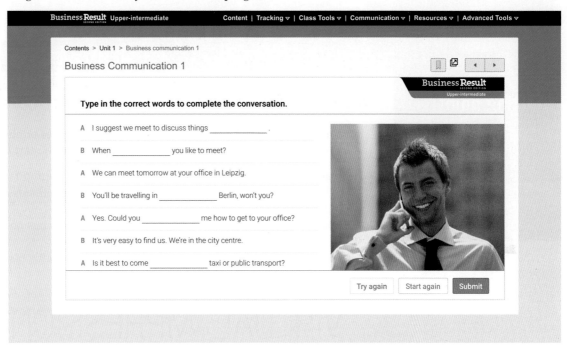

Additional resources

- watch and download all of the *Viewpoint* videos
- listen to and download all of the class audio
- sample emails for each unit

How to access your *Online practice*

To access your *Online practice,* you will find an access card on the inside cover of your Student's Book. This contains an access code to unlock all the content in the *Online practice.*

Go to **www.oxfordlearn.com** and activate your code, and then follow the instructions online to access the content.

1 First impressions

Starting point

1 Why are first impressions so important in business?

2 What gives us a first impression of a company or a person?

Working with words | Talking about first impressions

1 When you want to know more about other companies or about colleagues and clients before you meet them, where do you normally start looking?

2 Read this text about online impressions. Which paragraph (1–3) is about …?
   a how companies need to make sure their website maintains a visitor's interest ___
   b how people get their first impression of you or your business by going online first ___
   c how people looking for work need to check their digital history before applying for a job ___

VIRTUAL IMPRESSIONS

1 These days creating a good impression is more than just shaking hands and presenting a well-designed business card when you first meet someone. That's because before you even attended a meeting with a prospective client or a potential employer, you can guarantee that they've already searched your name, checked to see if your company has a good reputation via online review sites and even searched your personal online history.

2 To manage your online profile, start with your company's website. According to researchers at the Missouri University of Science and Technology, it takes under three seconds for an online visitor to start to form an opinion of your brand from the website. The researchers also tracked eye movements and discovered that visitors tend to gain their first impressions from the logo, photographs, menus and, in particular, the opportunity to make contact via social media. In other words, projecting the right kind of online image is not just about looking good, but companies should also make sure their customers can interact with them and start building a relationship.

3 Individuals such as freelancers and job-seekers also need to think carefully about their social media image before posting photos and comments online. A recent survey of 450 employers showed that more than 40% had taken a dislike to a potential employee as soon as they'd checked the person's Facebook page. One typical reason for rejection was finding out that the information on the CV didn't match the applicant's online profile. It's a good idea for anyone who is self-employed or looking for a job to think about how they come across to people and to make sure their online profile promotes a positive and truthful image.

3 Underline the answers to questions 1–3 in the text.
   1 What are the different ways we can find out more about companies/people?
   2 Which parts of a website are especially important to focus on?
   3 What might potential employers find out about you online? What can you do about this?

4 Complete questions 1–8 with the correct verbs from the list. Check your answers by finding the words in **bold** in the article.

build   come   create   form   have   manage   project   take

1 What kind of **impression** would your company like to _____ on its website?
2 What sort of **reputation** do you or your company _____?
3 How does your company _____ the right kind of **image** through its advertising?
4 How important is it to _____ your own online **profile**?
5 When you meet someone for the first time face-to-face, how do you _____ an **opinion** of them?
6 How do you think you _____ **across** to people you meet for the first time?
7 In your line of work, how important is it for you to _____ a close **relationship** with customers or clients?
8 Do you ever _____ an instant **dislike** to someone when you meet them for the first time? What are the reasons?

5 Work with a partner. Choose five of the questions in **4** to ask and answer.

6 ▶ 1.1 Listen to Zhifu Li, a website designer in Hong Kong, talking about adapting websites to local needs. Answer questions 1–2.
1 In what way is website localization like other forms of advertising?
2 What differences between Western and Asian websites does Zhifu mention?

7 Match each of these adjectives from audio script 1.1 to an adjective with a similar meaning from 1–12.

expensive   ineffective   arrogant   trustworthy   suspicious   complex   functional   modest   ostentatious   successful   wary   favourable

1 reliable _____
2 unsuccessful _____
3 showy _____
4 positive _____
5 costly _____
6 mistrustful _____
7 practical _____
8 complicated _____
9 simple _____
10 effective _____
11 over-confident _____
12 cautious _____

8 Work with a partner.
1 Which of the adjectives in **7** are positive and which are negative? Explain your choices.
2 Using as many of the adjectives as possible, discuss what makes an effective website in your culture.
3 What aspects of a website would give a negative first impression?

>> For more exercises, go to **Practice file 1** on page 106.

9 Work with a partner. Look at these things which can create a good or bad first impression of a company.
- uniform
- office / business premises
- telephone answering system
- reception area
- meeting / conference rooms
- quality of product / service
- warm greeting
- dress code
- website
- advertisements in the media
- brochures / printed materials
- price
- speaking customer's language
- reputation

1 Which four are the most important and why?
2 Choose two of the factors that create a good impression of your company. Explain how.
3 Choose two of the factors that are less successful at creating a good impression of your company. How could they be improved?

Business communication | Arranging a meeting

1 What percentage of your time is spent in meetings? What kinds of meetings do you attend? How do you normally arrange them (e.g. by email or by phone)?

2 Read this email from Ivan Formanek, owner of a translation agency in Prague.
  1 How did he find out about Sean McFee?
  2 Why is he contacting him?
  3 What does he ask Sean to do?

> **To:** sean.mcfee@sfdesign.com
> **From:** ivanformanek@sspeaking.cz
> **Subject:** Designer for new website needed
>
> Dear Mr McFee
>
> My name's Ivan Formanek and I have my own translation agency – Simply Speaking. I was given your details by one of your former colleagues, Ursula Vladikova. She recommended you to me as we are planning to renew our website.
>
> If you are interested in discussing this further, could you either call us or send an email in reply and we will arrange a meeting with you?
>
> Best regards
>
> Ivan Formanek

3 ▶ 1.2 Sean sends an email in reply to Ivan and then calls him. Listen to their conversation and answer questions 1–3.
  1 What is the purpose of the call?
  2 What is the outcome?
  3 Why is there a delay before the meeting can take place?

4 ▶ 1.2 Listen again and put sentences a–j in the correct order (1–10).
  a Yes. I, remember. ___
  b I'm calling about the email I sent you … _1_
  c Thanks for responding so quickly. ___
  d We can meet when I get back. ___
  e Let's say, provisionally, Tuesday the 13th at eleven o'clock. ___
  f See you in a couple of weeks. ___
  g I wondered if you'd had time to look through the portfolio I sent. ___
  h I suggest we meet to discuss things further. ___
  i When would you like to meet? ___
  j Fine, whatever's best for you. ___

Tip | *actually* and *currently*

Don't confuse *actually* with *currently*. Use *actually* as an alternative to *in fact* or *as a matter of fact*.

I'm **actually** going to be in Prague already.

Use *currently* to express something you are doing at the moment.

We're **currently** updating our corporate image.

Key expressions

Introducing self (email)
My name's ... and I (have / work for / represent) ...
I was given your details by ...
(She) recommended you to me as ...

Making a follow-up call
Hello ... This is ...
I'm calling about the email I sent you regarding ...
I wondered if you'd had time to ...?
I wanted to see if you are still interested in ...

Responding to a follow-up call
Yes, I remember.
Thanks for responding so quickly.
Thanks. I wanted to speak to you about ...

Arranging to meet
I suggest we meet to discuss things further.
When would you like to meet?
We can meet ...
Fine, whatever's best for you.
Let's say, provisionally, Tuesday the 13th at 11.00.
I'll get my assistant to call you later today to confirm.
See you (in a couple of weeks).

Discussing travel arrangements
You'll be travelling in from ..., won't you?
Can you tell me how I get to ...?
Is it best by taxi or public transport?
Let me know where you're staying and I'll email you a map and directions from your hotel.
There's a train that leaves at ...
Will I have time to catch that one?
It only takes ... to get to ...
Let me know if you need a taxi and I'll book one for you.

5 ▶ 1.3 Listen to a call Sean receives and answer questions 1–3.
1 Who is calling Sean and why?
2 How will Sean know how to find Simply Speaking?
3 What transport is he going to use to get to the meeting?

6 ▶ 1.3 Listen again.
1 What phrase does Sean use to ...?
  a enquire about transport
  b refer to the time of the train
  c discuss the possibility of catching the train
2 What phrase does Catherine use to offer help with ...?
  a directions
  b a taxi

>> For more exercises, go to **Practice file 1** on page 106.

7 Write a short introductory email to your partner, following steps 1–3.
1 Introduce yourself and your company.
2 Explain that your partner was recommended to you.
3 Suggest a meeting to discuss some future business.

8 Work with a partner. Exchange your emails from **7** and take turns to make a follow-up call. Remember to:
• introduce yourself and explain why you are calling
• arrange to meet
• discuss the travel arrangements

Practically speaking | Exchanging contact details

1 Are you good at remembering people's names and contact details? Do you have any special techniques for helping you remember names when you meet people for the first time? In what situations do you have to exchange names and contact details?

2 ▶ 1.4 Listen to three conversations and answer questions 1–2 for each one.
1 How does each speaker give their contact details?
2 Why do they want to keep in contact with each other?

3 ▶ 1.4 Listen again and match these phrases to each call in **2**.
1 Let me take your name and number. ___Call 1___
2 I have an email address for you, but I'm not sure if it's current. _____
3 I'll send you her contact details by text. _____
4 Can I have Suzy's number and email address? _____
5 It's probably easiest if I email you when I get back to the office. _____
6 Here's my card. _____

4 Match phrases 1–6 in **3** to categories a–c.
a asking for details _____
b giving details _____
c promising details _____

5 Stand up and walk around the class talking to each person. Ask each person for their contact details. Either give your details straightaway or promise to give them.

Language at work | Present simple and continuous

1   Work with a partner. Read sentences a–i and discuss why each sentence uses either the present simple or present continuous tense in **bold**.

   a   I**'m calling** about the email I sent you …
   b   Yes, I **remember**.
   c   We**'re** currently **updating** our corporate image.
   d   I **go** to Berlin once a month.
   e   It only **takes** 20 minutes to get to the station.
   f   I**'m leaving** the day after tomorrow.
   g   There's a train that **leaves** at 3.00.
   h   We can meet when I **get** back.
   i   I**'m covering** for a colleague who's on maternity leave.

2   Answer the questions in the *Language point*.

LANGUAGE POINT

In which sentence in 1 is the present simple used to refer to …?
1   a routine ___
2   something always or permanently true ___
3   a thought / feeling / reaction rather than an action ___
4   an item on a timetable ___
5   the future after a time word ___

In which sentence in 1 is the present continuous used to refer to …?
6   an action in progress at the moment of speaking ___
7   a current (unfinished) project ___
8   an arrangement in the future ___
9   a temporary situation ___

>> For more information, go to **Grammar reference** on page 107.

3   You want to find out this information from someone you meet for the first time. What questions would you ask?

who they work for	the department or area they work in
their responsibilities at work	a current project they are involved in
their daily routine	how regularly they need English at work
how their English studies are going	what their schedule is next week

4   Work with a partner. Ask and answer the questions in 3.

5   Which of these phrases would you normally use with the present simple, and which with the present continuous?

for the moment   at the moment   generally speaking   for the time being
on the whole   tomorrow afternoon   once a week   most of the time
every winter   right now   once in a while   as a rule   currently

6   Work with a partner. Use the phrases in 5 to make true statements about your activities in or out of work.

>> For more exercises, go to **Practice file 1** on page 107.

7   Give a short presentation about your company using these points.
   1   The industry as a whole:
     • how important it is and whether it employs a lot of people
     • current changes taking place and future developments
   2   Your company:
     • where it is based, what it does and who its customers are
     • current projects and future plans

The life overlap

These two Venn diagrams compare how the overlap between our working life and personal life can affect us. The first diagram highlights how frustrated we can become when we try to separate our personal life from our working life; there is very little overlap in the diagram and so this person is leading two separate lives which often leads to frustration. In contrast, the second Venn diagram shows a much larger overlap. This kind of person tends to be reconciled to the fact that their work is also part of their personal life; they don't change their character at work and in general they work on things that interest them and so aren't frustrated by their situation.

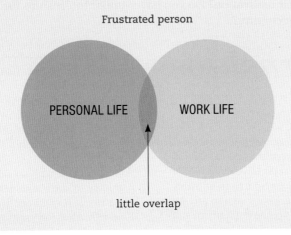
Frustrated person

PERSONAL LIFE   WORK LIFE

little overlap

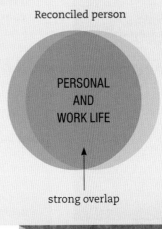
Reconciled person

PERSONAL AND WORK LIFE

strong overlap

Discussion

1 Are you able to stop working when you leave your place of work or do you often continue dealing with work from home (or on your phone)?

2 How easy do you think it is to separate your work and non-work life?

3 How much do you agree with the solution of allowing your personal and business life to overlap?

Task

1 Draw two Venn diagram circles to represent your personal life and your working life. Include the amount of overlap between the two circles which represents the relationship between these lives. Then show your partner and explain why you drew the circles in this way.

2 Work with a partner and draw two new circles to represent 'You' and your 'Partner'. With your partner, talk about your life at work and outside work, and find out what you both have in common. Make notes in the Venn diagram circles about 'You' and your 'Partner' while you speak. When you find something in common, note it in the overlap between the two circles; e.g. you both work in the same area of business or you both play tennis. Try to find as many things in common as possible.

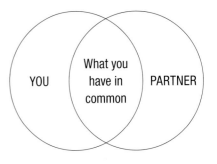
YOU   What you have in common   PARTNER

2 Motivation

Starting point

1 Which of these things motivate you in your job?
- colleagues
- interesting work
- gifts for achieving targets
- promotion
- training
- flexible hours
- money
- job security

2 What else would you add to the list?

Working with words | Motivation at work

1 Have you ever worked for no money? What was your motivation?

2 Read the text about internships. Why do interns often work for no money? What is their motivation? Do you have similar internships for people in your company or country?

Internships:
a step on the career ladder or unpaid labour?

The internship is a well-known starting point for any new graduate looking for their first step onto the career ladder. It's a good way to get hands-on work experience and a sure sign to any future employer that you have plenty of **self-motivation**. Many global companies now offer internship programmes: In the USA, Google recruits 3,000 interns in the summer, promising the chance to 'do cool things that matter'. The Bank of China runs an eight-week programme. In Japan, one software company runs a four-day internship with a cash **incentive** of ¥100,000. And the 'Big Four' audit companies – Deloitte, Ernst & Young, KPMG and PWC – employ more than 30,000 interns per year in offices in different countries, which may lead to a full-time position later on.

It is true that the majority of internships do not come with a cash **reward** or the promise of a job offer. For many, an internship can mean some unpaid hours spent making coffee and doing someone's photocopying. However, you have to start somewhere and in most cases, it will **benefit** you in the long-run. Alongside some menial tasks, you'll be learning about the professional work environment and meeting future contacts. One key piece of advice when you begin is to let the company know your areas of interest; find out if they can help you improve your **performance** in certain skills. Companies **appreciate** it when interns show interest in this way and they will reward your **enthusiasm** with a reference full of **praise** and **recognition** of your **achievements**. This could make all the difference at your first interview for a paid job.

3 Read the text again. Are these statements true (*T*) or false (*F*)?
1 Internships are not very common. ___
2 You can earn money on some internships. ___
3 At the end, most companies offer their interns a job. ___
4 Don't expect every aspect of an internship to be interesting. ___
5 It's a good idea to tell people what you are interested in learning about. ___
6 Good references from an internship can help you get a job. ___

4 Look at the words in **bold** in the article in **2**. Match each word in 1–5 to the correct definition, a or b.

1 enthusiasm ___ / self-motivation ___
   a a personal interest in doing something better or working harder
   b a strong feeling of excitement or interest in something

2 reward ___ / incentive ___
   a anything you receive for doing something well (e.g. money)
   b something offered that makes you want to work harder or do better

3 achievement ___ / performance ___
   a the things you have done successfully with your own effort and skill
   b how well or how badly you do something

4 benefit ___ / appreciate ___
   a to be useful to somebody or something.
   b to recognize the good qualities of somebody.

5 praise ___ / recognition ___
   a publicly saying that someone has done well
   b telling someone that you approve of or admire what they have done

5 Discuss these questions.

1 What incentives does your company offer?
2 What are some ways that managers can recognize good performance at work?

6 ▶ 2.1 Listen to three people talking about their jobs and answer questions 1–3.

1 What job does each speaker do?
2 What benefits, rewards and incentives does their company provide?
3 What other factors give them job satisfaction?

Claudia

Peter

Macie

7 Which of these words and phrases from the listening are material benefits? Which are non-material benefits?

~~profit-sharing scheme~~   *fulfilment*   company car   autonomy   feel valued
be acknowledged   commission   staff discount   attendance reward   appreciation
on-time bonus   compensation plan   positive feedback   (personal) development
praise   satisfaction   private medical insurance   non-contributory pension plan
(sense of) achievement

Material benefits: ____*profit-sharing scheme*____
Non-material benefits: _____*fulfilment*_____

8 Work with a partner and discuss questions 1–3.

1 Which of the material benefits in **7** are standard in an employment contract in your country? Which are additional benefits?
2 How does this vary according to profession?
3 How important to you are the non-material benefits? How do they compare to the material benefits?

>> For more exercises, go to **Practice file 2** on page 108.

9 Work in small groups. You are partners setting up your own company.

1 Decide on the type of company (service or product oriented) and how many employees you will need.
2 What benefits, rewards and incentives will you offer to your employees?
3 What effects will these have for both the employee and the company?
4 How will you make sure your employees receive some of the non-material benefits in **7**?

Business communication | Encouraging conversation

1 Work in small groups. When you meet someone for the first time, how do you encourage conversation? What kinds of topics normally motivate other people to make conversation?

2 Read these tips and decide which five are the most useful.

THE ART OF SMALL TALK

1 Introduce yourself and use a 'tag line', e.g. *Hi, I'm Jules from Munich*. This can get the conversation started as your colleague can ask a question about your home town or your trip.

2 When your colleague introduces himself/herself, try to repeat his/her name when you reply, or use their name later in the conversation.

3 Break the ice with a comment about a current news story or a remark about the event you're at, its location and the weather.

4 Avoid these topics of conversation: your health, your private life, gossip. The best conversation topics are sports, books, theatre, movies, food, museums and travel. Try and find a shared experience or something else you have in common.

5 Keep the conversation flowing by not monopolizing it. Ask a question and really listen to your colleague's reply. Then respond with comments from your own personal experience and ask another question.

6 Ask open questions which require more than a one-word answer. If your colleague asks a *yes/no* question, give some extra information.

7 Use sounds like *hmm* and words like *Really* to indicate that you are listening and interested. This will motivate your colleague to tell you more.

8 Share information about yourself, but keep it positive. People don't like colleagues who are negative or who complain a lot.

3 ▶ 2.2 Read the *Context*. Listen to four conversations from the first evening of the cruise. Work with a partner and answer questions 1–2 for each conversation.
1 Which of the tips are used or not used?
2 Is the conversation successful or unsuccessful? Why?

4 ▶ 2.2 Listen again and answer questions 1–7.

Conversation 1
1 What does Harry say to start the conversation?
2 What phrases does he use to end the conversation?

Conversation 2
3 What does Paolo say to start the conversation?
4 How does Sonia respond?

Conversation 3
5 What two phrases show that the speakers are interested in what the other person has said?

Conversation 4
6 What phrases do Adriana and Adam use to greet each other?
7 How does Adriana show that she is listening?

Context
A global media company has organized its annual incentive event to reward its most successful members of staff – a one-week cruise. Employees from all over the world have arrived on board and are now meeting on the first evening.

Tip | *well* and *so*
Use *well* to introduce a piece of information in a conversation.
Use *so* to indicate you're changing the direction of the conversation topic.
A *Are you here with colleagues?*
B *No.*
A ***Well***, *you'll soon get to know people.* ***So***, *would you like another drink?*

Key expressions

Starting a conversation
Hi, I don't think we've met.
Hello. It's Adriana, isn't it?
Hello, I saw you ... but I didn't
have a chance to speak to you.
I'm ...
Hello/Hi, I'm ... (from /
based in ...)
Is this your first (company
event)?
I thought I might see you
(here).
How lovely to see you here.
How are things?

Showing interest
Really?
I see.
What a coincidence!
That's amazing!
That sounds interesting.
Oh dear ...
Oh, I'm sorry to hear that.

Keeping a conversation going
By the way ...
Well, ...
Apparently ...
I've heard ... – is that true?
In fact ...
So ...
Don't you ...?

5 ▶ 2.3 Listen to a second conversation Adriana has later in the evening. This time the conversation is successful. Number the phrases a–j in the order you first hear them (1–10). How do the phrases help the conversation flow?
a Don't you … ___
b … by the way? ___
c What a coincidence! ___
d So … ___
e Really? ___
f In fact … ___
g I see. ___
h That sounds interesting. ___
i Well … ___
j Apparently … ___

▶▶ For more exercises, go to **Practice file 2** on page 108.

6 Work with a partner.
1 Read conversations 1 and 4 in audio script 2.2.
2 Discuss what each speaker could say to make the conversation more successful.
3 Now have two conversations similar to 1 and 4, using your ideas to make them more successful.

7 Work with a partner and have a conversation. Keep the conversation going as long as possible. Discuss as many of these topics as you can.
- hobbies
- TV/cinema
- work
- education
- vacation
- news
- sport
- food
- an interesting fact
- an enjoyable excursion nearby

Practically speaking | Ending and leaving a conversation

1 ▶ 2.4 When you end and leave a conversation, it is polite to give a reason and to promise future contact. Match the two parts of the phrases 1–5 to a–e. Then listen and check.
1 Is that the time?
2 Sorry, but I promised to meet someone.
3 I'm going to get some food.
4 Is that James over there?
5 Look, I have a meeting now.

a But it ends at five, so perhaps we can continue our conversation then?
b My parking ticket runs out in five minutes. Can we continue talking later?
c I missed lunch because of a conference call. So see you later.
d Excuse me, I really must go and speak to him.
e But I'll come back when I've seen them. Catch you later.

2 Work with a partner and practise each situation below. Have one or two minutes of small talk, then end the conversation appropriately.
1 You are at a conference making conversation. You have spoken for five minutes and have run out of small talk topics.
2 You are just leaving work after a long day when you bump into an old client in reception who's just arrived to see someone else. The client wants to chat.
3 You meet a work colleague by chance at the theatre during the interval. The bell for the second half has just rung.
4 You meet your old manager at your child's football match. You are with your family so you don't want to talk for very long.

Language at work | Question forms

1 Imagine you are at a conference. Which of these questions would you use to start a conversation with someone you think you might know?
   a It's Adriana, isn't it?
   b I'd like to know what time the next talk starts.
   c Aren't they based in Italy?
   d Didn't you work for them at one time?
   e Can you tell me which room the presentation is in?
   f We've met before, haven't we?

2 Match a–f in 1 to the question types in the *Language point*. Then answer questions 1–5.

LANGUAGE POINT

Indirect questions: ___, ___
1 What phrases make these questions sound more polite?
2 After the indirect phrase, does the verb come before or after the subject?

Negative questions: ___, ___
3 Do the questions use the full or contracted form of the auxiliary verb?

Question tags: ___, ___
4 What answer do you expect with a question tag?
5 When the main verb is positive, what is the verb in the question tag?

>> For more information, go to **Grammar reference** on page 109.

3 Work with a partner. Rewrite the question using the words given. Then take turns to ask and answer the questions.
   1 Do you come from Milan?
      _____*You come from Milan*_____, don't you?
   2 How much is the room per night?
      I'd like to know _____.
   3 You were with Unilever for a few years, weren't you?
      Weren't _____?
   4 Where do you buy your packaging from?
      Can you tell me _____?
   5 Do I know you from somewhere?
      I know you from somewhere, _____?
   6 What time does the exhibition hall open?
      Could you tell me _____?
   7 Do you want to meet us in the entrance after the next session?
      Why _____ in the entrance after the next session?
   8 Didn't they say they'd join us at seven?
      They _____ at seven, _____?

>> For more exercises, go to **Practice file 2** on page 109.

4 Work with a partner. Think of two questions to ask in these situations. Then practise the conversations using your questions.
   1 Your boss is sending you to work in Hong Kong. You want to know about travel plans and accommodation.
   2 You are about to order a product from a supplier and want to check these details are correct:
      Price: €200 / Delivery: 5 days / Delivery charge: €8 / Guarantee: 1 year
   3 You're at a conference and meet someone who you went to school with.
   4 You're waiting for a job interview. Talk to a person waiting with you.

Tip | Question use
Use questions to start and develop conversations in social situations
• to find out information
• to check or confirm information
• to show surprise or other emotions
• to encourage responses and keep the conversation going

Ten magically motivating words

Language is one of the most powerful tools when it comes to persuading customers. Certain motivating words and phrases will always have a magical effect on your customer's decision-making. Try any of these ten out in your next email, social media or blog post, and see which ones generate the best response.

1 **You (or Your)** Speak to the customer, about the customer, not about you.
2 **Because** Give a reason to take action.
3 **Free** Everyone likes 'free', don't they?
4 **New** Customers are interested in the newest or being the first.
5 **Easy** Let them know how easy life will be with your product or service.
6 **Sale** A traditional marketing word but it still motivates.
7 **Off** The suggestion of a discount always gets interest.
8 **Now** It's a call to action. Shop now, Act now, Subscribe now.
9 **Best sellers** People like to know they are buying what's popular.
10 **Thank you** Show your customer you love them!

Of course, you will want to use other words, including those specific to your product or service, but whatever you add, try to avoid words and phrases like *Hurry!*, *Look inside*, *Guaranteed*, and *Once in a lifetime*. These feel out-of-date and insincere, and definitely avoid *USING CAPITALS SO IT SEEMS LIKE YOU ARE SHOUTING AT YOUR CUSTOMERS!!!*

Discussion

1 How motivated do you think you are to buy products or services when you see adverts or read emails and social media from companies?

2 Think about your own company's advertising in English or in other languages. Does it often use the kinds of motivational words listed in the article?

3 Why do you think the writer says the words at the end can demotivate customers? How do you feel when you read an email or text using CAPITAL LETTERS?

Task

1 Think of five words that are specific to your product or service and that you think would motivate customers. Read them to your partner and explain your choices.

2 Work with a partner. Discuss and write a marketing email to send to customers announcing a new product or service. It could be from your own company or from a fictional business. Try to use as many motivating words from your list in 1 as possible.

3 Swap your email with another pair. Underline any words which you think are motivating and then give the other pair feedback on their use of motivational language. Did the email make you want to buy their product or use their services?

3 On schedule

Starting point

1 What projects are you currently working on?

2 Think of one project. What are some of the key stages?

Working with words | Managing projects

1 Work in groups. Look at the picture of a ride at a theme park. Try to list six stages in a project to build a ride like this, starting with 'Brainstorming'.

2 Join another group and list your stages. Add any new ideas to your list.

3 Read the article about planning and building theme parks. Which of your stages does it mention?

A RIDE THAT RUNS ON TIME

Theme parks are big business these days. Millions of visitors buy tickets to enjoy the rides at Universal Studios in Florida or Disneyland Paris and each year visitor expectations are higher. To survive in this competitive world, every major theme park needs its new attraction, which requires years of upfront planning.

Phase one in most projects begins with brainstorming. The theme park designers think about the story behind the ride and its imagined geographical location. No idea is considered too crazy at this stage as there are no budget constraints – yet. Once the basic idea is agreed, each part of the ride is storyboarded, like scenes from a film. The images from the storyboard are then transformed into a combination of 3D models of the ride and images on a computer. At this point, the design team presents the concept to the main project manager and tries to provide an accurate forecast of the time needed to complete the project and a realistic budget.

Once the project is given the go ahead, phase two begins and the project team starts to work with other engineers, model makers and sound and lighting designers. In order not to miss the deadline, the project will need a wide range of people with specialist skills, and many parts of the process are outsourced. This is a critical period when it's easy to run into problems. It would only take one of the teams to fall behind schedule or go over budget and the whole project could be delayed.

Assuming the construction phase stays on track, there then follows a long period of safety testing and assessment of the ride's performance. Having made the launch date, the park starts to monitor visitor feedback; they survey visitors, and the overall success of the new ride will be calculated over time by the number of visitors choosing to go on the ride every hour.

4 Work with a partner. Read the article again and answer these questions.
1 Why do theme parks need a new attraction every year?
2 How controlled are the early stages of a project?
3 What does the team have to present at the end of phase one?
4 In phase two, why does the number of people involved increase so much?
5 What can go wrong at this stage of the project?
6 How does the theme park know if the project is successful?

5 Match 1–10 to a–j to make phrases from the article.

1	upfront	a	constraints
2	budget	b	forecast
3	accurate	c	on track
4	realistic	d	budget
5	miss	e	planning
6	run into	f	launch date
7	stay	g	problems
8	go over	h	the deadline
9	fall behind	i	budget
10	make the	j	schedule

6 Work with a partner. Do you associate the phrases in **5** with successful (*S*) or unsuccessful (*U*) projects, or both?

7 Match the words in **bold** in 1–6 with a phrase with the same meaning from **5**.

1 To avoid problems later on, let's start with some **preparation before we do anything else**. _____*upfront planning*_____

2 Do we have a **sensible amount of money** or are we supposed to do this without spending anything? _____

3 Can I spend as much as I like or are there any **limitations to the amount of money I have**? _____

4 At this rate, we won't **meet the deadline to have it in the shops**.

_____

5 I need a **correct prediction** about timings and costs before I give the go ahead.

_____

6 The project **didn't stay on track with regard to the timings**.

_____

8 Choose a verb from the list that can go with all three phrases in each group.

miss   stay   go   run   make

1 _____ smoothly / on time / into problems
2 _____ the deadline / the launch date / the chance
3 _____ on track / within budget / the course
4 _____ over budget / ahead with the plan / out of control
5 _____ the deadline / a plan / a mess of it

» For more exercises, go to **Practice file 3** on page 110.

9 Work with a partner. Read the notes on a project review. Discuss and make a list of what went right and what has gone wrong for the project.

Example: The total cost of the work has gone over the original budget.

Project: increase plant space of factory by 25% and install new production line
Total cost of the work: estimate = €1 million; actual cost = €1.3 million
Time for completion of project = 18 months; actual time = 2 years

- project meetings not held on regular basis – communication often by email (not everyone copied in)
- clearing of site took place quickly and easily – met deadline
- production manager changed specification of production line equipment to increase capacity, but didn't tell project manager – software program had to be rewritten quickly – resulted in errors in program
- problems during construction – discovered length of new building 2 m short (due to changes in specification – suppliers not told of change)
- equipment for production line delivered two weeks late – not able to install power connections at scheduled time – loss of several weeks on schedule
- all other new equipment arrived on time
- kept to budget for first six months, but overspent after construction problems

10 Work with another pair and compare your lists.

Context

The Tech-Tariff project is a collaboration between MMT-Tec (service provider) and Anvikon (mobile phone manufacturer). The aim is to launch a hi-tech phone with new advanced features from Anvikon in combination with MMT-Tec's new tariff which includes free videophoning and multimedia message services. Sarah and Michelle from MMT-Tec and Ian from Anvikon are meeting to discuss the progress of the project.

Business communication | Running an update meeting

1 ▶ 3.1 Read the *Context*. Listen to Part 1 of the meeting and make notes about the items on the agenda.

TECH-TARIFF UPDATE MEETING   2 SEPT

Agenda

1 Update on marketing activities (MMT-Tec):
   - Launch date [1] *Set for 15th November*
   - Advertising campaign [2] _____
   - Launch party: Venue [3] _____
     Catering: [4] _____

2 Update on Anvikon activities:
   - Handset [5] _____

3 Project schedule [6] _____

---

2 ▶ 3.1 Listen again and answer questions 1–3.
1 What four phrases does Sarah use to ask for an update on the project?
2 What three phrases do Sarah and Michelle use to clarify the problem with the battery?
3 Turn to audio script 3.1 and <u>underline</u> all the phrases Michelle and Ian use to give an update on the project.

3 ▶ 3.2 Listen to Part 2 of the meeting and answer questions 1–3.
1 Why didn't Ian like the idea of finding another battery supplier?
2 Why didn't Sarah like the idea of not mentioning the battery life?
3 Which proposal did they finally decide on?

4 ▶ 3.2 Listen again. Complete these suggestions made by the speakers. What do the speakers say to respond to each of the suggestions?
a _____ another battery supplier?
   response: _____
b _____ keep the same battery but not mention its lifespan.
   response: _____
c _____ and see what the technicians suggest ...?
   response: _____
d Using a different phone for the launch _____.
   response: _____
e _____ look at what we can reschedule.
   response: _____

>> For more exercises, go to **Practice file 3** on page 110.

Tip | *things*

Use *things* to speak/ask about situations in general.
*How are **things** with you?*
*How does your side of **things** look?*
***Things** aren't running as smoothly as I'd hoped.*

Key expressions

Asking for an update
How does your side of things look?
How's the ... coming along?
How far are you with ...?
How are things with ...?
What's the current status of ...?

Giving an update
Up to now (the launch date) has been (set) ...
He (booked the venue) two weeks ago.
I've already ...
I haven't ... yet.
We're on track.
Things aren't running as smoothly as I'd hoped.
We've hit a problem with ...

Clarifying a problem
So what do you mean exactly?
So what you're saying is ...?
So the real problem lies with ...?

Making a suggestion
How about (+ -ing)
We could (+ verb)
Why don't we (+ verb)
... would be my proposal.
If you ask me, we should ...

Responding to a suggestion
That's a good idea.
It's worth a try.
I don't think that would ...
That's possible (but ...)
That's not an ideal solution.
I'm not convinced.
I suppose so.

5 Work with a partner. It is two days before the launch of the new Tech-Tariff phone. Student A, you are Michelle. Turn to page 136. Student B, you are Ian. Use the information below. Update each other on the progress of the project. Make sure you:
- clarify any information you're not sure about
- make and respond to suggestions as necessary

Student B
1 Read the 'To do' list you received from Michelle and the notes you have written under your tasks (I).
2 Michelle will call you. Answer Michelle's questions about your tasks.
3 Ask Michelle to update you on her tasks (M).
4 Make and respond to suggestions as necessary.

Launch date 'To do' list

- **Bring Anvikon merchandise to venue (I)**
  Done! Already sent. Suggestion: bring extras and leave in car?
- **Finalize timetable of day with sound engineers (M)**
- **Brief Anvikon staff about handset demonstration (I)**
  Problem – illness in office – rescheduled for tomorrow when all sales staff are present.
  Suggestion: time – mid-afternoon?
- **Check replies from the press – who's coming? (M)**
- **Send Anvikon PR manager's speech to MMT-Tec (I)**
  Not ready! Will contact him again today.
  Suggestion: PR manager emails it direct to MMT-Tec?
- **Make sure Sarah's briefed on everything (I/M)**
  On track! Have logged everything – will send brief to Sarah tomorrow p.m.

Practically speaking | Questioning a decision

1 When someone makes a decision, do you ever question it? What does it depend on? For example, do you ever question your manager's decisions? What might happen if we don't question decisions?

2 ▶ 3.3 Listen to three conversations and match each conversation 1–3 to the topics a–c.
a budget ___   b staffing ___   c schedule ___

3 ▶ 3.3 Listen again and tick (✓) the expressions you hear.
1 Are you sure that's the best way forward? ☐
2 I don't think that would work. ☐
3 That's not an ideal solution. ☐
4 Is that really the case? ☐
5 Sorry, but I'm not sure I agree. ☐
6 I'm not entirely convinced. ☐

4 Work with a partner. Make a list of three decisions you have made recently (either at work or at home). Then take turns to tell your partner about each decision. As you listen, question your partner's decision and make sure they have made the right decision.

Tip | softening

To sound less critical, you can soften your question like this:
I'm sorry, but I'm not sure I agree.
That's a good idea, but is it the only way forward?
I take your point, but is that really the case?

Language at work | Present perfect and past simple

1 Work with a partner. Read sentences a–f and decide if the tenses in **bold** are either present perfect or past simple.
   a Up to now, the launch date **has been set** for the 15th of November …
   b We**'ve hit** a problem with the handset battery life.
   c He **booked** the venue two weeks ago.
   d I**'ve already received** offers from various catering companies.
   e I **haven't made** a final choice **yet**.
   f I **sent** you a proposed agenda yesterday.

2 Answer the questions in the *Language point*.

LANGUAGE POINT

Which of the sentences in **1** refer to …?
1 a present situation resulting from a past action – we don't know or say when the action happened ___ ___
2 a finished past action – we know or say when it happened ___ ___
3 something that has/hasn't happened during an unfinished period of time ___ ___

Which words in sentences d and e mean that …?
4 something has taken place earlier than expected _____
5 we expect that something will take place _____

>> For more information, go to **Grammar reference** on page 111.

3 Which of these time expressions can we use …?
   1 with the past simple
   2 with the present perfect
   3 with either – but under what circumstances. Give examples.

   up to now   so far (this week)   since our last meeting   in the last month
   today   last week   a couple of weeks ago   this morning   yesterday
   to date   just   over the last few months

>> For more exercises, go to **Practice file 3** on page 111.

4 Work with a partner. Student A, turn to page 136. Student B, turn to page 137. Update each other on your project.

5 Work with a partner. Student A and Student B, turn to page 138. Follow the instructions and ask and answer questions about these 'To do' lists.

1 Print out and collate six copies of proposal to submit to management.
Contact office suppliers to check delivery date of latest order.
Email all staff with agenda for next team meeting.
Compile mailing list for this year's brochure.

2 Email colleague and ask for all the details about the conference.
Confirm acceptance of conference place with conference organizers.
Book return flights to Madrid – Friday to Monday.
Find two possible hotels in centre of Madrid.

6 Work with a partner. Think of five goals or plans you have had during the last six months. Tell your partner which of these you have achieved and when, and give some details. Which have you not achieved and why?

Five most common problems on projects

1

Not enough planning time

Lack of planning at the start of a project will always result in changes later on, eating up time and money.

2

Communication breakdowns

Breakdowns can occur between the teams, individuals within teams, third-party suppliers, and the end users.

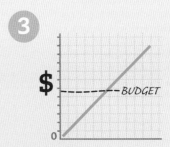

3

Unrealistic budget

Ineffective forecasting means you run out of money, departments fall behind, resources are slow to arrive, and the project goes out of control.

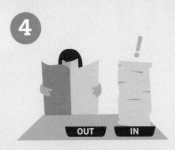

4

Not regularly checking progress

When you assume everything is going well, you might find you're suddenly faced with a huge list of problems just before the deadline.

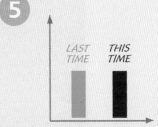

5

Not reviewing existing standards

If most of your projects run behind schedule and over budget, ask yourself why. If you keep doing the same thing, you'll get the same results.

Discussion

1 Do you agree with the list of the five most common problems on a project? Would you add any other problems to the list?

2 Which of these problems have you experienced on a project? What happened?

3 What have you learnt from your mistakes on previous projects? How do you do things differently now?

Task

1 Work in groups. Prepare a presentation entitled 'Five best solutions for Project Managers'. Use the list of the five most common problems and create a new list with the five best solutions.

2 Join another group and take turns to present your list of solutions. How similar or different were the five solutions in each group?

Preview

In this video lesson, you will watch an interview with Peter Tufano, the Dean of Saïd Business School which is part of the University of Oxford. He describes the role and purpose of the business school and the types of students who attend. He also talks about different ways of learning for business.

Focus

1 Where did you gain the qualifications and skills you need for your current job? What kinds of formal training do you still do? How important is it for your career?

2 ▶01 Watch a short video about Saïd Business School and make notes about the following:
- location and age
- facilities
- undergraduate and MBA programmes
- executive education and custom programmes
- world ranking

Profile

Peter Tufano is the Dean of Saïd Business School and a Professor of Finance. Before that, he was at Harvard Business School for 22 years. Peter Tufano is also a social entrepreneur and founded a non-profit organization which works with low-income households to manage their financial needs. He has also been advisor to business and government leaders.

Saïd Business School

3 ▶02 Watch the first part of an interview with Peter Tufano. Number topics a–e in the order he talks about them (1–5).
a the undergraduate students ___
b where students come from ___
c how Saïd is different to other business schools ___
d Saïd Business School and Oxford University ___
e executive students with experience ___

4 ▶02 Watch the interview again and answer these questions.
1 Peter Tufano describes Oxford University as 'large, complicated, old'. How does he describe Saïd Business School?
2 What do business schools, including Saïd Business School, teach you?
3 Peter Tufano thinks Saïd Business School helps students with the way the world is changing. What are some of those changes?
4 What are the characteristics of a typical student on the undergraduate programme?
5 What is the profile of a typical MBA student?
6 What is the profile of a typical executive student?
7 What is possible when you sit down next to a Saïd Business School student?

5 Work with a partner. Have you ever thought of going back to study? Would you like to study something to support your current career or something completely new? Give reasons for your answers.

Ways of learning

6 Match words and phrases 1–8 from the next part of the interview to the correct definitions a–h.

1 arm
2 synchronous
3 asynchronous
4 pedagogy
5 case method
6 critical thinking
7 tutorial
8 the core

a a method or approach to teaching and learning
b at the heart or centre of something
c analysing and evaluating information
d when two or more things happen at the same time
e a meeting between a student and a tutor, either one-to-one or in small groups
f a form of learning where you read and discuss a real situation and its outcome
g when two or more things happen at different times
h provide the skills that someone will need in the future

7 ▶03 Watch Peter Tufano talking about different ways of learning and answer these questions.

1 Which ways of learning does he contrast?
2 Why doesn't Saïd Business School insist on one pedagogy?
3 What is the benefit of using the case method (case study)?
4 How is critical thinking different from case method?
5 Why does Peter Tufano say 'getting your hands dirty is incredibly important'?
6 What conclusions does he make about different ways of learning?

Glossary
getting your hands dirty doing something directly yourself

A learning questionnaire

8 This questionnaire includes some of Peter Tufano's ideas and some other ways of learning. Answer the questions by ticking (✓) the appropriate boxes in the table.

Which of these ways of learning do you use to ...	learn a new language (e.g. English)?	learn a work skill (e.g. using new software)?	learn a hobby (e.g. a musical instrument)?
working with other people (e.g. in a team or group)			
working on my own			
in tutorials (or one-to-one with a teacher)			
in online courses (e.g. with an online tutor)			
by reading (e.g. articles and books)			
by listening (e.g. to lectures and podcasts with experts)			
by writing things down			
by doing a practical task (i.e. getting your hands dirty)			
by repeating the same thing many times			
by case method (case studies)			

9 Work in small groups. Compare and explain your answers in the questionnaire to the rest of the group. Have you used any other ways of learning in the past? How effective were they?

At the end of your discussion, summarize the group's feelings about the most effective ways of learning, and tell the class.

4 New ideas

1 What is the difference between an *invention* and an *innovation*?

2 What is your favourite invention, and why?

3 What innovation would improve the quality of your life at work? And outside work?

Working with words | Ideas and innovations

1 What kinds of awards do you have in your industry? Do you think industry awards are useful for new ideas and innovation in business?

2 Read the text and answer questions 1–2.
   1 What are the aims of the Ashden Awards?
   2 How does the charity achieve its aims?

The Ashden Awards for Sustainable Energy

The Ashden Awards for Sustainable Energy is a charity that rewards and promotes excellent sustainable energy solutions in the UK and the developing world.

Each year, the Ashden Awards holds a competition to find and reward organizations which have **carried out** practical and innovative programmes that demonstrate sustainable energy in action at a local level.

The charity raises international awareness of the potential benefit of local sustainable energy projects to deal with climate change and to improve the quality of people's lives.

It also aims to encourage more people and communities across the world to **take up** the challenge of making major breakthroughs in meeting energy needs.

The charity helps the development of sustainable energy projects in several ways. It gives cash prizes, to enable winners to **take** their work **forward**. It also publicizes the winners and their work through a worldwide media campaign, which aims to inspire others to follow their example.

This year, the winners of the award included a project to build footbridges in developing countries, and another to supply low cost solar-powered lighting.

3 ▶ 4.1 Listen to details of two projects that have won an Ashden Award.
   1 What is the main purpose of each project and how is it sustainable?
   2 How have the projects changed people's lives?

4 Match the adjectives in A to the nouns in B to make phrases used in the text in **2** and the listening in **3**. What other combinations are possible?

A	B
potential	approach
practical	benefit
cutting-edge	proposition
innovative	concept
commercially-viable	breakthrough
major	solution
key	technology

5 Work with a partner. Create a sentence for each phrase from **4**.

6 Match these phrasal verbs from the text and the listening to a verb 1–9 with the same meaning.

*carry out   come up with   pay off   take up   bring down
bring about   take forward   get round   set up*

1 avoid (a problem) _____
2 cause (something to happen) _____
3 create (an idea, a solution to a problem) _____
4 develop (a plan, a project) _____
5 have a good result _____
6 perform (an activity, research) _____
7 reduce (costs) _____
8 respond to (a challenge) _____
9 start (a business, a project) _____

7 Complete the texts with the correct form of a phrasal verb from **6**.

At the Barefoot College, we've ¹_____ an idea to ²_____ the problem of sustainable energy for cooking and heating in remote mountain villages in Nepal. We've ³_____ a project to supply solar power to these villages, and we train local people to install and maintain the systems. Many of our new engineers are women – they've really ⁴_____ the challenge of learning new skills. The main advantage of our training programme is that the new technology we install works properly and has a long life – so it can ⁵_____ real improvements to people's lives, and to the environment.

At KXN we've developed the technology to ⁶_____ a plan for improving the refrigeration of vaccines in northern Nigeria. Standard refrigerators are useless in remote areas because the electricity supply is so unreliable. After ⁷_____ research and trials, our solution was to build special refrigerators, using photovoltaic (PV) cells to generate and store electricity from sunlight. The initial investment was high, but it has ⁸_____. This type of refrigerator has excellent insulation, so it needs relatively little electricity to keep the contents cool. This has helped to ⁹_____ the overall cost of vaccination for people in these remote areas.

>> For more exercises, go to **Practice file 4** on page 112.

8 Work with a partner. Prepare to talk about an innovative idea for a new invention or new system. This can be connected with the place you work, live, or study. Choose at least eight words from **4** and **6** to use in your talk.

Business communication | Presenting a product or service

1 When you enter your place of work, what different types of security are used (e.g. CCTV, electronic name tags)? Do you think there is enough or not enough security at your company?

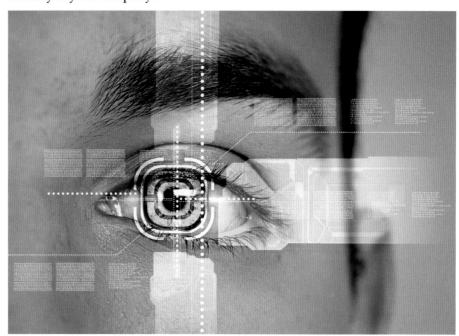

2 ▶ 4.2 Read the *Context*. Listen to Part 1 of Shireen's presentation and make notes to complete the slides.

Presentation to PharmaLab
Shireen Casey

1 _____

2 _____

3 _____

Questions

What is DiScan2?

A ^{4} _____ system,
based on ^{5} _____

How does DiScan2 work?

Employees ^{6} _____
The system ^{7} _____
and ^{8} _____

---

3 ▶ 4.2 Listen again and complete these phrases.
1 What I'd like to do in this presentation is _____.
2 First, I'll _____ the new DiScan product.
3 After that, I _____ a short video.
4 Does that _____?
5 Basically, DiScan2 _____ based on iris recognition.
6 _____? Well, it's a pretty simple concept.

Key expressions

Introducing a talk
What I'd like to do in this presentation is …
First, I'll give you a brief overview of …
Then I'll talk about …
After that I'd like to show you …

Introducing an idea, product or service
We call this new system (the DiScan2).
Basically, (DiScan2) is …
It is already being used in …
Well, it's a pretty simple concept.

Explaining the benefits
There are two main benefits of using (DiScan2).
The biggest potential benefit of (iris recognition) is …
This means that …
The other major advantage of (DiScan2) is …
And here is another great thing about (DiScan2) …

Comparing products and systems
… in comparison to your current system where …
However, with … it will/won't be able to …
Whereas you can/can't …

Checking and moving on
Does that sound OK?
OK, let's look at what (DiScan2) has to offer.
Now I'd like to move on to …

4 ▶ 4.3 Listen to Part 2. What are the main advantages of DiScan2?

5 ▶ 4.3 Listen again. What words and phrases does Shireen use to …?
a explain the benefits of DiScan2
b compare the current system with the new system
c move on to the next point

>> For more exercises, go to **Practice file 4** on page 112.

6 Work with a partner. Take turns to use the slides in **2** and the *Key expressions* to give a similar short presentation about DiScan2.

7 Prepare a short presentation about a new idea, a product, a system or a service that you know about, or are interested in. It doesn't have to be connected with work, but it can be. Make sure you:
• introduce your talk and the idea / product / service
• talk about the benefits
• compare the current situation with the new idea / product / service

Practically speaking | Referring to evidence

1 When you give presentations, is it important to support your ideas with evidence? Do you ever refer to the following types of evidence in your presentations? In what type of presentation would each one be useful?
• academic studies
• market research
• interviews and questionnaires
• examples of existing users
• medical evidence
• personal experience

2 ▶ 4.4 Listen to two questions from the audience after the presentation about iris recognition security in *Business communication*. Shireen answers each question by referring to evidence from different sources. Which of the types of evidence in **1** does she refer to?

3 ▶ 4.4 Listen again and write the verbs Shireen uses to refer to evidence.
1 Academic studies _____ that we feel more comfortable with iris scans than retinal scans.
2 All the medical evidence _____ that it's safe for the human eye.
3 Iris recognition is already being used in government security, which _____ how effective it is.

4 Think of one of your company's products or services, or a product or service that you know well.
• List the types of evidence you can give to explain the benefits of the product or service.
• Write some sentences using some of these reporting verbs for referring to the evidence:

shows   suggests   demonstrates   illustrates   proves   reports

5 Work with a partner. Take turns to read your sentences to your partner and refer to evidence. Does your partner's evidence make the benefits of the product or service sound more convincing?

Language at work | Present, past and future ability

1 ▶ 4.5 Listen to Richard Lake talking about his new business idea to some potential investors and answer questions 1–4.

1 What is Boatnet?
2 What is the current situation for boat owners who want to use the Internet?
3 What will Boatnet enable them to do in the future?
4 What protection does Boatnet have against competitors?

2 Read extracts 1–10 from the presentation. Which ones refer to …?

a present ability _____
b past ability _____
c future ability _____

1 I could see that there was definitely a market.
2 Boat owners want to be able to access the Internet.
3 You still can't access the Internet from your boat.
4 Our subscribers will be able to access the Internet for a basic monthly fee.
5 We were able to test the system extensively.
6 We can offer the service for £25 a month.
7 We'd like to be able to increase this.
8 Have you been able to get any sort of protection for it?
9 We couldn't get a patent.
10 So other companies won't be able to compete with you?

3 Use the extracts in **2** to help you complete 1–5 in the *Language point* with the words and phrases in the list.

> **LANGUAGE POINT**
>
> *has/have been able to   can   couldn't   was/were able to*
> *be able to   could   is/are able to   wasn't/weren't able to*
>
> 1 Use _____ or _____ to talk about general or present ability.
> 2 To talk about future ability, we use _____ after *will, might* and *may*, and verbs like *want to* or *would like to*.
> 3 Use _____ to talk about past ability with a connection to the present.
> 4 Use _____ to talk about general ability in the past, and before *hear, see, tell,* etc.
> 5 To talk about a specific situation in the past, if we mean 'tried and succeeded', we use _____. But if the sentence is negative we can use _____ or _____.

>> For more information, go to **Grammar reference** on page 113.

4 Work with a partner. Look at these rapidly-changing technologies and talk about past, present and future ability when using them.

*Example: In the past, I **wasn't able to** use my phone for taking photos – I could only text or make calls. With my current phone, I **can** take photos and video clips, play games and download music files. In the future, I'd like to **be able to** use my phone to park my car.*

>> For more exercises, go to **Practice file 4** on page 113.

5 Work with a partner and discuss similar changes affecting your own lives, in or out of work. Talk about technology, systems or methods of working, or choose from the list.

- electronic equipment
- work practices
- vehicles
- education
- travel
- medicine

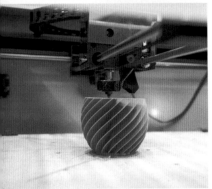

TALKING POINT

Are you a 'Yes, but...' or a 'Yes, and...' person?

In the working world, we are usually rewarded for getting things right and knowing the correct answers. For this reason, many business people are by nature careful and not big risk-takers. So when someone has a new idea or suggests a possible solution, colleagues might often respond positively, compliment the person on their idea, but then proceed to tell them why it might not work. These are 'Yes, but...' people. They like new ideas, but they often stop them before they can be fully explored. For new ideas to emerge, you need people who respond positively and then explore them in greater detail. The people who do this are 'Yes, and...' people.

Brainstorming meetings need 'Yes, and...' people. So that when a new idea is suggested, the next person follows on with a sentence starting with the words, 'Yes, and...'. Then the next person continues with another sentence starting, 'Yes, and...'. In this way, you can generate plenty of new ideas very quickly. To demonstrate how effective this type of brainstorming is, try the same activity with everyone in the meeting, but starting a sentence with 'Yes, but...' and see how quickly the new idea gets dropped.

That isn't to say we should never say 'no' in business, only that saying 'yes' is probably a better starting point – especially when it comes to new ideas.

Discussion

1 Read the text. Overall, would you say that you are more naturally a 'Yes, but...' person or a 'Yes, and...' person? Why?

2 Do you ever attend brainstorming meetings? What makes them successful? Why can they go wrong?

3 In your type of business or work, do you think most people are under pressure not to make mistakes and always to get the correct answer?

Task

Work in groups of four or five people. You work for a family company which manufactures traditional children's bicycles aimed at 4- to 10-year-olds. In the past, you were successful, but nowadays there are new competitors offering wider ranges of bicycles with innovative features. To try and find new ways to compete, your managing director has set up a brainstorming meeting.

1 Spend five minutes brainstorming new types of bicycles with new features. The first person begins with the words, *In my opinion, the new bicycle should* and then the next person continues with *Yes, and... (another idea)* and so on. From now on, the only rule of this brainstorm is start sentences with *Yes, and...*. One person should write all the new ideas down.

2 After the first brainstorming, the person who wrote the ideas down reads them all out. Then discuss and choose five or six of the best ideas.

3 Present your final list to the rest of the class. How different were your ideas from the other groups?

4 Repeat this activity for a product, service or problem connected to your business. Try to come up with new ideas and solutions.

5 Ethical business

Starting point

1 What effect (positive or negative) can companies have on the environment and the local community?

2 Do you know of any companies that are well known for their social responsibility? Is this a selling point for the company?

3 Do you know of any companies that have a public image problem because of their activities?

Working with words | Ethical business

1 Work with a partner. What are the characteristics of an 'ethical business'?

2 Read the text about a company called Patagonia. In what ways is the company an ethical business? How does this compare to your ideas in 1?

OUR REASON *for being*

Patagonia grew out of a small company that made tools for climbers. Mountain climbing is still at the heart of our business, but we also make clothes for skiing, snowboarding, surfing, fly fishing, paddling and trail running. All of these are silent sports. They don't require a motor or the cheers of a crowd – the rewards come from connecting with nature.

Our values reflect a business that was started by a band of climbers and surfers who love wild and beautiful places. This means that we act responsibly and take an active part in the fight to repair the damage that is being done to the health of our planet.

We acknowledge that the wild world we love best is disappearing. That is why we share a strong commitment to protecting natural lands and waters. Caring for the environment is very important to us. We donate our time, services and at least 1% of our sales to hundreds of environmental groups all over the world who are working to protect and restore the environment.

But we also know that our business activity – from lighting our stores to dyeing shirts – creates pollution as a by-product. So we work steadily to reduce the impact we have, and do more than simply comply with the regulations. We use recycled polyester in many of our clothes and only organic, rather than pesticide-intensive, cotton.

Staying true to our principles during thirty-plus years in business has helped us create a company we're proud to run and work for.

3 Read the text again and answer questions 1–5.

1 How have the company's founders influenced what the company does now?

2 What does the company have a commitment to? How do they show this commitment?

3 What points are made about the manufacturing process?

4 Why are the owners proud of the company?

5 Do you or would you buy products from companies like Patagonia? How important is it for you to buy products from ethical companies?

4 Match the words in A and B to make phrases to complete questions 1–7.

A	B
act	time
share	responsibly
take	the impact
stay	regulations
comply with	an active part in
reduce	true to its principles
donate	a strong commitment to

1 Do most companies in your country always _____ or do they sometimes bend the rules?
2 Do you know of any companies that _____, services or money to help local organizations?
3 How can businesses _____ they have on the environment?
4 Why should a company _____ and deal with any pollution that is a by-product of its business activity?
5 Does your company _____ the life of the local community. If so, what does it do?
6 Should a company _____ and values even if this means a loss of profit?
7 What companies in your country _____ protecting the environment?

5 Work with a partner. Ask and answer the questions in **4**.

6 ▶ 5.1 Listen to a radio presenter questioning Shamsul Aziz, a spokesperson for a leading gas and oil exploration company. Answer questions 1–4.
1 How would you describe the interviewer's style?
2 How does the spokesperson react to the questions?
3 What does the company do for …?
   a its staff   b the environment   c the local communities where it operates
4 Do you think the company is doing enough for the environment and local community?

7 Which of these nouns from audio script 5.1 do you associate with …?
1 an ethical company
2 an unethical company

bribery   ethics   deception   responsibility   fairness   generosity
values   corruption   prejudice   credibility   greed   discrimination

8 Work with a partner. Think of an action or a situation to explain the meaning of each noun.
   Example: *Bribery – paying money to a government official to get planning permission for a new building.*

9 Complete this table with the adjectives of some of the nouns in **7**.

Noun	Adjective	Noun	Adjective
deception	*deceptive*	ethics	
responsibility		corruption	
fairness		prejudice	
generosity		greed	
credibility		discrimination	

10 Work with a partner. Turn to page 136. Read about the two companies and discuss how ethical you think they are, using some of the nouns and adjectives from **7** and **9**.

>> For more exercises, go to **Practice file 5** on page 114.

Context

Hummingbird Teas focuses on speciality teas from countries such as China, India and South Africa. The unique selling point of the business is its ethos. It sources teas from small, local farmers and supports fair trade. It has recently brought in Clare, a PR consultant, to help raise its profile. Clare has been organizing a trip for reporters from ethical consumer magazines to see Hummingbird's operation. She is meeting with the reporters to give details of the trip.

1 When you have an overseas trip for work or you are preparing for someone to visit, how important is the planning stage? What can go wrong with the preparations?

2 ▶ 5.2 Read the *Context*. Listen to Part 1 of the meeting between Clare and the reporters. Make any necessary changes to these notes.

- Trip planned to China or South Africa (to be confirmed)

- Five days travelling around different tea plantations

- Opportunities for sightseeing will be provided

- Two possible dates for trip: February and March

- Two internal flights

3 ▶ 5.2 Listen again. Complete these phrases for explaining the plans and arrangements for the trip.
1 We _____ once you've decided what you'd like to see.
2 So, _____ how Hummingbird's operation works in China.
3 The _____ spend four days at one of the sites where the tea is grown.
4 You _____ accompany the workers in their daily work.
5 We've looked at all the options, and _____ two dates.

4 ▶ 5.3 Listen to Part 2 of the meeting.
1 What activities and visits can the reporters take part in?
2 What advice can Clare give about the guide?

5 ▶ 5.3 Listen again and complete these phrases.
1 We _____ watch the tea being prepared.
2 English isn't spoken so _____ with our guide.
3 On the subject of language – _____ a project set up to help build a new school.
4 That _____ really interesting. I _____.
5 … as it _____ travel with our interpreter.
6 A visit to the site _____.
7 I was there for the first time last month … It's _____.
8 Mmm … _____ I'm looking for.
9 Well, alternatively, _____ introduce you to the team who work for Hummingbird in China.
10 That would be great – _____.

6 Put phrases 1–10 in **5** into categories a–c.
a inviting _____
b recommending _____
c responding to an invitation or recommendation _____

>> For more exercises, go to **Practice file 5** on page 114.

Tip | advise and recommend

Advise and *recommend* are both quite formal ways of making a suggestion. Be careful with the word order.

*We **advise** you to set this up directly (with the locals).*
*We **recommend** (that) you stay with our guide.*

Key expressions

Explaining plans and arrangements
We'll email you the (final) itinerary.
We're planning to …
The idea is to …
We're going to arrange …
You'll get the opportunity to …
The flight leaves on …

Inviting
We'd like to invite you to …
You're welcome to …
Alternatively, we'd be delighted to …

Recommending
We strongly recommend you (stay) …
It would be a good idea to …
… is highly recommended.
It's well worth a visit.

Responding
That would be great.
That sounds really interesting.
Good idea.
That makes sense.
It's just the kind of thing I need.
That's not really what I'm looking for.

7 Work with a partner. Read this information about activities organized by Hummingbird Teas. Choose information A or B and take turns to invite and make recommendations of things to do or points to look out for. Decide for yourself if you want to accept or decline.

A

Hummingbird **Teas**

Invitation: Information day – How and why does Hummingbird Teas practise fair trade?

Recommended activities on the day:
- Presentation about the Slow Food movement in Europe and how Hummingbird Teas' activities complement this
- Tea tasting – rare and exotic teas

Advice: Arrive early for tea tasting – only ten people in each group

B

Hummingbird **Teas**

Invitation: Informal visit day, including presentation – The man behind Rooibos tea.

Recommended activities on the day:
- Hummingbird Teas help to make a difference – Slide show of tree replanting in the Himalayas
- Tea-making workshop – How to make the perfect cuppa

Advice: Taste teas at workshop before buying

8 Work with a partner. Your company has arranged an open day to give customers an insight into its operation. (If you don't work for a company, use the information on page 136.)
1 Make a list of:
  - the things you plan to show your guests on the day
  - any recommendations of things to do or points to look out for
  - things you hope to invite your guests to do
2 Find another partner (from a different company if possible). Take turns to:
  - explain your plans for the day
  - make any recommendations
  - invite your partner to do things
  - respond appropriately

Practically speaking | Responding to invitations

1 When someone invites you to do something, do you ever find it difficult to say 'no'? What are some ways to decline or delay your response?

2 ▶ 5.4 Listen to five invitations. Match each invitation 1–5 to how the other person responds, a–e.

invitation 1	a accepts
invitation 2	b declines
invitation 3	c partly accepts
invitation 4	d partly declines
invitation 5	e neither accepts or declines

3 ▶ 5.4 Listen again and write down any useful phrases the speaker uses in the responses.

4 Invite as many people as you can to these activities (or make up your own). When you receive an invitation, use some of the phrases from 3 to respond.
  - go to the cinema (to see?)
  - watch a football match (which team?)
  - go to the theatre (to see?)
  - go for dinner (where?)
  - hiking at the weekend (where?)
  - have a coffee (where?)

Language at work | Talking about the future

1 Read the sentences a–e. What tense is used in each sentence?
  a She**'s coming** in later on this morning to speak with you.
  b This **will give** you a real insight into their lives.
  c We've looked at all the options, and we**'re going to** arrange two dates.
  d The first morning flight **leaves** at 7.15.
  e A … it'd be a good idea to travel with our interpreter.
     B That makes sense. We**'ll speak** to our colleagues and let you know.

2 Match sentences a–e in 1 to situations 1–5 in the *Language point*.

> **LANGUAGE POINT**
>
> 1 someone making a decision as they speak ___
> 2 someone talking about a plan, intention, something they have already decided to do ___
> 3 someone talking about an appointment or arrangement ___
> 4 someone making a prediction ___
> 5 someone talking about a timetable or schedule ___

» For more information, go to **Grammar reference** on page 115.

3 Work with a partner. Decide which is the best option in *italics* in each sentence.
  1 I can't see you on Friday – I *'ll do / 'm doing* a training course in London.
  2 According to the weather forecast, it *'ll be / 's being* hot tomorrow.
  3 The next flight to Tokyo *arrives / is going to arrive* there at 10.45 tomorrow morning.
  4 A By the way, I'm out of the office tomorrow.
     B Are you? OK, I *'ll let / 'm letting* Christina know.
  5 I'm not in the office on Monday – I *'m going to go / 'll go* to an exhibition.
  6 I *meet / 'm meeting* Mrs Brasseler at 3.30 this afternoon.
  7 A Could you give me some information about Mr Ward's visit?
     B Of course, I *email / 'll email* the details now.
  8 I think Greta *is noticing / will notice* a lot of changes in the office when she returns from maternity leave.

4 Work with a partner. Ask and answer these questions using *will, going to,* the present continuous or the present simple.
  1 Have you got a busy weekend?
  2 Are you doing anything tonight?
  3 What's the weather forecast for the weekend?
  4 What time is the last train?
  5 What do you think about the threat of global warming?
  6 Are you free tomorrow afternoon?
  7 Have you booked your next holiday?
  8 What plans have you got for projects at work or home?

» For more exercises, go to **Practice file 5** on page 115.

5 Think of future work commitments, career plans or key events for your company. Write only the dates and times for these on a piece of paper. For example, *in 2025, 7.30 tonight, next Friday, next October, when I am 60,* etc. Compare your dates with a partner. Ask them to explain the importance of each date.
  Example: A *Why is 5th May 2025 important?*
            B *That's when the company **will** be exactly 50 years old. We're going to have a big celebration with all our major clients – it **will** be a big achievement for us.*

Rule 47: A set of personal standards

Richard Templar's book *The rules of work* provides 109 rules to follow in order to be successful in business. Rule 45 requires that you know the ethics of your industry. Ask yourself, what does your industry or company contribute to society? Is the contribution positive and beneficial, or negative and damaging? How much a part of that industry are you?

If your answers to these questions lead you to believe that your industry stinks, that doesn't (necessarily) mean you have to hand in your notice today. After all, you can always try to change things from the inside. However, if you are ever faced with the ethical dilemma of crossing the line and doing bad things, then you will need to set personal standards. This is Rule 47. Rule 47 requires you to set personal standards which you won't break for any reason, such as:

- I will not break the law in order to further my career.
- I will share my skills and knowledge with anyone who would benefit in the same industry.
- I will not be jealous of anyone else's success in the same industry.
- I will always put my family first (before work).
- I will not work evenings or weekends, unless it is an emergency.

Discussion

1 Do you think it's always necessary to contribute something to society in business? Why/Why not?

2 What do you think the terms 'your industry stinks' and 'crossing the line' mean in the article?

3 If you think the industry you work in is unethical, which do you think is better: to hand in your notice, or to try and change things from the inside? Give reasons for your answer.

4 Do you think it's a good idea to have a set of personal standards at work? Why might it be difficult not to break them sometimes?

Task

1 Look at the list of five personal standards in the article. Which ones would you include in your list of personal standards? Which would be difficult to follow?

2 Work in groups. Tell the group your answers for 1 and give your reasons.

3 As a group, write a list of between eight and ten more personal standards to follow at work. You can use some (not all) of the standards in the article and add your own. Start each standard with the words 'We will …' or 'We will not …'

4 Present your list to the other groups.

6 Making decisions

Starting point

1 Think of one or two good decisions you have made. How much were you guided by facts and figures? How much did you follow your intuition?

2 Does having more time to think produce better decisions? Or do you decide faster *and* more wisely when under pressure?

Working with words | Personality and decision-making

1 How much do you think our personalities affect our decision-making?

2 Read this text about personality and decision-making. Which personality type …?
   1 thinks it's important to be on time
   2 enjoys an argument
   3 finds it hard to concentrate on one thing at once
   4 is more interested in the future than the past

ALL IN THE MIND

Are you an extrovert or an introvert?

Extroverts are often **outgoing** and enthusiastic. They are good with people and enjoy a public role. They prefer to do lots of things at once and can be easily distracted. They're talkers rather than listeners and can be **impulsive**.

Introverts are often **self-contained** and reserved. They can be very **focused** when working on tasks and prefer to focus on one thing at a time. They are good listeners, they think before they act and prefer to be behind the scenes.

Are you a sensor or an intuitive?

Sensors are often sensible and **pragmatic**. They are good on details and remembering facts and specifics. They are reliable and **methodical** and work at a steady pace. They trust their own experience and use established skills.

Intuitives are often energetic and **creative**. They like to focus on the big picture and on future possibilities. They like things that are new and different and prefer to learn new skills. They are **thoughtful** when making decisions and trust their instincts.

Are you a thinker or a feeler?

Thinkers usually take a **rational** approach to decision-making and prefer to remain **detached**. They are honest and direct, valuing fairness. They can be ambitious and critical. They take few things personally and like-arguing and debating issues for fun.

Feelers are often **instinctive** in their decisions rather than relying on facts or reasons. **Tactful** and diplomatic, they avoid arguments and take many things personally. They appear warm and friendly, like to be appreciated and are good at complimenting others.

Are you a judger or a perceiver?

Judgers often make decisions easily and quickly. They appreciate plans, rules and schedules and are usually punctual. They are **determined**, keep to their deadlines and like to complete projects. They are serious and **conventional**, and like decisiveness in others.

Perceivers are often **indecisive**; they like to be **flexible** and to keep their options open. Being unconventional, they dislike rules and deadlines. They like to start projects and prefer to play now and work later.

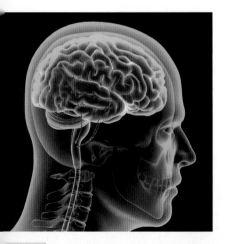

3 Match the adjectives in **bold** in the text to the statements 1–16.

1 I am not influenced by other people or my emotions. _detached_
2 I do things in a careful and well-ordered way. _____
3 I find it hard to make up my mind about things. _____
4 I focus on what I want to do and don't let anyone stop me. _____
5 I do things based on my own feelings. _____
6 I am happy to change my plans when necessary to suit my friends. _____
7 I am confident and friendly. _____
8 I like to think about things carefully. _____
9 I can produce new things using my imagination. _____
10 I do what is normal and acceptable. _____
11 I make decisions objectively. _____
12 I don't do things that will upset or annoy people. _____
13 I depend on myself. _____
14 I pay careful attention to what I'm doing. _____
15 I do things as I think of them without considering the consequences. _____
16 I like to find practical solutions to problems. _____

4 Work with a partner. Choose five of the adjectives in **3** and explain what kind of people you like to work with and why. Then choose another five adjectives and explain what kind of people you don't like to work with and why.

5 Work with a partner.

1 Find things in the text that the personality types:
a are good at/with   b like/prefer to do
2 What are you good at/with? How do you like/prefer to approach decision-making?

6 Decide which personality type you are most like in each section in the text in **2**.

1 Write down the first letter of the type you choose in each section:
• extrovert (E) or introvert (I)? ___   • thinker (T) or feeler (F)? ___
• sensor (S) or intuitive (N)? ___   • judger (J) or perceiver (P)? ___
2 Turn to page 139 to find out what your choice reveals about you.
3 Share the information with a partner. Say if you agree or disagree with it and why.

7 ▶ 6.1 Listen to four people talking about decision-making. Which personality type best applies to each speaker?
Speaker 1: extrovert (E) or introvert (I)? ___
Speaker 2: sensor (S) or intuitive (N)? ___
Speaker 3: thinker (T) or feeler (F)? ___
Speaker 4: judger (J) or perceiver (P)? ___

8 Match the verbs in A to the noun phrases in B to make phrases from **7**.

A		B	
weigh up	consider	(my) own judgement	different perspectives
delay	have confidence in	my decision	all the options
rely on	get	two things	my instincts
trust	decide between	feelings	information

9 Work with a partner. Use the phrases in **8** to talk about the way you made one or two recent decisions in or out of work.

>> For more exercises, go to **Practice file 6** on page 116.

10 Work with a partner. What personality types would be most suitable for these jobs and why?
• sales manager   • office administrator
• website designer   • accounts controller
• human resources manager   • training consultant

Tip | *good at/with*
Use *good at* to talk about a skill or activity.
*Marc is **good at** languages / speaking Italian.*
Use *good with* to talk about using something or dealing with someone.
*Joel is **good with** computers / people.*

Business communication | Decision-making

1 Why is it sometimes difficult to reach decisions in a meeting? To make the meeting effective, what does the leader of the meeting need to do?

2 ▶ 6.2 Read the *Context*. Listen to the meeting and tick (✓) the points discussed.
  1 Freeze recruitment ☐
  2 Cut back on overtime ☐
  3 Reduce office resources ☐
  4 Change phone provider ☐
  5 Reduce client expense accounts ☐
  6 Cut back on business trips ☐

3 ▶ 6.2 Listen again and complete the phrases in 1–8.
  1 Yes, well, _____ our costs for personnel are very high.
  2 … number of employees. _____ the overtime figures. They're _____, and they're costing us …
  3 The _____, we need to look at why we have so much overtime.
  4 … a lot of waste. _____ printing emails out on expensive copy paper.
  5 So _____ is monitoring the office supplies …
  6 I'm _____.
  7 As far as _____, we'd make hardly any savings …
  8 Matt _____. But _____ cut expense accounts …

4 Sinead is leading the discussion. Turn to audio script 6.2 and <u>underline</u> the phrases she uses to:
  1 set the agenda for the discussion
  2 manage turn-taking
  3 invite people to express their opinions
  4 move on to a different topic
  5 manage the timing
  6 monitor action points

>> For more exercises, go to **Practice file 6** on page 116.

Tip | *getting at*

Use *getting at* to talk about what someone means.
*What are you **getting at**?*
*So what you're **getting at** is …*

Key expressions

Presenting an argument
If we look at the facts, we'll see ...
Look at ... They're here in black and white ...
The fact is ... / The thing is ...
The advantage/drawback is ...
If we ..., it'll mean ...
A classic example is...

Giving an opinion
I (don't) think (we should) ...
If you ask me, we should ...
..., that's my view
In my opinion ...
As far as I'm concerned ...
I think it would be crazy to ...

Responding to opinions
Exactly/Absolutely.
You're / X is right.
What X says is right.
Yes, but ...
I'm not convinced.

Clarifying
Could you give us some detail, please?
What I mean is ...
So what you're getting at is ...
In other words ...

Leading the discussion
Today, I'd like to establish ...
I'd like to discuss the pros and cons first.
(Jens), could you start us off, please?
What's your position on this?
Hang on. Let's hear what (Jens) has to say ...
I don't want to spend too long on this point.
Can we move on to ...?
Let's turn to the next item ...
Let's look into it ... and discuss it again at our next meeting.
Let's draw up some action points on ...

5 Work in small groups. You are going to continue the meeting from **2**.
1 Look at this agenda item and decide on your opinion of each suggestion. Add two extra suggestions to the list.

Reduce staff benefits / activities

- reduce subsidies in staff cafeteria
- cancel annual staff away day
- restrict Christmas event to staff only
- introduce a PIN number for photocopying and limit number of copies per person
- _____
- _____

---

2 Choose eight phrases from *Key expressions* that you have never used or are not very familiar with. Write these on separate cards. (Don't include expressions from *Leading the discussion*.)
3 Continue the meeting from **2**. As you participate, 'play' your phrase cards by placing them in front of you when you use the phrase correctly. Your colleagues will return the card to you if the phrase is not used correctly.
4 The winner is the first person to play all their cards correctly.

6 Work in groups of four. You are at a departmental meeting. You have €50,000 left in your annual budget. As a group, try to decide how to spend the money.
1 Before the meeting do the following:
- Decide on what type of department you are.
- Make a list of five suggestions for spending the money (the money can be divided between more than one idea).
2 Prepare for the meeting with a partner. Decide which suggestions on the list you agree/disagree with and think of arguments to support your opinions.
3 Hold the meeting, taking turns to lead the discussion.
4 Report back to the class on any decisions you made.

Practically speaking | Talking about social plans

1 During the break in a long meeting, there's often time for small talk. What kinds of topics might you discuss with your colleagues? Think of three questions you might ask.

2 ▶ 6.3 Listen to five short conversations during the break in a meeting. The first speaker asks about the other person's plans. In which conversation is the second speaker ...?
a certain about plans ___
b certain about plans but unhappy with them ___
c certain about having no plans ___
d fairly certain about plans ___
e uncertain about plans ___

3 ▶ 6.3 Listen again. For each conversation, make a note of the phrases used to:
1 ask about plans
2 respond to a question about plans
3 react to someone's plans

4 Take a short break and talk to as many people as possible in the class. Ask and answer questions about your evening / weekend / holiday plans.

Language at work | Countability | Expressions of quantity

1 Read sentences 1–6 and match the nouns in **bold** to a–c.

1 We'll find there's a lot of **waste**.
2 It's a **problem** we've come up against again and again.
3 We'd make hardly any **savings**.
4 We need to look at why we have so much **overtime**.
5 We should look carefully at client travel **expenses**.
6 I don't want to spend too long on this **point**.

a singular countable noun _____
b plural countable noun _____
c uncountable noun _____

2 Decide if these nouns are countable (C), uncountable (U), or both (B). If the noun can be both, is there a difference in meaning between the two options?

news   product   colleague   expenditure   paper   information   suggestion
business   travel   experience   time   fact   accommodation   journey   software
correspondence   proposal   money   equipment   insurance   document   advice

3 Complete the table in the *Language point* with nouns from **2**. Make the nouns plural if necessary.

LANGUAGE POINT

Expression of quantity	+ noun
a, an, the, one	product
too many, not many, a few, fewer, very few	facts
lots of, plenty of, more, most, some, not enough, hardly any, not any, no	news
too much, not much, a little, less, very little	

>> For more information, go to **Grammar reference** on page 117.

4 Complete sentences 1–8 with the expressions of quantity from the list.

too much   any   enough   very little   a   some   too many   fewer

1 There's _____ money left in the budget, so we can't buy that new software.
2 There were _____ points of disagreement than expected in the meeting.
3 The project is late because we spent _____ time on the planning stage.
4 I need _____ information about hotels in the area.
5 They didn't take _____ of my suggestions on board at all.
6 We haven't got _____ chairs for the meeting – could you get two more?
7 Currently we're employing _____ people – we have to make some cuts.
8 Would you like _____ drink?

>> For more exercises, go to **Practice file 6** on page 117.

5 Work with a partner. Compare these situations, using as many of the quantifiers in **3** as you can.
• working for a multinational company versus working for a small family firm
• communicating by video-conference versus communicating face to face
• working with an experienced colleague versus working with a trainee
  Example: With a small family firm, I have lots of contact with the owners …

6 Work in small groups.
1 Discuss how you could improve the services and facilities in the building or local area where you work.
2 Present your ideas to the class and give reasons for the improvements.

Tip | *most (of the)*
Use *most* to refer to something in general.
***Most** people have jobs.*
Use *most of the* to refer to a more specific group.
***Most of the** people I know have jobs.*
(NOT: *the most people.*)

The decision gap

When it comes to travel, when do you make that final decision to book your flight? Six months before flying? A month in advance? A week? The day before?

Research using data from 6.4 million business flight bookings shows the following:

- Women book nearly two days earlier than men.
- The older the traveller, the earlier he or she books it (though in every age group, women always book before men).
- The more frequently someone travels, the shorter the booking time before they fly.
- The difference in decision-making virtually disappears between the genders when it comes to more than 20 flights per year.

The differences in gender decision-making when it comes to travel aren't easily explained, but it certainly has financial implications. On average, women save about $17 per trip, or 2% of the ticket price by booking earlier; so maybe for international businesses with high travel costs, letting an older woman decide on the travel arrangements could bring substantial savings.

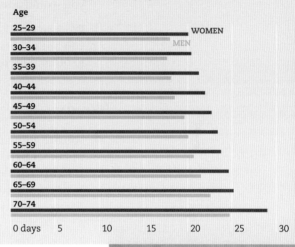

Advance booking (in days) by age of traveller

Discussion

1 When do you normally make your final decision to book a flight? How does your answer compare with the information on the chart?

2 Are you surprised by the results in the chart with regard to gender and age? Why/Why not?

3 How much do you trust the information from research like this? Give reasons for your answer.

Task

Work in small groups of three or four.

1 You have been asked by your company to do more research into how different people make decisions. Make a list of five or six everyday workplace tasks that involve people making decisions (e.g. when to recruit more staff, when to place an order, when to book your annual leave, etc.).

2 Design a questionnaire about these decision-making tasks that will find out more about people's decision-making process. For example, questions might include 'How far in advance do you normally decide to book your annual leave?'

3 When your questionnaire is ready, interview people in the other groups in the class. Try to interview as many people as possible.

4 Return to your group and compare your questionnaire results. Create a chart showing all the data collected by the group. Present it to the class and draw any conclusions.

Focus

1 Think about a product you bought recently. As a consumer, which of the factors in the list below do you think affected your decision to buy the product? Score each factor between 1 (no effect) and 5 (very big effect).
- the price (e.g. discounts, special offers, etc.) ___
- the need (e.g. something you needed for daily life or something you wanted rather than needed) ___
- the location (e.g. convenience of the shop, position on the shelf, online shopping, etc.) ___
- the brand (e.g. it's the brand you always buy) ___
- the colour and design of the packaging ___
- the mood you were in at the time (e.g. feeling relaxed, feeling unhappy) ___

2 Are there any other important factors that affect your decision-making that you would add to the list in **1**?

3 Work in small groups and take turns to tell the other people about the product you bought and what factors affected your decision-making. When you listen to other people, ask further questions about why they bought the product.

Mood

4 You are going to watch an interview with Professor Nancy Puccinelli about customer behaviour. Before you watch the video, match the words and phrases 1–12 to their definitions a–l.

1 undercurrent	a	scientifically
2 innate ability	b	preference, often not based on fair judgement
3 visceral	c	powerful effect
4 subtle cues	d	based on strong emotional feelings instead of careful thought
5 impact	e	a skill you are born with
6 salient	f	hidden activity or cause
7 empirically	g	important or noticeable
8 bias	h	signs that are not obvious
9 procurement	i	purchasing/buying
10 default attentional system	j	something which makes us make a decision based on our 'common sense' or general experience
11 left and right visual fields	k	a natural way the brain always pay attention to something
12 heuristic cues	l	the range of vision humans tend to have either to one side or the other

5 01 Watch the first part of the interview with Nancy Puccinelli. Number topics A–C in the order she talks about them (1–3).
A how some people are good at recognizing other people's moods ___
B how our everyday moods affect our decision-making as consumers ___
C how a sales person can respond to customer moods effectively ___

6 ▶01 Watch the video again and answer questions 1–5.
1 What 'undercurrent' affects our decision-making all the time?
2 Why might we be 'down in the dumps'?
3 What can have dramatic effects on how we're perceiving and interacting with our environments?
4 In her example of the wine store, what mistake does the sales person make?
5 If the sales person had noticed the customer's anxiety, how should they have responded?

7 Have you ever made a bad decision because you were anxious, tired or 'down in the dumps'? What happened? Tell the class.

Price

8 In the next part of the interview, Nancy Puccinelli comments on the best position to show the price. Before you watch, look at the advert for a fizzy drink and circle where you think the best position for the price is.

9 ▶02 Now watch the second part of the interview with Nancy Puccinelli and check your prediction in **8**.

10 ▶02 Try to remember if statements 1–5 are true (*T*) or false (*F*). Then watch the video again and check.
1 Before the study, Professor Puccinelli expected the position of the price to make no difference. ___
2 It was found that all retailers tend to put their prices in the same position. ___
3 The right side of the brain controls our attention so we tend to notice things more on the left side of what we see compared to the right side. ___
4 It is thought that the dominant visual field also affects how we read words and numbers. ___
5 Professor Puccinelli and her team have only tried this experiment once. ___

11 Work in small groups and discuss these questions.
1 When you go shopping, where do you normally see the prices?
2 How much do you think the location of prices affects your decision to buy something?

Gender

12 ▶03 In the third part of the interview, Nancy Puccinelli describes some research into how men and women make decisions when shopping. Watch the video and <u>underline</u> *men* or *women* in these conclusions from the research.
1 *Men / Women* spend more time examining and reading an advertisement.
2 In most households, *men / women* are responsible for around 80% of the household purchasing.
3 *Men / Women* use physiological 'short-cuts' to decide if something is a good deal or not.
4 *Men / Women*'s judgement is influenced if the colour of the price is red.
5 *Men / Women* have a greater ability to remember the price of a product.

13 Work in small groups and discuss questions 1–3.
1 Are your company's products or services aimed more at either men or women?
2 Overall, are men or women usually responsible for ordering and buying your products?
3 Do you think the research into gender could have any implications for your business?

Applying the research

14 Work in small groups. Prepare a proposal for a retail business with a chain of shops that is looking to improve its customer experience. Having listened to Nancy Puccinelli's research findings, hold a meeting to discuss what action can be taken in your client's outlets. Discuss each item on the agenda and draw up a plan with a list of action points.
1 customer moods and how sales staff should respond
2 location and colours of prices on products
3 advertising to men and women

15 Form new groups. Present and compare your list of action points.

Glossary
across the board in every case
all over the map different in every way
down in the dumps feeling unhappy
fine print detailed information that you have to read carefully
I should pass I shouldn't do/buy something
lo and behold an idiomatic expression to introduce surprising news
set me back informal phrase meaning 'cost me'

7 Outsourcing

Starting point

1 What is outsourcing?

2 Does your company or a company you know outsource any of its production or services?

3 What kinds of work do you think a company can outsource?

Working with words | Outsourcing

1 Work with a partner. Look at the title of the article below. Discuss what you think it will say about outsourcing.

2 Read the article and find out if your predictions in 1 were correct.

THE RISE AND FALL OF OUTSOURCING

China probably provides the majority of outsourcing for global manufacturing firms, but when it comes to **offshore locations** for service industries, no other country comes close to India. Take the IT industry. A whole range of products such as cars, Disney animation and Windows software rely on the **skilled workers** of India. It's estimated that about two thirds of all offshore IT work is carried out in India. Similarly, nearly fifty per cent of all **business process outsourcing** (BPO) services are now based in India.

The growth of outsourcing in India began in the early part of the twenty-first century when western businesses realized they could outsource routine work in order to concentrate on their **core activities**. India offered the **outside expertise** needed because of its ready supply of highly qualified graduates with English-language skills. The **sector** grew quickly, and by 2010 it employed around a million people.

Since then, an estimated two million business-services jobs have shifted overseas from the USA and Europe to countries such as India, China and Brazil. The revenue from **export growth** in a country like India also allowed greater investment in **infrastructure** and **training facilities**, so that now the country is able to offer even greater expertise to multinational companies, especially in IT.

However, there are now signs that the outsourcing opportunities are slowing down. There are three key reasons for this: one reason is that salaries in the sector have risen very quickly – ironically – because of its financial success. As a result, western businesses don't make the **cost-savings** they once did. In addition, a lot of companies have already outsourced all the IT and BPO work they can – there is nothing left to outsource. Finally, and perhaps more worryingly for the **outsourcing vendors** in countries like India, their clients are starting to relocate parts of their business **closer to home** where they believe they have greater control over areas such as quality, and where their IT and BPO operations are not several time zones away from head office.

Some analysts are predicting that outsourcing as we have known it might come to an end by 2025.

3 Read the article again and answer questions 1–4.

1 How is outsourcing in India different to China?

2 Why were businesses attracted to India in the early part of the twenty-first century?

3 What did the profits from outsourcing allow India to invest in?

4 What are the three reasons why outsourcing might slow down?

4 Match the words in **bold** in the article to the definitions 1–12.
1 part of a country's economy _____
2 basic systems like transport that a country needs to work properly _____
3 a company's main area of work _____
4 companies that sell outsourcing services _____
5 places where people can learn new skills _____
6 an increase in products sold abroad _____
7 people with the training and experience to do a job well _____
8 contracting a business task to an outside service provider _____
9 knowledge or skills provided by an external supplier _____
10 based in a foreign country _____
11 when you find ways to cut your overheads _____
12 nearer to where you are based _____

5 Work with a partner. Make a list of the advantages and disadvantages of outsourcing based on the information in the article and your own ideas.

6 ▶ 7.1 Listen to three people talking about outsourcing. What advantages and disadvantages do they mention? Are any of them the same as your list in **5**?

Speaker	Advantages / Disadvantages
Paula Dale, Politician	
Christian Amiel, Sales Manager	
Chitra Sampat, Call Centre operative	

7 Find the verbs in the list in audio script 7.1 and check which nouns they collocate with. Then complete questions 1–9 with the verbs.

improve   lead to   take   streamline   achieve
develop   get through   gain   free up   create

1 Do you think outsourcing business process tasks will _____ serious job losses in the EU?
2 What strategies could governments _____ to cope with job losses and to _____ more jobs in the EU?
3 What factors cause a company to _____ cost-cutting measures?
4 How do companies that outsource _____ lower overheads?
5 How does outsourcing help companies to _____ their operation and become more efficient?
6 What tasks could they outsource to _____ resources for their core activities?
7 Why can companies that outsource _____ a bigger volume of work?
8 How can a company _____ a competitive edge over rival companies?
9 In what ways can outsourcing _____ quality of life for workers in emerging economies?

8 Work with a partner. Ask and answer the questions from **7**.

>> For more exercises, go to **Practice file 7** on page 118.

9 Work in small groups. Read about Company X.
1 What are the advantages and disadvantages of outsourcing for this company?
2 Present your ideas to the class.

Company X is considering how it can reduce some of its costs and free up resources to concentrate on its core activities. It has recently reviewed the quality and efficiency of its IT section. It has experienced difficulties recruiting experienced IT operatives. In addition it needs to reduce its IT budget. It is currently considering outsourcing the IT section, including its customer help desk, to a specialized computer company in an offshore location which operates 24/7. This will involve cutting 70 jobs in its home office. The offshore company (based in one of the emerging economies) would charge an annual fee for salaries, and administration and maintenance costs. This would be a saving of 45% for Company X.

Business communication | Presenting factual information

Context

Sanjit Kundu works for Business Initiatives Bangalore. The Bangalore region has been singled out as a prime area for European companies to outsource to. Sanjit's role is to inform potential clients about Bangalore's business connections and its IT industry. Sanjit is 'on tour' in Europe and has been invited to make a presentation to GSV Chemicals in Belgium. This international company is considering outsourcing its IT department to a cheaper location.

1 Read the *Context*. Why is Sanjit visiting GSV Chemicals? What reasons do you think he might give to convince them?

2 ▶ 7.2 Listen to Part 1 of Sanjit's presentation and answer questions 1–2.
  1 What are Bangalore's key selling points as a location for outsourcing?
  2 What presentation technique does Sanjit use to keep the audience's attention?

3 ▶ 7.2 Listen again and answer questions 1–2.
  1 What two phrases does Sanjit use to prove his information comes from factual data?
  2 What phrases does Sanjit use to explain the cause of …?
    a Bangalore's educational institutes having international recognition
    b Bangalore becoming the fastest growing city in Asia

4 ▶ 7.3 Listen to Part 2 of the presentation and answer questions 1–3.
  1 Is Bangalore's ability to attract industry a recent development?
  2 What do these figures relate to?
    a 25–28%   b 512   c 64   d 1,000
  3 What is Sanjit's final argument for investing in Bangalore?

5 Complete these sentences from Sanjit's presentation with the pairs of words in the list.

go + leave   looked + move   mentioned + earned   look + figures
notice + chart   looking + see   resulted + changes   turn + attention

  1 I've briefly _____ at the background, so let's _____ on to some business facts.
  2 You will _____ on this _____ the breakdown of traditional industries.
  3 As I _____ earlier, this has _____ us the name 'India's Silicon Valley'.
  4 Let's _____ our _____ to some specific facts on the IT sector.
  5 _____ at this slide, we can _____ it is expected that Indian IT services will continue to grow …
  6 And have a _____ at these _____: more than 1,500 software and outsourcing companies …
  7 Before I _____ today, I'd like to _____ you with some food for thought.
  8 Investment in Bangalore has _____ in dramatic, positive lifestyle _____ for its people.

6 ▶ 7.3 Listen again and check your answers in 5.

>> For more exercises, go to **Practice file 7** on page 118.

Tip | food for thought

Use the phrase *food for thought* with *leave* and *give* when you are giving someone some information which you would like them to consider carefully.

*I'd like to leave you with / give you some **food for thought** … this has resulted in dramatic lifestyle changes for its people.*

Key expressions

Presenting factual information
Statistics show ...
Recent data / Research indicates ...

Explaining cause and effect
Due to ...
As a result of ...
The effect of this is ...
(This) has resulted in ...
Subsequently, ...
A knock-on effect of this ...

Referring to visuals
You will notice on this chart ...
Looking at this slide, we can see ...
Have a look at these figures ...

Moving from one point to another
Let's turn our attention to ...
I've (briefly) looked at ... so let's move on to ...
A further point to mention is ...

Referring backwards
... which relates back to ...
As I mentioned earlier ...
... which I referred to earlier.

Concluding on a strong note
Before I go today, I'd like to leave you with some food for thought ...
The message I'd like to send you away with today is ...

7 Work with a partner. Use these slides to prepare a short presentation about the benefits of outsourcing to Bangalore. Give your presentation to another pair.

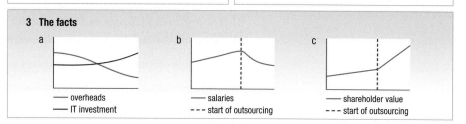

> **1 Advantages of Bangalore**
> * cheap location
> * labour force
>   – skilled
>   – strong work ethic
>   – multilingual
> * established international community

> **2 Your benefits for outsourcing**
> * reduce costs
> * become more international
>   – better communication
>   – networking and synergies
> * invest early in emerging market

> **3 The facts**
> a
> b
> c
> —— overheads
> —— IT investment
> —— salaries
> --- start of outsourcing
> —— shareholder value
> --- start of outsourcing

8 Prepare a short presentation about one of topics 1–3 below.
1 changes in your company or in the economy of your country
2 why a particular company should relocate to your town / city
3 why a potential investor should invest in your company

Make sure you:
* introduce yourself and the topic
* include some facts and figures (these don't need to be true / accurate)
* refer to any changes and explain cause and effect
* conclude on a strong note

Practically speaking | Asking questions after a presentation

1 Work in groups and discuss these questions.
1 When you give a presentation, do you prefer your audience to ask questions during the presentation or at the end? Why?
2 People in the audience have different reasons for asking questions or making a comment. What are some of the different reasons?

2 ▶ 7.4 Listen to four people in the audience at the end of a presentation. Which speaker (1–4) ...?
a refers to a specific point in the presentation ___
b expresses concern and asks the presenter to comment ___
c thanks the presenter and then asks a question ___
d asks the presenter to repeat and give more detail on something ___

3 ▶ 7.4 Listen again and write the three missing words in 1–8.
1 I'd like to _____ _____ _____ a point you made about ...
2 First of all, I'd like to _____ _____ _____ giving us such an interesting presentation.
3 I think everyone _____ _____ _____ .
4 One _____ _____ _____ is this: How long ...?
5 Can I ask you to _____ _____ the slide _____ with the overhead estimates?
6 Could you _____ _____ _____ them in a bit more detail?
7 I'd like to _____ _____ _____ , if that's OK.
8 I was wondering if you'd like to _____ _____ _____ ?

4 Work in small groups. Take turns to give a one-minute presentation to the rest of the group. You can use your ideas from *Business communication* or part of a presentation from your job. After the one-minute presentation, each person in the group must ask a question or make a comment using some of the phrases in **3**. The presenter must answer or comment.

Language at work | The passive

1 Read these two sentences. Which is in the active form and which is in the passive form? Why is each form used?
   1 Thousands of European back-office jobs have been outsourced to India.
   2 EU companies have outsourced thousands of back-office jobs to India.

2 Read these sentences and <u>underline</u> the passive form.
   1 Bangalore's educational institutions have been awarded international recognition by a number of organizations.
   2 It is said that Indian IT services will continue to grow over the next 5 years.
   3 The arguments for outsourcing weren't presented convincingly enough.
   4 Next, the call is automatically transferred overseas to a call centre in Bangalore.

3 Match the sentences in 2 to categories a–d in the *Language point.*

> **LANGUAGE POINT**
>
> The passive form (*be* + past participle) focuses on what happens to something, not who does something. We often use it:
> a when the 'doer' is unimportant or mentioned using *by* ___
> b to describe a process or how something is done ___
> c to avoid saying who is responsible for failure or a mistake ___
> d to make information (e.g. in the news) more impersonal ___

>> For more information, go to **Grammar reference** on page 119.

4 Read these sentences. Which sound natural in the active form? Which would sound more natural in the passive form? Change them into the passive.
   1 Somebody stores a lot of our sensitive information in secure remote sites.
   2 Somebody phoned you while you were out at lunch.
   3 Somebody must know where Jason has gone.
   4 Workers will close the road for repairs for two weeks.
   5 You can't use the lift today because someone is servicing it.

5 Use the passive to rephrase sentences 1–5 to avoid saying who is responsible.
   Example: *I'm afraid I didn't get your email – my colleague deleted it by mistake.*
   I'm afraid I didn't get your email – **it was deleted** *by mistake.*
   1 I'm afraid you're being made redundant. *I have made the decision and it's final.*
   2 I can't make a copy of the letter because *Jo hasn't fixed the photocopier yet.*
   3 *John in the post room sent the package yesterday,* so it should arrive today.
   4 These cuts are unavoidable, and *I am making them to try and save money.*
   5 I can assure you that *someone will deal with your complaint.*

6 Use the passive to rephrase these sentences so they are more impersonal.
   Example: *They think that the company will open an office in Electronics City.*
   It is thought *that the company will open an office in Electronics City.*
   1 *People say* that Singapore's very nice, but I've never been there myself.
   2 *Everyone knows* that Indian software engineers are extremely skilled.
   3 *Most people think* that property in London is a bit overpriced.
   4 *People believe* that Microsoft is interested in expanding its operations in China.
   5 *Some people expect* that outsourcing overseas will decrease in the next five years.

>> For more exercises, go to **Practice file 7** on page 119.

7 Work with a partner. Think of recent news in the media. Then rewrite 1–3 to report the news impersonally.
   1 People at work think …
   2 A lot of people believe that …
   3 Everyone says that …

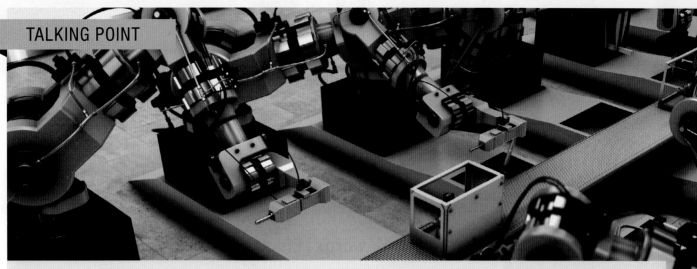

TALKING POINT

Outsourcing to robots

Although robots in the workplace are common in routine manufacturing processes, we have yet to see the robot revolution really take off. However, it is thought that around 35% of current jobs are at risk over the next 20 years from automation. The jobs most at risk include call centre workers and telephone sales people, basic accounting roles such as bookkeeping, and routine secretarial work.

At-risk jobs also tend to be those which are outsourced and so businesses are starting to compare the costs of outsourcing with the costs of using robotic software and hardware. In a study by the management consultancy Deloitte called *The robots are coming*, it's estimated that an offshore full-time worker is 35% cheaper than a worker based in the UK. However, a robot could be around 90% cheaper. Unlike humans, robots also work 24/7 with very few errors.

How do I know if my job is at risk from robots in the future?

At work, do you need to ...?

1 complete the same tasks every day ☐
2 negotiate with clients ☐
3 work in small spaces ☐
4 help other people ☐
5 assemble objects ☐
6 persuade people ☐
7 write reports and work on spreadsheets ☐
8 have new ideas and be creative ☐

If you mainly ticked the odd numbers, your job is at risk. If you ticked the even numbers, your job is probably safer.

Discussion

1 Does your industry make use of robots in any way? How?

2 As more robots are used in the future, how might your industry be affected?

3 According to the article, what kind of financial savings could be made by using robots? Do you think this will be the main consideration in the future? Why?

Task

1 Work with a partner. Answer the questions in the text above. Then tell your partner what the answers say about your job in the future? Do you agree with the results of the test? Why/Why not?

2 Work in groups of four. Your company manufactures and exports clothing. It is planning to replace 50 employees with robots over the next three years. You are going to take part in a discussion and negotiation.

Work in two separate pairs.

• Pair A: You are the managers. Make a list of reasons why using robots will be good for the company and why the redundancies are necessary. Be prepared to convince the other pair why it's good for the company.

• Pair B: You represent the employees. Make a list of reasons why replacing humans with robots is not good for the employees and the company. Try to convince the managers to change their minds.

3 When both sides are ready, present your arguments and try to reach an agreement.

8 Employees

Starting point

1 Why do employees leave a company?

2 What are some of the ways employers can encourage them to stay?

Working with words | Employers and employees

1 Have you ever worked for a business and owned shares in it? As an employee, do you think it would change your attitude to working for the company?

2 Read the article and answer questions 1–4.
   1 Why were the employees at Classic Motor Cars surprised?
   2 Why didn't the owners sell it to another company?
   3 How will the new company be organized?
   4 Why does Luke Martin think employees will work a little bit harder?

EMPLOYER GIVES AWAY CLASSIC CAR COMPANY TO EMPLOYEES

Sixty employees, including seven apprentices, received quite a surprise when they arrived at work the other day. They all work for Classic Motor Cars, a business set up in 1993. Owners and employers, Peter Neumark and Nick Gold Thorpe announced their plans for retirement and then went on to say that instead of selling the profitable business (last year's turnover was £5.2 million) to new owners, they would give the company to the employees. Peter Neumark said that he 'couldn't think of a better set of owners' to run the firm.

The new company will be run as an employee-ownership trust which means that each member of staff owns shares in the company. There is an operational board in charge of the day-to-day management, but all staff have a say in the running of the company. Luke Martin, who was first employed by the company as an apprentice 12 years ago, summed up the feeling: 'We are all a bit shocked. It took a while to sink in. We've got this amazing opportunity to put ideas on the table and shape a business.

Ex-employer Peter Neumark with the new employee-owners

It gives everyone drive to work a little bit harder when it's your own business.'

The company plans to continue growing and will offer apprenticeships and new employment to six people every year for the next three years. They will start as normal employees and then join the trust after a certain period of time.

3 Do you think this kind of employee-ownership could work in every type of business? Why/Why not?

4 Work with a partner. Find the four forms of the word *employ* in the article. Identify the word form (verb, adverb, adjective or noun) and define each one. Now complete the table with the word forms and definitions of these other forms of *employ*.

	Word form	Definition
self-employed		
unemployed		
employable		
unemployable		
employability		
unemployment		

5 Work with a partner. Look at the words in the list. <u>Underline</u> other forms of these words in the article and identify the form (verb, adverb, adjective or noun). Then write a short definition for each.

apprentice (x2)   *retire*   *profit*   *own*   *operate*   *manage*

6 How common is it for people to change jobs and relocate in your country? What does it depend upon?

7 ▶ 8.1 Listen to two employees talking about their employment history and answer the questions.

Speaker 1
1 What was his job and what is his job now?
2 Why did he change his job?
3 How did he go about getting new employment?

Speaker 2
1 Why was she thinking of changing her job?
2 How did the employer convince her to stay?
3 What has she learnt about people's reasons for staying and leaving their job?

8 Find these pairs of phrases in audio script 8.1. Explain the difference in meaning between the phrases in each pair.
1 career prospects / job opportunities
2 full-time employment / apprenticeship
3 job security / job satisfaction
4 taking early retirement / being made redundant
5 relocate / redeploy
6 being laid off / being unemployed
7 a sideways move / a change of direction
8 a glass ceiling / an opportunity for advancement
9 training / personal development

» For more exercises, go to **Practice file 8** on page 120.

9 Tell your partner about a job change you have made. Why did you make it? How did you go about it?

10 Work in small groups and discuss the statements below. Then present your views to the rest of the class, giving examples from your own experience as appropriate.
1 It is better to persuade people over 55 to take early retirement than to make people redundant based on the length of time in the company.
2 It is better to redeploy staff or promote internally than to appoint outside candidates.
3 Opportunities for advancement and personal development at work lead to greater job satisfaction than a rise in pay.

Business communication | Negotiating with colleagues

Context

Johanna and Dermot are leaders of two different teams in a financial services company. They have been given the task of creating a third team from their existing staff to set up a new branch in another country.

1 When we talk about negotiating, we often think of negotiating with clients and customers. However, we also negotiate with colleagues at work. Which of these things do you discuss and negotiate at work? Who do you negotiate them with?

- when you can take your holiday
- your department's annual budget
- which staff you want in your team
- a pay rise
- flexible working hours
- something else?

2 ▶ 8.2 Read the *Context*. Listen to the first part of a meeting with Johanna and Dermot and answer questions 1–3.

1 What is the problem with choosing the most capable workers to make a third team?
2 How many people would they choose from their two teams, based on individual strengths?
3 Why don't they decide to use contract workers?

3 ▶ 8.2 Who says expressions 1–10? Listen again and tick (✓) Johanna (J) or Dermot (D).

		J	D
1	What we need to decide on today is …	☐	☐
2	The areas we need to discuss are …	☐	☐
3	Let's look at what our options are.	☐	☐
4	What I propose is …	☐	☐
5	If we did that, we'd end up with …	☐	☐
6	How about we look at …?	☐	☐
7	Supposing we stretch the budget a little …	☐	☐
8	That'll solve the problem.	☐	☐
9	It just wouldn't work if …	☐	☐
10	OK, I'm happy with that.	☐	☐

4 ▶ 8.3 Listen to the second part of the meeting. Johanna and Dermot are negotiating the new team. Correct the notes Johanna made at the meeting.

Tip | what

Use *What* at the beginning of a statement to explain what you're going to say
***What** I propose is …*
***What** I suggest is …*
***What** I think is …*

Meeting with Dermot – Team for new branch

Two people to be transferred from my team:

Brett will do the trainees' work if necessary

Timo (trainee) will join the new team

Sabrina – good, has international experience

Deadline from HR: team to be decided by next Monday

Key expressions

Outlining the points for discussion
What we need to decide on today is ...
The areas we need to discuss are ...
Let's look at what our options are ...

Putting forward proposals
One option would be to ...
How about we (look ...)?
What I propose is ...
Let's keep our options open ...
Supposing we (stretch ...), why don't we (take on ...)?

Stating consequences
We'd (have) ..., if we did that.
That'll solve the problem.
It just wouldn't work if we (took on ...).
Unless we (get ...), we won't (be sending ...).

Bargaining
I could offer you ..., but I'd expect ...
If you guarantee ..., I'd let you have ...
I'll be happy (for/to) ... provided you ...

Reaching agreement
I'm happy with that.
I can live with that.
That sounds like a plan/deal.

Summarizing the situation
Let's just summarize the situation ...
So (what) have we got so far?
So, a quick recap ... If I ..., you'll ...

5 ▶ 8.3 Listen again. Number these sentences in the order you hear them (1–8).
Let's just summarize the situation. _1_
I'll be happy for Brett to be on the team, provided you replace one of the trainees with someone experienced. ___
Unless we get this list to HR before Friday, we won't be sending anyone. ___
I can live with that. ___
I could offer you three, but I'd expect three from your team, too. ___
So, a quick recap: if I send Brett ..., you'll send Sabrina ... ___
If you guaranteed Brett, I'd let you have Jamie, Pascale and Timo. ___
That sounds like a plan! _8_

>> For more exercises, go to **Practice file 8** on page 120.

6 Work with a partner. Student A is the employer. Student B is the employee. Read this information and think about your position. What will you negotiate?

> A major new client has been acquired and your employer needs you to help with some training. Unfortunately, this coincides with a holiday you have booked.
>
> **Employer:** Decide why you need this employee for the training at this time. What alternatives can you offer your employee?
>
> **Employee:** What alternatives can you offer your employer so you don't have to rearrange your holiday? Or if you do have to change the holiday, what will you want in return?

Start your negotiation. Use the stages and phrases in the *Key expressions* box.

7 Work in groups of four.
1 Pair A, turn to page 137. Pair B, turn to page 139. Read the information and prepare for the negotiation.
2 When you are ready, carry out the negotiation. Report the results to the class.

Practically speaking | Making quick requests

1 When you need help with something at work, who do you ask first? Why?

2 ▶ 8.4 Listen to six short conversations. What help does the first speaker want in each conversation? Does the second speaker agree to help?

3 ▶ 8.4 Listen again. How does the second speaker respond to each request 1–6? How does the first speaker reply when the response is negative?
1 Do you have a minute? _____
2 Could you just have a quick look at my computer? _____
3 Would you mind checking ...? _____
4 Excuse me, am I disturbing you? _____
5 Could you spare a few minutes? _____
6 Can you give me a hand with ...? _____

4 Which of the phrases in **3** are more formal (*M*) or less formal (*L*)?

5 Work with a partner. Read these situations and have short conversations. Decide on the appropriate level of formality.
• You need a client's email address.
• You need confirmation whether a business trip is taking place.
• You need help opening an email attachment.
• You need ideas for a retirement present for your boss.
• You want to swap shifts.
• You need to make an appointment for an appraisal.

Language at work | *If* clauses

Time · IF · Cost · **Quality**

1 Read about the *IF triangle*. Why is it called this? Do you think it's a useful way to look at negotiating?

> **The 'IF triangle'**
> When you start a negotiation, it's always useful to start a sentence with 'if'. The 'IF triangle' shows that we usually negotiate three types of things: time, quality and cost. You can usually be flexible on two of these, but never on three. For example, you can have something made quickly at good quality, but you will have to pay more for it.

2 Read these sentences from different negotiations. Which parts of the *IF triangle* are they negotiating in each one? Write *time*, *cost* or *quality*.

a I'll work over the weekend if you pay me overtime. _____

b If you don't fix this fault by the end of today, we won't pay the balance. _____

c If we included a five-year lease instead of two, would you sign the agreement today? _____

d I'd need some kind of money-back guarantee this time if the response rate to the advert was as low as this again. _____

3 ▶ 8.5 Which word or words in a–d in **2** can the words in the list replace? Listen and check.

unless   provided   supposing   in case

4 Answer the questions in the *Language point*.

> **LANGUAGE POINT**
>
> 1 Which sentences in **2** refer to a situation which has a high possibility of happening? Which sentences refer to a situation which is more imaginary?
> 2 Which sentences in **2** use the first conditional and which sentences use the second conditional? Which verb forms are used in each conditional?
> 3 Match the four alternative ways of saying *if* in **3** to the meanings a–d.
>   a if not _____
>   b if and only if _____
>   c just imagine _____
>   d because something might happen _____

>> For more information, go to **Grammar reference** on page 121.

5 Work with a partner. Take turns to complete these sentences from negotiations using the words in *italics* and your own ideas.

1 I could probably get you a better discount *provided* …
2 We can't give you a guaranteed delivery time *unless* … / *in case* …
3 *Supposing* I agreed to an extra 14 days' credit, would …?
4 *Unless / Provided* you take out a year's subscription …
5 We offer free customer support *in case* … / *as long as* …
6 *Supposing* I finished those sales figures for you …?

>> For more exercises, go to **Practice file 8** on page 121.

6 Work with a partner. Turn to page 137.

1 Read the information. Work together to think of arguments that both the manager and employee could make.
2 Choose to be the manager or employee. Have a discussion and try to reach an agreement.

Flow

Staff turnover and staff retention is one of the biggest challenges (and costs) in any business. Retaining employees is about matching the task to their level of skills and abilities. When employees are not challenged, they become bored and unproductive. When they are challenged too much, they become frustrated and give up. So managing employees is all about achieving 'flow'. Flow happens when an employee is challenged at or near their maximum skill level. Employees in a state of flow lose track of time and experience true job satisfaction.

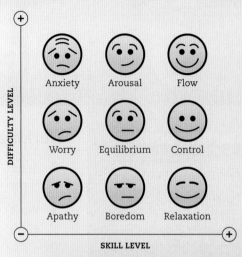

Discussion

1 In your type of business, is there high staff turnover? How much of a challenge is staff retention?

2 What are some of the different ways in which employers can retain staff?

3 Do you think it's always possible for a manager to give employees a task where they achieve 'flow'? Why/Why not?

Task

1 Work with a partner. Read about three employees. Discuss their situation and match them to a face on the diagram.

- Ryan has just started working in a restaurant. He has completed a two-year course in catering and applied for the job in order to work as an assistant to the head chef. For the first month he has been chopping vegetables every night and washing up.

- Susan has worked as an assistant for a year in the marketing department. She's been responsible for basic clerical duties. Recently the events manager left and a suitable replacement has not been found yet. With no background or training, Susan has been asked to take on many of the organizational duties, including setting up promotional events.

- Ian has worked in the design department of an IT company for three years. He's a good team worker and clients like his work. For the first time, he's been put in charge of planning a project with a key client in which he can select his own team.

2 List four or five tasks which you regularly do in your job. Then place those tasks on the diagram in terms of difficulty level and skill level and decide which face represents how you feel about each task. Which tasks make you feel in a state of 'flow'?

3 Work with a partner. Tell each other about your answers in 2 and give your reasons. If your partner doesn't feel challenged enough at work, try to give him/her some advice.

9 New business

Starting point

1 Why do people start their own business?

2 What are the challenges of setting up a new business?

3 What kind of person starts a new business? What makes a successful entrepreneur?

Working with words | Starting up a new business

1 Before you start a new business, how can you test if your idea is likely to be successful?

2 Work with a partner. Look at the title of the article and discuss what 'start-up' and 'pop-up' might mean. Now read the article and compare your ideas.

START-UPS WITH POP-UPS

In 1999 three friends saw a **gap in the** drinks **market**. They spent six months and £500 developing fruit smoothies and then they sold their drinks from a **pop-up stall** at a weekend music festival. Above the stall was a sign which said: 'Should we give up our jobs to make these smoothies?' and people were asked to throw their empty cups into bins marked 'Yes' or 'No'. 'Yes' won and the Innocent brand was born.

The story of Innocent drinks is one that brings hope to all **would-be entrepreneurs**. The three founders saw an immediate **return on their investment** in a pop-up, and the business now **turns over** £100 million a year and the company employs 275 people. It was taken over by Coca-Cola in 2013, which has at least a 90% share. As for the three original founders, they still own part of Innocent and have set up an **investment fund** called 'Jam Jar Investments' to give **financial backing** to new businesses. It's all a long way from that pop-up at the music festival.

A pop-up is defined as anything from a burger van to a market stall that serves as a **temporary outlet**. Companies like Innocent have proved that pop-ups can form part of a serious **business model** and a recent UK study found that many entrepreneurs now include pop-ups as part of their marketing strategy. Launching a pop-up store is a cheap way to test the market and it can also generate quick sales to help with **start-up capital** without necessarily relying on investment from a **venture capitalist**.

Typically, pop-ups should be located anywhere with crowds such as at football matches or rock concerts. Another option is to rent an empty shop for a few weeks on a high street. Pop-up stores are proving especially popular with online businesses because it's an effective way to meet new customers face-to-face. Collecting their details allows a start-up to email afterwards with news about the products and – of course – invite customers to the next pop-up.

3 Read the article again and answer questions 1–4.
1 How did the founders of Innocent get customer feedback on their smoothies?
2 Nowadays, how do the founders help other new businesses?
3 How does a pop-up reduce a new business's costs?
4 What advice does the article give about where to locate a pop-up?

4 Would the idea of a pop-up work in your business? Why/Why not?

5 Match the words in **bold** in the article to the definitions 1–11.

1 money to help and support someone's business _____
2 money to set up a business _____
3 a place to sell something for a short period of time _____
4 people who would like to try and start their own business _____
5 the way a business operates to make money _____
6 an amount of money from people who will invest in a business _____
7 to do business worth a particular amount of money _____
8 opportunity to sell something not yet available _____
9 temporary place to sell your products _____
10 someone investing in a business in return for part of its profits _____
11 profit from putting money into a business _____

6 Complete the advice about funding a start-up using the words from **5**.

For any would-be [1]_____, the first challenge is to spot a gap in the [2]_____. When you think you have your new product or service, the next challenge is to raise enough start-up [3]_____ to set up the business. A bank loan is one option if you can show you have a good business [4]_____ for the operation of your business plus a well-written plan with financial estimates. Another option is to get support from an investment [5]_____. By working with investors, you get the financial [6]_____ you need and you can also draw on the experience of the investors. The downside is that they will want a share of the profits. To minimize your spending at the beginning, consider doing a pop-up by renting a temporary [7]_____ during a busy event. It's a good way to get started and may even get a useful return on your [8]_____.

7 ▶ 9.1 Listen to James Murray Wells talking about his business. Make notes on:

- type of business
- start-up finance
- biggest challenge
- marketing
- advice

8 ▶ 9.2 Listen to extracts from 9.1. What adjectives follow adverbs 1–6?

1 completely _____
2 very _____
3 absolutely _____
4 extremely _____
5 incredibly _____
6 totally _____

9 Read the *Tip*. Study the adverbs + adjectives in **8** and answer questions 1–2.

1 Which adverbs are used with gradable adjectives such as *good*?
2 Which adverbs are used with ungradable adjectives such as *perfect*?

Tip | Gradable and ungradable adjectives

Gradeable adjectives describe qualities that can exist in different strengths: *good, kind, nice, important, expensive, generous, helpful, risky, profitable, difficult*.
Ungradeable adjectives describe qualities that already express an extreme (or limit): *perfect, terrible, fantastic, impossible, outrageous, useless, ridiculous, wonderful*.

10 Work with a partner. Use adverbs and adjectives to respond to the statements.
Example: It's absolutely ridiculous that the bank won't lend us any money!

1 The bank has refused to give us a loan.
2 What's it like working for yourself?
3 I've just been nominated for the 'Entrepreneur of the Year' award.
4 Our business start-up is losing €50,000 a week.
5 The investors wanted an 80% share of my new business in return for the money.

>> For more exercises, go to **Practice file 9** on page 122.

11 Work in small groups. Choose one of these business ideas or your own idea.

A collapsible scooter that you can take on the train or put in the boot of your car to use in busy cities to avoid traffic. You plan to import these scooters from the US and sell them to customers in your own country.

A fleet of self-service, pay-as-you-go cars for urban commuters. Users are given a special PIN number to access the cars (which are located in designated parking places). Users pay a membership fee and then have to pay a fee based on the amount of time they use the car.

1 What's your opinion of the business idea? How successful could it be?
2 What help might someone need setting up this business? Who could they approach for finance? What advice would you give?
3 What problems or challenges might the business face?

Context

Maintaining contacts with business colleagues is important as their help or expertise may be useful at a later date. Three business people have contact with former colleagues and ask for assistance with a business venture.

Business communication | Maintaining contacts

1 Think of the last time you had a chance encounter with someone you hadn't seen or heard from for a long time. Describe the meeting. How did you feel? What did you talk about?

2 ▶ 9.3 Read the *Context*. Listen to three conversations and choose a piece of information from each category in the table to describe each one. Write the number of the conversation in the correct space. There are two extra pieces of information in each column.

Situation		Relationship	
A phone call at work	___	College friends	___
At a trade fair	___	Ex-work colleagues	___
In a taxi queue	___	Business acquaintances	___
At an airport	___	Customer/supplier	___
In a coffee shop	___	Competitors	___

Recent past information		Favour requested	
Found present job by chance	___	Contacts in Internet insurance business	___
Married a French woman	___	New local member of staff	___
Had a promotion	___	Business contacts	___
Business has lost customers	___	A new job	___
Works in car industry	___	Venture capital	___

3 Which conversation is …?
a more formal ___
b neutral ___
c less formal ___

4 Match 1–8 to a–h to make phrases.

1 I'm not sure … ___
2 I haven't … ___
3 What have … ___
4 How's … ___
5 It's good to … ___
6 That's actually … ___
7 The thing is, I'm … ___
8 I'll certainly … ___

a work?
b looking for someone to work with us …
c the reason why I'm calling.
d think about it.
e seen you for ages.
f you been doing?
g hear from you.
h if you remember me.

5 ▶ 9.3 Listen to conversation 1 again and check your answers.

6 Put the phrases in **4** into these categories.
a greeting an old friend/colleague _____
b asking about work/life _____
c changing the subject to introduce a favour _____
d asking a favour _____
e responding to a request for a favour _____

7 Turn to audio script 9.3. Underline all the phrases in conversations 2 and 3 which match the categories in **6**. Compare the level of formality of the phrases used in all three conversations.

>> For more exercises, go to **Practice file 9** on page 122.

Tip | *anyway*

Use *anyway* to return to an earlier topic, change the subject or end the conversation.

***Anyway**, you mentioned changes. What's been happening?*
***Anyway**, what have you been up to?*

Key expressions

Greeting old friends/acquaintances

I'm not sure if you remember me.

I haven't seen you for ages …

It's lovely to hear from you.

What are you doing here?

When was the last time we saw each other?

It's been a long time since we've been in contact.

Asking about life/work

What about you?

What have you been doing / up to?

How's work?

How's life treating you?

How's business with you?

Are you still …?

Changing subject

That's actually the reason why I'm calling.

By the way, could you do me a favour?

With that in mind, maybe I could ask you a favour.

Asking a favour

The thing is, I'm looking for someone to …

Could you put me in touch with … since you …?

We are looking for… and I wondered if …

Responding to a request

I'll certainly think about it.

Let's chat/talk about that over dinner.

It sounds an interesting proposal.

Send me the details …

That isn't something I can decide on right now.

---

8 Work with a partner. Have two conversations using the flow chart. Take turns to be Student A. Use the prompts numbered 1 for the first conversation and the prompts numbered 2 for the second.

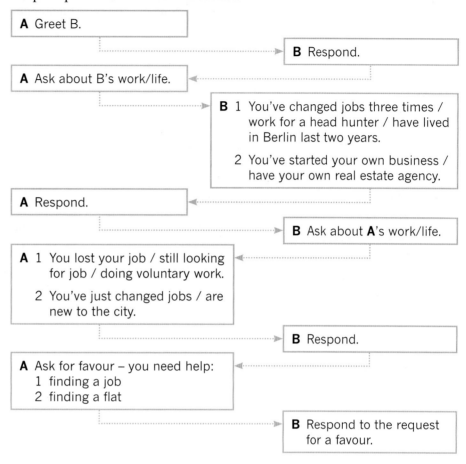

A Greet B.

B Respond.

A Ask about B's work/life.

B 1 You've changed jobs three times / work for a head hunter / have lived in Berlin last two years.

2 You've started your own business / have your own real estate agency.

A Respond.

B Ask about **A**'s work/life.

A 1 You lost your job / still looking for job / doing voluntary work.

2 You've just changed jobs / are new to the city.

B Respond.

A Ask for favour – you need help:
1 finding a job
2 finding a flat

B Respond to the request for a favour.

9 Write down three true and three untrue events which have happened to you over the last few years.

1 Work with a partner. Have a conversation. Greet each other and find out as much information about your partner's recent past as possible.

2 Decide which information was true/untrue.

3 Check with your partner if you were correct.

Practically speaking | Avoiding saying 'no'

1 In some cultures, people avoid saying 'no' directly. When someone makes a request, how easy is it for you to say 'no'? What does it depend upon?

2 ▶ 9.4 Listen to three people making requests. Tick (✓) four expressions they use to avoid saying 'no'.

I'd love to help, but I think I'm away … ☐

You know I'd normally help, but at the moment … ☐

I'm afraid I don't have any spare time … ☐

Can I get back to you on that one later? ☐

Have you tried asking anyone else in the office? ☐

Try me again in a few months' time. ☐

3 Work with a partner. Take turns to request and respond to situations 1–4.

1 Do you think you could have a look at the results from our customer survey and prepare a report for the team meeting on Monday?

2 I'm supposed to be making a presentation at the investor relations meeting next Friday, but I want to take a day's leave. Could you stand in for me?

3 Could you stay late tonight and help with the stock taking?

4 You're just the person we need for helping out at the conference next weekend. Are you free?

Language at work | Present perfect simple and continuous

1 Underline the present perfect simple and continuous verbs in 1–5.

1 Our company has secured a huge contract with Mobelitec.
2 GBF have been keeping me very busy.
3 Since you left GBF, life's been extremely hectic.
4 Since last month, I've been commuting between France and Belgium.
5 She's lived in Brussels for years.

2 Answer the questions in the *Language point*.

> **LANGUAGE POINT**
>
> Match the tenses in sentences 1–3 in **1** to situations a–c.
> a a continuous activity that started in the past and is still going on
> b a state that started in the past and is unchanged.
> c a finished activity with an end result
>
> Compare sentences 4 and 5 in **1**, and answer questions d–e.
> d Which tense suggests something is temporary?
> e What is the difference between the use of *for* and *since*?

>> For more information, go to **Grammar reference** on page 123.

3 Choose the best ending (a or b) for each sentence and explain your choice.

1 I've worked out a final price   a but I'm still waiting for some figures.
   I've been working out a final price   b and it's lower than the original estimate.

2 I've been calling Mrs Fischer   a but I can't get through to her
   I've called Mrs Fischer   b and left her a message.

3 I've worked with Karen   a because her supervisor is on sick leave.
   I've been working with Karen   b for over 30 years.

4 We've been hiring   a a manager and three supervisors.
   We've hired   b people for the new factory.

>> For more exercises, go to **Practice file 9** on page 123.

4 Complete the sentences with information about you. Then tell your partner.

1 a I've been working on …   b I've worked on …
2 a I've been trying to …   b I've tried to …
3 a I've been reading …   b I've read …
4 a I've been thinking about …   b I've thought about …
5 a I've been watching …   b I've watched …

5 Work with a partner. You have been doing various tasks for setting up a new business. Student A, turn to page 137. Student B, use the information below.

1 Use these prompts to ask questions about the progress your partner has made.
   - sort out insurance?
   - decide on company name?
   - do anything about accounting system?
   - set up website?
   - phone solicitor?

2 Use the information in the table to answer your partner's questions. Say what you have been doing this week and what tasks you have/haven't done.

Ongoing this week	Done	Not done
• Contact estate agents in all locations. • Check local newspapers for business premises to rent. • Research transport links.	• Discuss required features of business location with adviser. • Make list of possible locations.	• Go to any of the possible locations.

6 Give a short presentation about a current company project. Say how long it has been going on, what has already been achieved and what remains to be done.

TALKING POINT

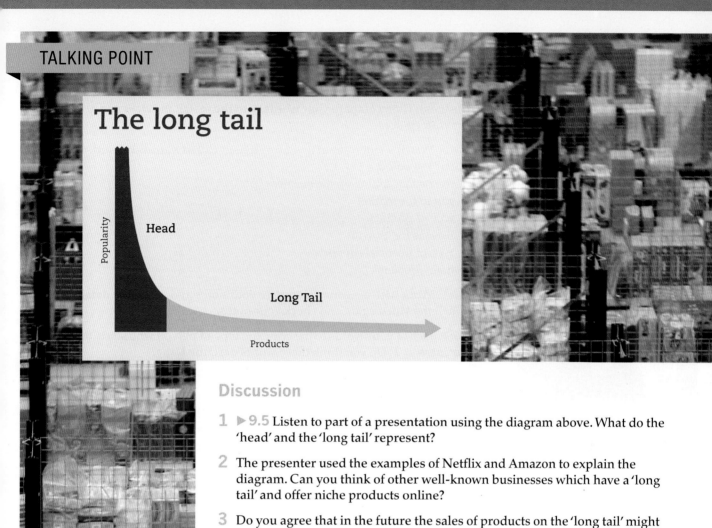

The long tail

Discussion

1 ▶ 9.5 Listen to part of a presentation using the diagram above. What do the 'head' and the 'long tail' represent?

2 The presenter used the examples of Netflix and Amazon to explain the diagram. Can you think of other well-known businesses which have a 'long tail' and offer niche products online?

3 Do you agree that in the future the sales of products on the 'long tail' might become more profitable than the 'head' for many businesses? Why/Why not?

Task

1 Work in groups of four. You are consultants giving advice to three small businesses with shops on the high street. Read each profile and discuss what products and services are part of the 'head' and how they could develop more products or services that are niche (but still profitable).

- A shop which sells posters, photographs and picture frames. Their best-selling products are usually posters of popular musicians and posters of well-known films.

- A shop which sells kitchen appliances and stocks some spare parts for recent models of refrigerators and cookers. It also does some repairs and stocks spare parts for newer models.

- A musical instrument shop with two rooms at the back for music lessons. The shop also sells books on how to learn to play instruments and books of modern music by popular bands.

2 Work with another group. Present and compare your ideas. How similar or different are they?

3 Think about and make notes on your own company by answering these questions.

- Which of your products or services are part of the 'head'?

- Do you already offer niche products or services which are part of a 'long tail'?

- How could your company increase the length of its 'long tail' and therefore create new business in the future?

4 Present your ideas in 3 to the rest of the class.

Preview

In this video lesson, you will watch a short video about Katia Burghard who set up her own business. Then you'll watch an interview with Professor Thomas Hellmann from Saïd Business School talking about what it takes to become an entrepreneur.

Focus

1 Think of three words that describe the type of person who starts their own business. Then compare your words with the rest of the class and give reasons for your choices.

2 ▶01 Watch a video about an entrepreneur called Katia Burghard. Make notes about 1–6 below.
1 reasons for setting up the business
2 gap in the market
3 type of product
4 reasons for growth
5 type of financial support
6 main problems

3 ▶01 Work with a partner. Compare your notes and add more details. Then watch the video again and check your notes.

4 Look back at your words to describe the type of person who starts their own business in **1**. Do you think these words describe Katia?

Being an entrepreneur

5 You are going to watch an interview with Professor Thomas Hellmann about being an entrepreneur. Before you watch the video, match the pairs of words 1–7 to the correct definitions (a or b).
1 characteristic ___ / tendency ___
   a always behaving in a particular way
   b personal quality
2 grit ___ / risk ___
   a situation where you face danger
   b courage and bravery
3 equity ___ / debt ___
   a share of a business
   b amount borrowed and owed
4 grant ___ / crowdfunding ___
   a finance given (e.g. by government) to a business that does not have to be repaid
   b finance raised from large numbers of people via a website (e.g. Kickstarter)
5 loan ___ / lone ___
   a on your own
   b money that has to be repaid (usually with interest)
6 venture capitalists ___ / angel investors ___
   a firms that invest other people's money in new businesses
   b individual people who invest their own money in businesses
7 inspiration ___ / perspiration ___
   a sweat caused from heat, exercise or hard work
   b sudden brilliant new ideas

6 ▶02 Watch the whole interview with Thomas Hellmann. Number topics a–f in the order he talks about them (1–6).
a tendencies of entrepreneurs ___
b reasons for failure ___
c the type of people who become entrepreneurs ___
d the most important characteristic of entrepreneurs ___
e tips for being successful ___
f ways of financing a new business ___

Profile

Professor Thomas Hellmann is the Academic Director of the Entrepreneurship Centre at Saïd Business School. He is a leading international expert in entrepreneurship.

7 ▶03 Watch the first part of the interview again and answer these questions.

1 How easy is it to define the type of person who makes a good entrepreneur?
2 What different types of people become entrepreneurs?
3 What is the attitude of most entrepreneurs towards risk?
4 How do control and optimism relate to being an entrepreneur?
5 How does the work of an entrepreneur compare with someone who works for a company?

8 Thomas Hellmann used the words in the list below. Work with a partner and discuss the ones which you think describe you. Based on your answers, do you both think you would make good entrepreneurs?

risk-taker   hard-working   risk-tolerant   optimistic
willing to take control   risk-seeker

Finance, failure and success

9 ▶04 Look at the list of possible sources of finance, 1–9. Watch the second part of the Thomas Hellmann interview again. Tick (✓) the forms of financing he is positive about. Put a cross (✗) next to those he is negative about. Put a question mark (?) next to those he doesn't comment on.

1 your bank manager ___   6 venture capitalists ___
2 debt ___   7 angel investors ___
3 equity ___   8 crowdfunding ___
4 credit cards ___   9 family and friends ___
5 loans or grants ___

10 Discuss these questions as a class.

1 Why might Thomas Hellmann think that Katia Burghard's form of financing her business was not typical?
2 If you needed finance for a new business, which forms of financing in **9** would you use? Why?

11 ▶05, 06 Watch the last two parts of the interview, in which Thomas Hellmann compares failure and success in entrepreneurship. Make notes in the table and then compare your notes with a partner.

Two reasons for failure	Three reasons for success
1	1
	2
2	3

Glossary

an ecosystem of investors a community of people who put money into businesses

create a dent in the world affect or change the world in some way

enjoy the ride refers to the idea of a ride at a fairground or theme park that is exciting and fun

entrepreneurship is 10% inspiration, 90% perspiration success is mainly due to hard work and not only about having a good idea

pull the plug on this end a project or plan

the lone hero, the lone cowboy someone who always succeeds alone, such as the main character in old American 'Western' films

you have to roll up your sleeves you have to work very hard

Three steps to entrepreneurial excellence

12 Prepare a two-minute inspirational presentation to a group of would-be entrepreneurs entitled 'Three steps to entrepreneurial excellence'. Using the information from the videos and your own ideas, think about the key points and recommendations you will include in each part. Structure your presentation in three parts:

- tendencies and qualities of all entrepreneurs
- choosing the right kind of financing
- success and dealing with failure

13 Give your presentation to the class.

Starting point

1 Is the world a better place with communication technologies? Why/Why not?

2 What communications technology could you personally not live without? Why?

Working with words | Communications technology

1 Look at the chart of some results from a survey. Do you think the results are similar for you? What might be different?

Which online and digital tools are most important for workers?

Email	61%
The Internet	54%
Landline phone	35%
Cell or smartphone	24%
Social networking sites like Twitter, Facebook or LinkedIn	4%

2 ▶ 10.1 Listen to a report on the survey in **1** into the impact of technology on workplace communications. Answer questions 1–4.

1 What percentage of workers in the survey used the Internet in their job?
2 With regard to email and social media, what hasn't happened, despite some predictions in the past?
3 What did the results show with regard to online distractions affecting productivity in the workplace?
4 How have company management attitudes changed towards the Internet in recent years?

3 ▶ 10.1 Complete questions 1–8 with the phrases in the list. One of the phrases is split into two parts. Then listen again and check.

*impact on   integrate into   policy on   limits on
bring about   access to   collaborate with   focuses on*

1 How much do you need to _____ the Internet and mobile technology _____ every part of your workplace?
2 In what ways does digital technology _____ _____ your daily working life?
3 For your job, do you have to have _____ _____ the Internet 24/7, even when you aren't at work?
4 The survey _____ _____ adult Internet users at work. Do you think the results in the chart would be similar for people's home life?
5 Do you often use video communication tools such as Skype to _____ _____ colleagues in other parts of the world on different projects?
6 What is your company's _____ _____ personal use of the Internet?
7 Does your company put any _____ _____ what employees can say or post online?
8 What other changes do you think the Internet will _____ _____ in the future?

4 Work with a partner. Ask and answer the questions in **3**.

5 Read the two articles. Add the missing sentences a–e to 1–5 in the texts.
   a Around 22 million users in Kenya regularly send money this way.
   b Both are good examples of how technology can bring new business to local economies.
   c It delivers free health care to developing nations around the world.
   d That's because so many people rely on mobile phones for daily communication and everyday tasks.
   e They can provide an immediate diagnosis or consultation by email or video link.

Mercy Ships

The global charity Mercy Ships provides the largest floating hospitals in the world. ¹___ One key item of technology used on the ships is the Nikon Coolscope. It's a type of microscope which allows the volunteer to analyse blood and tissue samples in distant locations around the world. Images of the samples obtained from patients are loaded onto the Internet for medical experts to study in land-based hospitals. ²___ The Coolscope can also be used for 'live' sessions during an on-board operation in which a doctor can control the microscope as if he or she is on board with the patient.

Mobile Entrepreneurs

There's a new generation of tech entrepreneurs in Africa who are developing apps for every aspect of life. Ironically, the lack of infrastructure in some parts of the continent (such as no phone landlines) has driven this tech innovation. ³___ For example, instead of using cheques, cash or credit cards, people use money transfer systems such as M-pesa on their mobiles. ⁴___ Another growing business is Sendy which is a Nairobi-based start-up. The app connects local people to motorcycle riders and van drivers who will deliver packages. ⁵___.

6 Work with a partner. Read the articles again and answer questions 1–2.
   1 How has technology improved the service Mercy Ships can provide?
   2 Why is there a new generation of tech entrepreneurs in Africa?

7 Complete the word families in the table for the words from the texts.

Verb	Noun (person)	Noun	Adjective
		technology	technical/technological
analyse			
		consultation	
			developmental/developing
		innovation	
		communication	
connect			
transfer			
		economy	

» For more exercises, go to **Practice file 10** on page 124.

8 Work in small groups. Discuss the changes that communications technology has brought about in your job / company / industry. Make notes under these two headings.

Positive changes	Negative changes

9 Present your views to the class, giving examples from your own experience.

Business communication | Dealing with information on the phone

Context

JC Office Supplies is an international company located throughout Europe. Departments are centralized in certain countries, e.g. Internal Procurement is based in Poland, so employees have to communicate regularly with colleagues overseas as well as with their external clients.

1 How do you prefer to communicate with colleagues and clients, e.g. by email or phone? When is one type of communication better than the other?

2 ▶ 10.2 Read the *Context* then listen to three phone conversations and complete the three forms.

1

PROCUREMENT DEPT. INTERNAL ORDER FORM

Name: *Paola*

Dept: ¹ _____

Country: *Italy*

Order for: ² _____

Order no.: ³ _____

Action: ⁴ _____

2

IT HELP DESK CALL LOG

Caller: *Johann*

Country: *Denmark*

Problem: ⁵ _____

Action: ⁶ _____

3

CUSTOMER SERVICES COMPLAINT FORM

Customer: *Donna Fitzpatrick*

Company: ⁷ _____

Order no.: *560H*

Complaint: ⁸ _____

Action: ⁹ _____

3 ▶ 10.2 Listen again and match the expressions to each conversation 1–3.
a What seems to be the problem? _1_
b How can I help you? ___
c What can I do for you today? ___
d Could you give me the order number? ___
e You mean the screen goes blank? ___
f I'll look into it. ___
g If I understand you correctly ... ___
h Can you tell me when ...? ___
i Could you explain exactly what the problem is? ___
j Let me get this straight. ___
k Could I just clarify what you're saying? ___
l Talk me through it. ___
m What you're saying is ...? ___
n What I'll do is check the figures. ___
o I'll get back to you shortly. ___
p I'll fax it straight to them. ___
q As soon as I've looked into it, I'll call you back. ___
r Will it be ready in time for the deadline? ___

≫ For more exercises, go to **Practice file 10** on page 124.

Tip | *by* and *until*

Use *by* to refer to a deadline or the latest date when something must be finished:
*I need the report **by** Friday.*
Use *until* to refer to a period of time to do something in:
*We have **until** Friday to finish the report.*

Key expressions

Requesting information
What seems to be the problem?
How can I help (you)?
What can I do for you (today)?

Establishing the facts
Can you tell me when (this happened)?
Could you explain exactly what the problem is?
Could you give me (the order number)?
Talk me through (it / what happened).

Clarifying/checking facts
Let me get this straight.
What you're saying is …
You mean …?
If I understand you correctly, …
Could I just clarify what you're saying?

Promising action
I'll look into it.
What I'll do is … and …
I'm going to have to look into this.
I'll get back to you (shortly).
Once I've (checked the details) / As soon as I've (looked into it), I'll call you back.

Referring to time/deadlines
by (Friday) at the latest
by tomorrow / lunchtime / the end of the week
in time for the deadline
as soon as
shortly

4 Work with a partner. You are going to deal with a phone call from a colleague. Student A, turn to page 138. Student B, use the information below. Read your information and take turns to make and receive the call. Make sure you:
- request information about the problem or situation and establish the facts
- clarify the information and check that it is correct
- promise action and confirm deadline

Student B
1 You work in the Sales Department and call the Departmental Administrator.
  Problem: the dates for your business trip have changed.
  Further information: you need the original flight cancelling and a new one booking; this also applies to the hotel.
  Deadline: by next week
2 You work in the Travel and Logistics Department and receive a call from the Customer Services Department.
  Action to promise: email new details as soon as you have them

5 Work with a partner. Decide what phrases the caller and receiver might use in these situations. Then take turns to make and receive a call.
1 A team leader from Operations calls Human Resources. The employment contracts for two new workers are needed by the end of the day – there's already been a delay of six weeks.
2 The Communications Officer from a company calls a printing company. The in-company magazine hasn't arrived and it is due to be sent out to employees tomorrow.

Practically speaking | Resolving problems on the phone

1 What do you say when you answer your mobile phone to a colleague or client in these situations?
- you're on a train and the signal is unreliable
- you can't hear the other person because of the noise around you
- you are about to leave work for the day

2 ▶ 10.3 Listen to three conversations. Answer questions 1–2 for each conversation.
1 What is the situation?
2 How is each situation resolved?

3 ▶ 10.3 Match statements 1–4 to the response a–d. Listen again and check.
1 Sorry, but this'll have to be quick, René, I'm about to board a plane!
2 You're breaking up. I'm afraid I didn't catch that last bit.
3 It's a really bad signal.
4 Look, I'm sorry, but I'm just on my way out. Can I call you back tomorrow?

a Yes, I'm around in the morning. ___
b So now's not a good time to call? ___
c OK. I'll hang up and call you on your landline. ___
d I said, any chance of getting it to me by tomorrow? ___

4 Which statements in **3** indicate there is a problem in communication? Which statements indicate that it isn't a good time to call?

5 Work with a partner. Practise making phone calls in these difficult situations.
1 You're on holiday when your manager calls about an unfinished report.
2 You've gone to visit a client in a remote country location where there is unreliable mobile reception. You call your PA for some figures.
3 You're at the cinema and have forgotten to turn off your mobile. Your colleague calls to remind you about an appointment.
4 You're at a noisy, crowded sports event. A colleague calls to rearrange a meeting.

Language at work | Phrasal verb word order

1 Underline the phrasal verb (verb + particle) in sentences 1–8.
1 Can you call Peter back?
2 Let me read the message back to you.
3 Look through this report, please.
4 Let's put off the decision until next week.
5 Sorry, but you're breaking up.
6 I'll hang up and try your landline.
7 I'd like you to look into this problem before we meet again next week.
8 This new initiative should bring about some positive changes.

2 Match the phrasal verbs in 1 to their meanings, a–h.
a end a phone call ___
b make happen ___
c repeat aloud a message you've taken ___
d have a bad phone connection ___
e read something ___
f return a phone call ___
g investigate ___
h postpone ___

3 Match the phrasal verbs in 1 to categories A–D in the *Language point*.

LANGUAGE POINT

A Some phrasal verbs are <u>not</u> usually followed by an object.
_____ _____

B With some phrasal verbs, the particle usually goes <u>before</u> the object.
_____ _____ _____

C With some phrasal verbs the particle usually goes <u>after</u> the object.
_____ _____

D With some phrasal verbs, the particle can go <u>before or after</u> the object with no change in meaning. The particle goes <u>after</u> the object when the object is a pronoun; e.g. *it*. _____

» For more information, go to **Grammar reference** on page 125.

4 Work with a partner. Make sentences with the phrasal verbs in the list. Then match them to categories A–D in the *Language point*.
Example: *I deal with customer enquiries. = Category B*
deal with   eat out   look out!   put through
look for   come across   write down   speak up

5 Put the words in 1–10 in the correct order. Four sentences have two answers.
Example: *How did you come across in the interview?*
1 How / did / come / in / the / interview / you / across ?
2 fell / project / The / schedule / behind
3 He / carry / instructions / out / my / didn't
4 You / take / challenge / up / should / their
5 Can / deal / you / this / problem / with ?
6 up / Let's / and / cons / weigh / the / pros
7 The / it / consultants / drew / up
8 I'd / to / to / the / next / like / turn / point
9 speed / We / need / to / up / the / team
10 When / the / entrepreneurs / did / set / the / company / up ?

» For more exercises, go to **Practice file 10** on page 125.

6 You'd like a colleague to help you with some work. Write a short email and explain what you'd like her to do. Use four or five phrasal verbs in your email.

7 Work with a partner. Swap your emails and read your partner's email. Now reply to your partner's request for help using some more phrasal verbs.

The telephone card game

Work in small groups. You are going to play a game with lots of different telephone conversations. Each player places a counter on START. Flip a coin to move.
Heads = Move 1 square. Tails = Move 2 squares.

♦ **DIAMONDS** make a question with the phrase and then telephone another player to ask your question.

♣ **CLUBS** move to the nearest player's square and start the telephone conversation.

♥ **HEARTS** choose any player and have a short telephone conversation using the two phrasal verbs.

♠ **SPADES** follow the instructions.

The player who lands on END first is the winner.

START

♣ Move to another player's square and telephone him/her. Ask him/her to solve a problem for you at work.

♦ Can you talk me through …?

END

♦ **2** Could you explain exactly what …?

♥ **9** Choose any player. Have a conversation using:
read back / speak up

♣ **12** A client left a voicemail complaining about a faulty product. Move to another player's square and call him/her back.

♠ **19** You can't get a signal on your phone. Miss a go.

♠ **3** You solve a customer's problem on the phone. Have another go.

♣ **8** Move to another player's square and telephone him/her. Request information about their latest products or services.

♠ **13** Your mobile has a good Wi-fi signal. Have another go.

♥ **18** Choose any player. Have a conversation using:
eat out / write down

♥ **4** Choose any player. Have a conversation using:
break up / call back

♠ **7** The Internet is down. Miss a go.

♥ **14** Choose any player. Have a conversation using:
fall behind / speed up

♦ **17** Can you give me …?

♦ **5** Can you tell me …?

♣ **6** Move to another player's square and telephone him/her. Explain that you are going to be late for the meeting. Explain why.

♦ **15** Can you describe what …?

♣ **16** Move to another player's square and telephone him/her. Check you have his/her correct contact details (numbers, emails, etc.)

11 Change

Starting point

1 What has been the biggest change in your job in the last year?

2 How easy or difficult has it been for you (and the people you work with) to deal with the change?

3 Overall, do you think the change was beneficial?

Working with words | Talking about change

1 When a business or organization proposes changes, what can go wrong?

2 ▶ 11.1 Listen to a presentation about change management and the five steps of the ADKAR® model. Write what each letter stands for.

A _____

D _____

K _____

A _____

R _____

3 ▶ 11.1 Match each step in the ADKAR model in 2 to explanations 1–5. Then listen again and check your answers.

1 People need to accept that change is necessary and feel motivated to support the change. _____

2 Make sure people don't revert to their old ways of working by monitoring processes and recognizing successes. _____

3 Let people know what is changing and how it will affect them. Explain the dangers of not changing at all. _____

4 Check if everyone is able to change, and remove any remaining barriers. _____

5 Your staff need to know how to change and what to do. This might include training in new skills. _____

4 Work in groups and discuss these questions.

1 Do you think the ADKAR model would work in your company/organization? Why/Why not?

2 Which of the five ADKAR steps do you think would be most challenging?

5 Match each pair of verbs from the listening in 2 to the correct definition, a or b.

1 oppose ___ / react ___
   a respond to something by showing feelings or taking action
   b disagree strongly with something

2 resist ___ / prevent ___
   a not accept something and try to stop it from happening
   b stop something from happening

3 implement ___ / revert ___
   a start doing something in the same way you used to do it
   b make something start to happen

4 maintain ___ / support ___
   a make something continue at the same level or standard
   b show you agree with something or someone

5 achieve ___ / affect ___
   a produce a change in someone or something
   b succeed in doing something in a difficult situation

6 Complete the missing words 1–8 in the article. Then look back at exercise **5** to check your answers.

When you first try to ¹i_____ change in an organization, people are naturally concerned about how it will ²a_____ them personally. They tend to ³r_____ to proposals for change in three ways.

The supporters are in favour of change, and will be receptive to your plans. Use their enthusiasm and optimism to persuade others to ⁴a_____ change.

The ambivalent are anxious about change and they may ⁵o_____ some of the plans at first. Be prepared for this resistance by offering the right guidance and training. In the end, they will usually ⁶s_____ your plans.

The opponents will ⁷r_____ any kind of change. They may even be hostile and try to ⁸p_____ you from putting your plans into action. Accept that you will face criticism and that you will need to convince some people more than others.

7 Which of these words and phrases from the article in **6** describe …?
1 worry and uncertainty *concerned*
2 opposition to change _____
3 support and a positive attitude _____

~~concerned~~ anxious in favour of resistance ambivalent
hostile receptive enthusiasm criticism guidance optimism

❯❯ For more exercises, go to **Practice file 11** on page 126.

8 Work with a partner.
1 Which of the three categories of person in **6** would you put yourself in?
2 Use some of the words from **5** and **7** to make statements about how you react to change.

9 Work in groups. Choose ONE of the following changes in your company:
- a new system of flexible working hours and shift system to replace the traditional 9 to 5 working day
- a camera monitor system to increase security in the workplace and to monitor staff behaviour and time-keeping
- a compulsory car-sharing system to reduce the number of people travelling on their own to work

Discuss how you will implement the change. Use the ADKAR model and the questions below.
A How will you make staff aware of the need for the change?
 What resistance do you expect?
D How will you make everyone in favour of the change?
K What training or guidance will you need to offer?
A How will you check if everyone is ready?
 How will you deal with any staff who are not able to change?
R How will you monitor the change and recognize success?

Tip | *affect* and *effect*

Affect (verb) and *effect* (noun) are used to talk about something or someone which has caused a change in something or someone else.
A *How will the takeover **affect** you?*
B *The changes won't **affect** me directly, but they will have an **effect** on the workforce in Spain and Italy.*

Context

FGR is a textiles company based in the UK. Due to fierce global competition, FGR's management called in business consultants to see what changes could be made to help the company work more efficiently. Rachel and Imran are department leaders and have attended the consultants' final meeting. Their task now is to present the consultants' proposed changes to the other heads of department.

Business communication | Presenting future plans

1 Some teams, departments or companies operate a bottom-up management approach where employees are involved in decision and policy making. Work in small groups and discuss questions 1–2.

   1 Who proposes ideas for change and makes the decisions in your company?
   2 What role, if any, do employees play in helping implement change?

2 ▶ 11.2 Read the *Context*. Listen to the presentation given by Rachel and Imran. Complete the missing information 1–5 in these notes.

Consultant's findings

Job losses? _Yes_

How will job cuts be made? [1]_____

Pay freeze? _Probably_

How will we be informed? [2]_____

New management model: _bottom-up management_

When will it be implemented? [3]_____

Friday afternoon ideas forum – potential problem:
[4]_____

Will employees get remuneration? [5]_____

---

3 ▶ 11.2 Match 1–10 to a–j to make expressions from the meeting. Then listen again and check your answers.
   1 As you all know, ___
   2 We'd like to ___
   3 Decisions will definitely ___
   4 Over the next few weeks, we'll be hosting ___
   5 Starting from next month, we'll be putting ___
   6 We're proposing a ___
   7 You may be wondering ___
   8 It's crucial to get the employees ___
   9 This last point is probably going to ___
   10 We're calling ___

   a departmental meetings.
   b Friday afternoon ideas forum.
   c it is likely …
   d on our side.
   e be difficult to administer …
   f if this will work.
   g assure you that …
   h have been made by March …
   i regular updates on our Intranet.
   j on you to be positive …

4 Turn to audio script 11.2. What do the speakers say to …?
   1 hand over to someone else
   2 expand on an idea

   ≫ For more exercises, go to **Practice file 11** on page 126.

Tip | Let's

Use *Let's (do)* rather than *I'd like to (do)* in a presentation to involve your audience and make the situation more personal.

Let's *digress for a few minutes and look at this idea in detail.*

Key expressions

Explaining future events

Over the next few weeks, we'll be …

We plan to keep you informed about …

Starting from next month, we'll be …

Our idea is to …

We're proposing …

Later this year we'll be …

Making predictions

Decisions will definitely have been made by …

Hopefully, the new model will be in place by …

We are fairly certain this will have been carried out by …

This is probably going to be (difficult to …).

Referring to audience concerns

We're well aware of your concerns regarding …

As you all know …

We'd like to assure you that …

Many of you have asked about …

You may be wondering if …

Call for action

It's crucial to …

We're calling on you to be …

Giving more detail

Let's digress for a moment and look at this in more detail.

Handing over to someone

I'd like to pass the next point over to …

(John) will now deal with …

5 Work with a partner. Take turns to present situations 1–6 using an appropriate phrase. Each person should use a different phrase for each situation.

1 Explain a future planned event, e.g. increase of staff numbers by 5%.

2 Make an informed prediction about the financial status of your/a business area.

3 Refer to your staff's concerns that the company may close and reassure them.

4 Indicate that you are going to expand on a point about a new flexitime system.

5 Hand over the presentation about your department to a colleague from a different department.

6 You've made a presentation about new, higher sales targets. Give your audience a 'call for action'.

6 Choose one of the topics below and prepare a mini-presentation (two minutes) about proposed changes. Include at least one phrase from each category in *Key expressions*. The content doesn't have to be true for your job or company.

- your department
- holiday procedure
- use of the Internet in work time
- overtime rules
- your company's product/service
- working hours

7 Give your presentation to a partner. Your partner should listen and check which phrases you used from *Key expressions*.

Practically speaking | Giving both sides of the argument

1 When discussing changes at work, why is it important to consider both sides of an argument, for and against? Give an example of when you have to understand the other point of view at work.

2 ▶ 11.3 Listen to four short conversations about new proposals at work. For each conversation, make notes about the arguments for and against.

	For	Against
1 Changing the team meeting		
2 Restructuring		
3 Learning Spanish		
4 Extending office hours		

3 ▶ 11.3 Listen again and write down the phrases the speakers use to give both sides of the argument.

4 Work with a partner. Take turns to ask each other for your opinions on these proposals. Respond by giving both sides of the argument, using some of the phrases you noted down in **3**.

- introducing a new car-sharing policy and reducing the number of car parking spaces
- providing only decaffeinated coffee and tea in the company cafeteria
- introducing a shift system to make communication easier with clients worldwide
- changing from business class to economy class for all business trips

Language at work | Future tenses and probability

1 Read sentences 1–3 and <u>underline</u> the future verb forms.

1 A final decision will definitely have been reached by March.

2 Over the next few weeks, we'll be hosting departmental meetings.

3 I probably won't be going anywhere on that day.

2 Answer the questions in the *Language point*.

> **LANGUAGE POINT**
>
> Match sentences 1–3 in **1** to the tenses and situations a–c.
> Use the future continuous to talk about:
> a an activity that is part of a future programme ___
> b an activity that will/won't be in progress at a particular time in the future ___
>
> Use the future perfect to talk about:
> c an action that will be finished by a particular time in the future ___
>
> What is the normal position of an adverb of probability (e.g. *definitely*, *probably*, *possibly*) in the future continuous and future perfect in …?
> d a positive sentence ___
> e a negative sentence ___

>> For more information, go to **Grammar reference** on page 127.

3 Work with a partner. Look at the picture and answer questions 1–2. Use the prompts and/or your own ideas.

1 What will be happening over the next six months?
   clear / ground   cut down / trees   take on / temporary workers

2 What will have happened by this time next year?
   complete / project   build / new supermarket   create / local jobs

4 ▶ 11.4 Listen to extracts 1–3. What is being discussed in each extract?

5 Turn to audio script 11.4. Find the phrases in the table that the speakers use to talk about the probability of things happening. Complete the table with *0%*, *25%*, *50%*, *75%* or *100%* to show how probable the things are.

Extract 1	Extract 2	Extract 3
might ___50%___	it is doubtful _____	definitely won't _____
bound to _____	is certain to _____	'll probably _____
probably won't _____	are likely to _____	perhaps _____
there's a good chance _____		will definitely _____

>> For more exercises, go to **Practice file 11** on page 127.

6 Work with a partner. Using the phrases from **5**, talk about your activities in and out of work.

1 What activities will / might / won't you be doing …?
   • next week   • next month   • in six months' time   • next year

2 What do you think you will / might / won't have achieved …?
   • by the end of next week   • between now and the end of the year

7 Work with a partner. What developments do you predict in your industry? What will be happening in 20 years? What changes will have taken place?
   *Example: A lot more people **will be working** from home.*
   *The retirement age **will have been raised** to 75.*

8 Work with another pair. How probable are their predictions in **7**?

Fun theory

Changing people's behaviour can be challenging. Typically, incentives such as money and bonuses are offered to make people do something new. Alternatively, threats and penalties are issued to those who fail to behave properly. 'Fun theory' offers an alternative approach, believing that 'fun is the easiest way to change people's behaviour for the better.' Thefuntheory.com, which was set up by Volkswagen, suggests some ways to apply change through fun.

How do you encourage commuters to take the healthy option?

For many people, the daily commute doesn't involve much physical exercise. So one train station transformed one of their staircases into a piano keyboard; when you walked on each step it played a different note. As a result, two thirds more people than usual took the stairs instead of the escalator.

How do you get people to recycle more?

The challenge of getting people to recycle more plastic and glass is one that has encouraged innovation. In Beijing, machines take your plastic water bottles, calculate the value, and give you credit towards your train ticket. 'Better day' recycling machines in Canada give cash in return for recycling along with a fun message like 'You are a wonderful person'. But perhaps the most fun idea is the invention of a bottle bank in Sweden where you could win points like playing on an arcade game.

Discussion

1 Do you think you would change your behaviour because of the ideas in the article? Why/Why not?

2 When are incentives such as money and bonuses effective in making people change their behaviour? Can you think of examples from your workplace?

3 Do you think threats and penalties are more or less effective than incentives for changing behaviour? Give reasons for your answers.

Task

1 Work in groups of three. Read about three situations and discuss how you could change the employees' behaviour, using fun theory, financial incentives, penalties, or any other method.

- You have recycling bins around the offices for all types of rubbish (e.g. paper, plastic, glass, etc.). Recently you have noticed that employees have become less careful and started to throw the wrong type of rubbish into the different bins. How can you change this behaviour?

- Most people in your company work with computers and rarely have any face-to-face communication with each other. So once a month, your company holds a social event at lunchtime where people have the chance to meet and talk to people from other departments. Unfortunately, only about 15% of the staff ever attend. How can you improve staff attendance?

- You often send out emails to your customers inviting them to complete a feedback form about your company. Unfortunately, very few of your customers ever fill it in. How can you encourage more customers to complete and return it?

2 Present your best ideas for each situation in 1 to the rest of the class and explain how this will change behaviour.

3 Can you think of any other behaviour you would like to change in your company (either with employees or customers)? How could you apply fun theory?

12 Data

Starting point

1 How important is it for your company to get data and information about your customers?

2 How does your company collect customer data?

Working with words | Dealing in data

1 What are some of the ways people or companies can find out information about you online? What can you do to protect your identity and personal information online?

2 Read the article. Which paragraph, A–C, describes how to …?

1 protect customer data ___
2 use customer data ___
3 gather customer data ___

CUSTOMER DATA

A In this information age, companies are obsessed with data, but with so much data available the challenge is to make sense of it all. So many businesses now need staff who can both analyse the data and then turn it into profit. To understand just how important data analytics is, consider its real-world applications. Amazon uses information on our previous purchases – known as 'basket analysis' – to make further recommendations. The telecommunications firm EE monitors customer behaviour and can offer perks to high value customers. And before opening another coffee shop, Starbucks studies traffic flows and demographics in order to identify potential new store locations.

B As so much decision-making becomes data-driven, we also need to know how to gather quality data effectively. That will still involve using the traditional questionnaires and surveys to find out data such as age, profession, gender, and marital status, but if you sell products online, then it's also important to keep records on a customer's transactional history telling you not only what a customer buys, but also when, and how often. Increasingly, businesses also buy data from specialist companies who have sophisticated forms of data gathering. Online advertisers can analyse an individual's web activity through technologies such as cookies in order to target users with certain adverts. And social media sites like Facebook and Twitter know all about our friends and interests through the 'Like' and 'Tweet' buttons. There is even software to track the movements of our mouse on the screen.

C Whatever the ways you deal in data, make sure the approach is legal. When customers disclose their personal and financial information to you and your business, they trust that you won't lose it or abuse that trust – either by accident or otherwise. So protect yourself by giving customers access to your privacy policy. The policy should state who is collecting the data and how it's going to be used. Also remember that data such as passwords and credit card numbers needs to be encrypted. A data breach will do more long-term damage to a business than not collecting it in the first place.

3 Read the article again and answer questions 1–5.

1 Does the writer suggest there is a shortage of people with data analytics skills?
2 What are the real-world applications of data for Amazon, EE and Starbucks?
3 Does the writer think questionnaires and surveys have no purpose anymore?
4 What examples of sophisticated online data gathering does the writer give?
5 What is the writer's main advice to companies who use customer data?

4 Find one/two-word nouns in paragraphs A–C to match the definitions 1–10.

Paragraph A

1 a period in history where people have access to lots of information
   information age

2 the study of facts and information (often from a computer)
   _____

3 how people act and what they do when they make buying decisions
   _____

4 data relating to a particular group of people _____

Paragraph B

5 affected by the information and facts you have collected _____

6 the timeline of customer activity when buying products from a website
   _____

7 the collection of information _____

8 small files which a website sends to your computer to track what you click on
   _____

Paragraph C

9 a statement explaining how a company will use a person's data
   _____

10 when you lose, or someone steals, your customer data _____

5 Write the missing words in questions 1–6.

1 Does your company need to employ people who are skilled in data _gathering_
   and data _____?

2 How much of your decision-making is data-_____?

3 What are the typical _____ of your business's customers, e.g. their age,
   lifestyle and background?

4 If someone read your online _____ history, what would they find out about
   your buying habits?

5 Has your company ever had a data _____ and had customer data stolen?

6 When you buy something from a website or use its services, do you check and
   read its _____ policy? Why/Why not?

6 Work with a partner. Ask and answer the questions in **5**.

7 Match verbs 1–9 to nouns a–i. Then check your answers in the article in **2**.

1 analyse ___   a recommendations
2 monitor ___   b trust
3 offer ___   c personal information
4 make ___   d users
5 keep ___   e credit card numbers
6 target ___   f perks
7 disclose ___   g data / activity
8 abuse ___   h records
9 encrypt ___   i behaviour

» For more exercises, go to **Practice file 12** on page 128.

8 Work in groups. Imagine you are a consultancy giving advice on two different
   businesses' proposals below. Discuss and list what types of data you will need
   and how you will gather it.

1 Finding a good location to open another fast food restaurant for a well-known
   chain.

2 Increasing the online traffic to the website of a company which plans to start
   selling its products online.

9 Join another group. Take turns to present your ideas and make
   recommendations to each of the businesses.

Business communication | Discussing data

1 Do you look at the ads and pop-ups that you see on websites or do you ignore them? How influential are they?

2 ▶12.1 Read the *Context*. Listen to Caroline reporting back on the seminar. What do these figures refer to?
  1 18–30 _____
  2 198.4% _____
  3 81.4% _____
  4 $300.4 million _____
  5 154.4% _____

3 Match 1–10 to a–j.
  1 Could you fill us … ___
  2 Roughly … ___
  3 Apparently, a recent … ___
  4 What's that … ___
  5 Simon claimed … ___
  6 So how should we … ___
  7 Can we look … ___
  8 According to a recent … ___
  9 So the bottom line … ___
  10 The overriding trend … ___

  a in terms of growth?
  b is that user-generated media will be our new advertising platform …
  c speaking, by 2025 it'll only comprise 39.7%.
  d interpret this drop?
  e in on the most relevant information from the seminar?
  f is for technology, car and media brands to use this.
  g that last year blog advertising accounted for …
  h at the figures?
  i study shows a huge increase in advertising investment via this media …
  j survey, total projected expenditure …

4 ▶12.1 Listen again and check.

  >> For more exercises, go to **Practice file 12** on page 128.

Key expressions

Asking for / checking data
Could you fill us in on …?
Could you give us the low-down on …?
Can we look at the figures …?
So what are the facts and figures?
How do these figures compare to/with …?
What's that in terms of (growth)?
How should we interpret (this drop)?

Reporting information
According to (a recent survey), …
Apparently, a recent study shows …
Supposedly, …
Roughly speaking …
(Simon) claimed that …
(Simon) assured us that …

Summarizing findings
The bottom line is …
The overriding trend is …
In general, …
Overall, things are looking positive / up / gloomy.

5 Work with a partner. You have been researching the popularity of blog advertising and have collected some information. Student A, turn to page 138. Student B, use the information below. Report your information to your partner. Request the missing information 1–8.

	Facts and figures	Comments
No. people surveyed	1 _____	
Type of people	professional, global companies, different jobs / industries / segments	provide reliable results – a good cross section
Survey results		
read blogs	2 _____	3 _____
read blogs once a week	51% (approx. 2,300)	
read blogs weekly for business information	53%	need more information about who these people are and which blogs
read weekly on technology topics	4 _____	
pass on information or content from blogs	5 _____	6 _____
indicate that blogs influence their purchase decisions	53% (approx. 2,385)	very important information for us!
are thinking of starting their own blogs	7 _____	8 _____

Practically speaking | Describing trends

1 When you receive advertising emails, do you usually …?
- delete them straightaway
- open the email, and read it before deciding what to do
- click on the email, read it, then click through to the company's website

Does your business use email advertising campaigns? How effective are they?

2 ▶ 12.2 Listen to an extract about an email campaign. Answer questions 1–3.
1 How many emails did they send this month?
2 Was the response better or worse than last month?
3 What was the reason for this?

3 ▶ 12.2 Listen again and match phrases 1–4 to the information a–d they refer to.
1 a noticeable rise
2 stayed roughly the same
3 went up significantly
4 gave a substantial boost

a click rate (number who opened the email)
b the offer of a 20% discount
c overall response to this month's campaign
d click through (number who opened the link)

4 Put the trend phrases in **3** on this scale.

```
●────────────●────────────●────────────●────────────●
fast/big fall   slow/small fall   no change   slow/small rise   fast/big rise
```

5 Work with a partner and add these other phrases to the scale. Then think of three more trend phrases and add them to the scale.
significant jump   slight drop   remain steady   steady increase   plummet

6 Work with a partner. Use phrases in **3** and **5** to describe recent changes in:
- the rate of inflation
- your company's turnover
- the price of petrol
- rates of unemployment
- the strength of your currency
- interest rates on borrowing

Example: Last quarter showed a substantial boost in interest rates from 1% to 2%.

Language at work | Reporting

1 How do you usually listen to music? For example, streamed online or on CD?

2 Read this article on the music industry and answer questions 1–2.
  1 What is the overall trend in sales for the music industry?
  2 What is one surprising trend? What are some of the reasons for this?

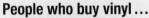

People who buy vinyl ...

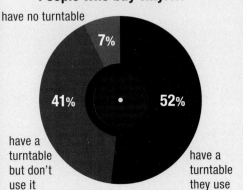

have no turntable — 7%

41% — have a turntable but don't use it

52% — have a turntable they use

During a period of slow decline of sales in the music industry, the rapid growth of vinyl record sales has been one of the big surprises. For the eighth year in a row, it was reported that sales of vinyl albums have increased dramatically and a recent consumer survey concluded that music streaming sites are boosting this growth rather than competing against it. The majority of these record buyers are young adults aged between 25–34 who listen to music online before buying.

The survey also asked them how much they had listened to the record after they bought it. 48% admitted that they hadn't played it at all and 7% said they didn't even own a turntable. One student explained, 'I have vinyls in my room, but it's more for décor. I don't actually play them.' Another 18-year-old told a reporter that it was nice to have an object you could hold and physically play. She added, 'I also think it's important to support artists financially if you can.'

3 <u>Underline</u> eight sentences in the text in **2** which report what someone said.

4 Answer the questions in the *Language point*.

LANGUAGE POINT

Look at the eight sentences you underlined in the article in **2**.
1 Which sentences use direct speech? Which ones use reported speech?
2 What reporting verbs are used? What verb is used to report questions?
3 What is the word order in the reported question?
4 What comes after *tell/told*, but not after *say/said*?
5 Compare the two sentences below. In sentence **a** why is the underlined verb still in the present? In sentence **b** why is the main verb in the past perfect?
   a A survey concluded that music streaming sites <u>are boosting</u> this growth.
   b 48% admitted that they <u>hadn't played</u> it at all.

>> For more information, go to **Grammar reference** on page 129.

5 Complete the sentences to report the direct speech in 1–6.
  1 'We sold over six hundred thousand records in the first three months of this year.'
    The music industry said that they _____ of last year.
  2 'We are currently selling more than ever before.'
    He says that they _____ more than ever before.
  3 'In the USA, vinyl sales are worth $416 million.'
    Two years ago it was reported that _____.
  4 'What do you think about the level of service from mobile phone companies?'
    The survey asked consumers what they _____.
  5 'I prefer watching videos online to watching TV.'
    One person tells us that she _____.
  6 'The results don't tell us about downloads among the over 50s.'
    She explained that the results from last months' survey _____.

>> For more exercises, go to **Practice file 12** on page 129.

6 Think of a conversation you had recently with a customer or colleague. Make notes about who said what. Then report the conversation to your partner.
   Example: *The customer said he was happy with the service he'd received that day.*

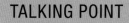

TALKING POINT

Statisticulation

Statistics are often used to try and convince consumers about a product. When used honestly, statistics can be a very effective and persuasive tool. However, using statistics in a misleading way is called 'statisticulation'. Here are some commonly used tactics:

A non-representative group: If a survey finds that '80% of all customers would use mobile app if available' then a company might invest heavily in the development of such an app. However, if the survey was only carried out with customers using mobile devices, then the survey isn't representative.

Small sample size: The statistic that people are 25% happier when they work for small organizations than for large organizations might affect your future career decision-making; unless of course the sample only included ten companies in total.

False connections: If one study finds that the average vegetarian earns 10% more than a meat-eater, would you assume that by cutting out meat you increase your income? Probably not, but that doesn't stop some researchers making such connections.

Using visuals to create an impression: Visual communication is often used to present data and it can affect the way we see the results. The two graphs on the right show the same statistics, but the upwards trend in one seems more dramatic than in the other.

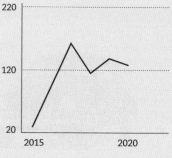

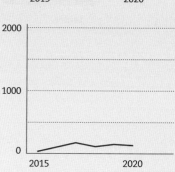

Discussion

1 To avoid being misled by statisticulation, what kinds of questions should you ask about any statistics before you use them? For example, how many people were surveyed?

2 Have you ever come across the tactics described in the article? What were the statistics and the conclusions?

3 Does your business ever use statistics to convince its customers? How effective is this kind of approach?

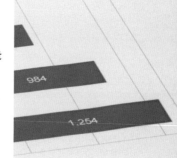

Task

1 Work in groups. Read these four statistics reported in the *Harvard Business Review*. What questions could you ask about each one to check for statisticulation? e.g. In the first, how many research participants took part? How did they test for creativity?
   - In one study, research participants were found to be more creative when they were exposed to a low background noise of 70 decibels compared to virtual silence.
   - A group of right-handed consumers were shown pictures of a bowl of yoghurt with the spoon on the right or left side. 29% of them were more likely to buy the yoghurt when the spoon was on the right.
   - Workers who sit at tables of 10 or 12 people for lunch perform more effectively than those who sit at tables for 4.
   - A sample of people were offered the chance to buy a discounted coffee mug. Some consumers were also told that they had been randomly selected to get the discount. These people were three times more likely to buy the mug than the people who believed everyone got a discount.

2 Discuss how each statistic might influence the way a company works with its staff or persuades its customers.

Preview

In this video lesson, you will watch an interview with Professor Andrew Stephen about using social media for marketing and advertising.

Lemon.

Profile

Professor Andrew Stephen is one of the world's leading academic marketing experts with a particular emphasis on issues of marketing and technology. He is head of the marketing faculty at Saïd Business School.

Focus

1 Work in small groups and discuss these traditional forms of advertising. Think of one advantage and one disadvantage for each one.

Example: You can target the type of people who buy a particular type of newspaper or magazine. / TV advertising is expensive and people often avoid watching the adverts.

- newspaper or magazine
- posters, leaflets and billboards
- television
- radio

2 Form new groups. Share your ideas and add any more advantages and disadvantages to your notes.

Social media marketing

3 You are going to watch an interview with Professor Andrew Stephen talking about advertising on social media. Before you watch the video, match words and phrases 1–12 to the correct definitions a–l.

1 interactive	7 dissemination
2 tracking	8 social media platforms
3 intrusive	9 hallmarks
4 high-consideration goods	10 synergistically
5 utilitarian	11 silos
6 hedonic	12 touch points

a following the clicks of the consumers online ___
b different things working together like one ___
c separate or isolated areas ___
d products that customers have to think a lot about before deciding to buy ___
e something that gets in the way of everyday life ___
f not necessary but enjoyable ___
g useful and necessary ___
h allowing two-way flow between a person and the advert ___
i key moments on the customer journey to buying a product or service ___
j websites such as Facebook, Instagram, Twitter, etc. ___
k important symbols ___
l spreading information to many people ___

4 ▶01 In the first part of the interview, Andrew Stephen talks about how social media has changed marketing. Watch the video and decide which words or phrases 1–9 refer to traditional forms of advertising (*T*) or social media advertising (*S*).

1 mass communication model ___	6 sparks a conversation ___
2 one-way ___	7 brands 'talking to people' ___
3 two-way ___	8 not as valuable ___
4 interactive ___	9 less intrusive ___
5 allows tracking and measuring ___	

5 ▶01 Work with a partner. Compare your answers in **4** and try to explain how the answer refers to each form of advertising. Then watch again and check your answers.

6 ▶02 In the second part of the interview, Andrew Stephen describes in what ways social media advertising can be more effective and less effective. Watch and make notes in the table.

Types of products social media advertises …	How social media can work …
more effectively	more effectively
less effectively	less effectively

7 ▶02 Compare your notes in **6** with a partner. Then watch the second part of the interview again and add any missing information.

8 Work in small groups and list the different types of social media platforms you all use. Then answer these questions.
1 Which of these platforms have a lot of advertising? How much do you respond to the adverts (as a consumer)?
2 How much does your business advertise on these platforms? In what ways?

The media mix

9 ▶03 Watch the third part of the interview with Andrew Stephen and answer questions 1–4.
1 With social media, how does the return on the investment compare with traditional forms of advertising, like TV?
2 How does he compare the 'reach' of social media with TV advertising?
3 How could your social media advertising start a conversation? How has this influenced other forms of advertising?
4 What are some of the ways you can mix different types of media as part of your advertising campaign? How can they work together, synergistically?

10 ▶03 Work with a partner. Compare your answers to the questions in **9**. Then watch the video again and add further details.

11 What different types of advertising does your business use? How could they work together, synergistically? Discuss with your partner.

Developing a social media strategy

12 ▶04 In the final part of the interview, Andrew Stephen says there are three points to consider when developing a social media marketing strategy. Watch and number a–c in the order he talks about them.
a audience ___   b content ___   c dissemination ___

13 ▶04 In his description of the three points, Andrew Stephen lists the types of questions you need to ask yourself when developing a strategy. Watch the video again and write the different questions you have to ask when planning each stage.

14 Work in small groups. You are going to plan a new digital media strategy for your company's product/service or a product or service that you know well. Plan your strategy by discussing the three points in **12** and the questions in **13**. Then present your strategy to the rest of the class.

Glossary

back in the day idiomatic phrase used to refer to a period in the past when something was good

compare apples to apples comparing two similar things

get a backlash receive a negative response/reaction

jarring when two things don't work well or go well together

jog your memory remind you of something you may have forgotten

my gut says (it's good) my intuition tells me

ROI return on investment

try to nut it out at a micro level try to analyse something very specific

13 Culture

Starting point

1 A common piece of advice for people living or working in another country is *When in Rome, do as the Romans do.* What do you think this expression means?

2 How much do you change your behaviour if you visit another country for work or as a tourist? Why?

Working with words | Cultural differences

1 If you do business with a different culture, what is it useful to know about that culture? Read the text and compare your ideas.

Working across cultures

Professor Geert Hofstede of the Netherlands conducted a study of how values in the workplace are influenced by culture. His research, based on a large database of employees' values collected by IBM, covers 74 countries and regions.

Working, entertaining, negotiating and corresponding with colleagues from different cultures can be quite difficult. One misunderstanding could have a negative effect on months of work. Understanding intercultural differences can help communication with colleagues from other cultures. According to Hofstede, if we compare the key factors in our own culture with those in another culture, we can predict possible difficulties.

HIERARCHICAL OR EGALITARIAN?
Some cultures, like Malaysia and Indonesia, are **hierarchical** with a caste or class system; there is often a big difference in wealth between individuals. At work, employees respect authority, don't usually take responsibility and have a **formal** relationship with their manager. Other cultures, like Australia and Denmark, are more **liberal** and **egalitarian**. Managers give their employees responsibility and often socialize with them.

INDIVIDUALISTIC OR COLLECTIVIST?
Individualistic cultures, such as the USA and the Netherlands, think that individual rights and freedom of speech are important. Personal goals, choices and achievements are encouraged. In more **collectivist** cultures, such as Korea and Colombia, this self-centred

approach is discouraged. The group, such as the family, has a big influence on people's lives and is often seen as more important than business. Companies have a strong work group mentality and praise is given to teams rather than individuals.

MASCULINE OR FEMININE?
In 'masculine' societies, like Brazil and Mexico, the male dominates the power structure. Competitiveness and assertiveness are encouraged, and the accumulation of wealth is important. Many employees 'live to work' and take short holidays. In 'feminine' societies, such as Sweden and Finland, family, personal relationships, and quality of life are more important. Conflicts are resolved through negotiation, and people 'work to live', enjoying longer holidays and flexible working hours.

CAUTIOUS OR RISK-TAKING?
Some cultures, especially those with a long history such as Greece and Portugal, are quite **cautious**. They often have religious backgrounds and resist new ideas. At work, people prefer to follow **strict** rules and do things as they always have been done. Other cultures, like Jamaica and Singapore, often have a younger history and are willing to take risks. They are more **open** to new ideas, and are more **accepting** of change.

2 Read the text again. According to Hofstede, which cultures …?
1 think family life is important
2 like to be very polite to their manager and/or follow rules and regulations
3 adapt easily to change

3 Discuss questions 1–2 as a class.
1 Look at the four pairs of key factors in the text. Which of the key factors would you use to describe your culture?
2 Based on your experience of working with and meeting people from other cultures, would you agree with Hofstede's conclusions? Why/Why not?

4 Work with a partner. Match the adjectives in **bold** in the text to definitions 1–10.
1 very polite _____
2 organized in levels _____
3 classless _____
4 careful _____
5 receptive of new ideas _____
6 allowing freedom _____
7 shared by all the group _____
8 something which must be obeyed _____
9 willing to tolerate something _____
10 focusing on one person _____

5 Discuss how each adjective in **4** could be seen as positive and negative.

6 ▶ 13.1 Listen to two people talking on the subject of culture.
1 Summarize the main points of the first speaker's story.
2 What type of course is the second speaker talking about? What do people learn about on the course?

7 Complete sentences 1–8 with the words from the list from audio script 13.1.
aware   sensitive   familiar   respectful   tolerant   informed   adjust   used

1 People from Finland don't like to offend other people, so they're always very _____ to their guests' feelings.
2 I found it quite hard to _____ to the hierarchical culture in Thailand – my culture is much more egalitarian.
3 I wasn't very _____ with the way business is done in Romania, so I was surprised by the amount of bureaucracy.
4 I wasn't _____ of the custom of greeting the oldest person first in China, so I'm afraid I offended my host.
5 Mexico is a hierarchical culture, so it's important to be _____ of people of a higher rank.
6 My boss sent me on a cross-cultural training course, so I was _____ about business etiquette in Brazil before I was seconded there.
7 I'm _____ to people being direct in my own country, so the indirect communication of Singaporeans seemed strange to me.
8 My colleague is always very punctual, so he wasn't very _____ of the Greek custom of arriving late for dinner!

8 Work with a partner. Use five of the words from **7** to ask each other questions.

>> For more exercises, go to **Practice file 13** on page 130.

9 Work with a partner. Prepare some information for someone from a different culture who is coming to work in your company. Think about the things below and explain how aspects of your culture influence behaviour.
• how people behave in meetings
• relationships between different members of staff, e.g. formality
• individual efforts and teamwork
• responsibility
• company policy
• social events

Business communication | Narrating past events

1 ▶13.2 Listen to two conversations describing critical incidents. Which two of these situations are mentioned in each conversation?
   1 importance of punctuality
   2 questioning an authority figure
   3 importance of seniority and titles
   4 small talk before meetings
   5 saying 'yes' to avoid loss of face

2 ▶13.2 Listen again. Complete sentences 1–10 with the phrases from the list.

in the end   that's   but then   it came about because of   as time went by
so that was   it wasn't until   due to   so what   that was when

Critical incident 1
   1 … for years. _____, I noticed that things weren't being done that I'd requested …
   2 … it wasn't done. _____ I was aware we had a problem.
   3 Well, _____ understandable.
   4 And _____ I talked to a Korean friend that I realized what was wrong.
   5 My team didn't want to refuse my request _____ respect for my seniority.

Critical incident 2
   6 Yes … _____ I realized they hadn't actually told him this.
   7 … authority figure. _____ the first problem solved.
   8 _____ did you do?
   9 Well, _____ I asked Anna, a Polish colleague.
   10 Yes. _____ the lack of information about why we were questioning them.

3 Which of the phrases in 2 do the speakers use to …?
   a help to tell the story of the incident and indicate the sequence of events
   b explain the reason for the incident
   c show they are listening / encourage more information

>> For more exercises, go to **Practice file 13** on page 130.

Key expressions

Giving an explanation
... due to ...
It seems that ...
The reason being that ...
It came about because of ...

Linking the narrative
It wasn't until ... that ...
Luckily ...
And/But then ...
What's more ...
Despite ...

Time expressions
While/When ...
At first ...
After that ...
As time went by ...
In the end ...

Encouraging more information
So what did you do?
What had you done?
And what did (she) say?
What happened (next / then / after that)?
That's (understandable).
Go on. / Oh?
What was (her) view?
So how did you ...?

Summarizing the narrative
That was when ...
So that was the first problem ...
All in all ...
It really surprised me (but it worked).
I was extremely disappointed.

4 Work with a partner. Read the text about doing business in Indonesia. Use the pictures and prompts to tell the story of the critical incident.

DOING BUSINESS IN INDONESIA

It's important to offer refreshment to guests. This is seen as respectful and polite. Guests should wait before drinking – their host will indicate when drinking can commence.

Often there is a pause between receiving the drink and being asked to drink. The sign to drink may indicate that business is over. Make sure you wait and follow your host's example.

Last year / Indonesia / colleague / negotiate contract

Picked up cup / colleague / wait

Near end of meeting / refreshments

Negotiation complete / host / invited

5 Work with a partner. Think of a situation where there was a misunderstanding between you and someone from a different culture, e.g. on business or on holiday. Tell your partner about the incident. Use these ideas if necessary:
- in a restaurant – ordering food and drink
- talking about own country/background
- being unaware of traditions/culture
- asking for directions
- deadlines/dates
- on the phone

Practically speaking | Talking about news and gossip

1 Why do people enjoy reading or watching news and gossip about other people such as celebrities? Do you enjoy hearing news and gossip about other people at work? Why/Why not?

2 ▶ 13.3 Listen to three short conversations about news. Which one is about ...?
a relationships ___   b a missing item ___   c leaving the company ___

3 ▶ 13.3 Listen again. Which of the phrases 1–10 can you use to ...?
a introduce the topic of news ___ ___ ___
b repeat news you have heard ___ ___ ___ ___ ___
c respond to news ___ ___

1 Rumour has it ...
2 Surely not!
3 I spoke to (Robert) and he told me that ...
4 Did you hear the latest about ...?
5 According to (Sam), ...
6 That's nonsense!
7 (Anna) says that ...
8 Have you heard the news?
9 Apparently, ...
10 You'll never guess what I heard ...

4 Work in groups of four. Think of two pieces of news each. Work with a partner and share your first piece of news. Respond to your partner's news appropriately. Change partners and share your second piece of news.

One evening in December, an American billionaire was being driven down the motorway in New Jersey. It was raining hard, but the road was busy as thousands of people were leaving for their Christmas holidays.

Suddenly, the car got a flat tyre, and the chauffeur pulled over to the side. When he opened the boot, he realized that he had left the tool kit behind. While he was standing there in the rain, wondering what to do, another motorist saw him and stopped. Together, they changed the wheel, and as the man was leaving, the billionaire wound down the window. He asked if there was anything he could do to thank him, and the man said his wife might like a small bunch of flowers.

Two weeks later, a bunch of flowers arrived at the man's house. With it there was a small note thanking the man for his help and telling him that the whole of his mortgage had been paid off.

Language at work | Narrative tenses

1 Read this story about a billionaire entrepreneur. Do you think it's true? Why/Why not? Discuss your ideas with a partner.

2 Work with a partner. Number events a–i in the order they happened (1–9).
a The chauffeur and the motorist changed the wheel. ___
b The car had a flat tyre. ___
c The billionaire set off down the motorway. ___
d The chauffeur realized he couldn't change the wheel. ___
e The chauffeur didn't put the tool kit in the boot. ___
f The billionaire paid off the man's mortgage. ___
g A passing motorist stopped to help. ___
h Some flowers arrived at the man's house. ___
i The billionaire spoke to the man. ___

3 Answer the questions in the *Language point*.

> **LANGUAGE POINT**
>
> <u>Underline</u> the verb forms in the story and match them to these tenses:
> Past continuous / Past simple / Past perfect
>
> Complete the explanations with the correct narrative tense from 1.
> Use the _____ to describe background information at the beginning of the story.
> Use the _____ to describe the main actions and events in the story.
> Use the _____ to talk about an action in progress, interrupted by another action.
> Use the _____ to talk about an action that happened before another past action.

>> For more information, go to **Grammar reference** on page 131.

4 Complete sentences 1–6 with the correct form of the verbs in brackets.
1 They cancelled my flight because it _____ (snow) so I _____ (sleep) in the airport lounge.
2 I didn't want to interrupt my colleague while he _____ (talk) on the phone so I _____ (send) him an email instead.
3 I felt very embarrassed when I realized that I _____ (forget) my host's name, so I _____ (apologize) quickly.
4 During the time I _____ (stay) in Denmark, I didn't know whether to arrive on time for dinner so I _____ (decide) to arrive five minutes late.
5 My host offered me a small gift just as I _____ (leave) for the airport and I _____ (give) her a souvenir from my own country.
6 I didn't know if the party was formal or informal because I _____ (lose) my invitation, so I _____ (wear) a smart outfit.

>> For more exercises, go to **Practice file 13** on page 131.

5 Work with a partner. Take turns to talk about one of the situations below. Give some background information about the situation, explain how it came about, what happened and how it was resolved.
• a time when you were dressed inappropriately for something
• a time when something unexpected happened at work
• a time when you were unsure how to behave culturally in another country
• a time when you had a minor accident or injury of some kind
• a time when you had transport problems and were extremely late for something

The power of storytelling

Everyone loves a good story. That's because stories are emotional. While we'll listen to facts and then forget them, we'll listen to a good story and retell it.

So in business, stories are powerful. A good story is a well-delivered sales pitch. It's a CEO presenting a company's future vision to the employees. It's explaining how you came up with an exciting innovation to a group of potential investors. And it's a word-of-mouth recommendation from one satisfied customer to another.

Whatever your story, learn how to tell it.

Discussion

1 Do you agree that storytelling is a powerful tool in business? Why/Why not?

2 ▶ 13.4 Listen to a person talking about the history of a company in two different ways. Which version did you find more interesting? Which told you more about the company culture?

3 ▶ 13.4 How much of the first story can you remember? Work with a partner and try to retell it. Then listen to the first story again and find out how much you remembered.

Task

1 Work on your own. Plan a story (of 2–3 minutes) about your company. Include some or all of the following:
   • how it first began
   • who set it up
   • how the company grew
   • who the customers are
   • something that demonstrates your company's values and beliefs

2 When you are ready to tell your story, work in groups of four. Decide who is Student A, B, C and D. You are going to take turns to tell your stories to each other. Listen carefully because you will have to retell your partners' stories.
   Step 1   Tell your partner your story: Student A works with Student B, and Student C works with Student D.
   Step 2   Retell the story you have just heard in Step 1 to your next partner: Student A works with Student C, and Student B works with Student D.
   Step 3   Retell the story you have just heard in Step 2 to the story 'owner': Student A works with Student D, and Student B works with Student C.

   How much of your story did your partner tell correctly?

3 Think about the different stories you have just shared. Which parts of the stories were most memorable? Why?

14 Performance

Starting point

1 What criteria could you use to measure the performance of a company / a project / an employee?

2 Which criteria are the most important for each one?

3 Which criteria are the easiest to measure?

Working with words | Staff appraisals

1 How is staff performance measured where you work? How do you receive feedback on your performance?

2 Read the article and answer questions 1–3.
1 Paragraph 1 describes a typical procedure for appraisals. Is it similar to your company's procedure?
2 The first sentence in paragraph 2 refers to a 'mixed response' from employees. What were the responses?
3 In what ways are the systems of giving feedback at General Electric and Adobe different from the traditional approach to appraisals?

The end of the annual performance review?

If your company conducts annual appraisals, the following procedure might sound familiar: You receive an email from your boss inviting you to an appraisal with a form attached. You fill a series of tick boxes, rate objectives on a scale, and express your views on certain issues. Then you have your meeting, agree your objectives for the coming year, and plan to meet again in another 12 months' time.

That's the standard annual performance review for many companies and it gets a mixed response from employees. In one survey of 2,900 workers, 29% thought annual appraisals were a waste of time and 21% even described them as 'unfair'. Many more were positive about the experience, but felt that receiving constructive feedback on a more regular basis would be more beneficial.

It's this kind of viewpoint which has led to some businesses moving away from the once-a-year format towards a 'give feedback anytime' approach. General Electric, for example, which employs around 300,000 people worldwide, has an app which allows employees to read regularly updated feedback on their phone. It allows managers to address any immediate concerns and it gives employees the opportunity to raise any issues or respond to criticism.

But if you already dread the approach of your annual performance review, then isn't the prospect of your performance being monitored twenty-four seven even worse? Supporters of a more fluid approach to appraisals don't think so. The software company Adobe offers employees frequent face-to-face 'check-ins' with their managers where they can discuss their current role and plan their future careers. Since implementing this system, there has been a 30% drop in employees leaving the company. So perhaps rather than waiting a whole year to find out if something can be improved, more regular updates mean employees can learn from any mistakes immediately.

---

3 Do you think the General Electric and Adobe approach to appraisals would work at your company? Would you benefit from such an approach? Why/Why not?

4 Look for these words in the text and match the verbs in A to the noun phrases in B to make phrases.

A		B	
conduct	address	issues	objectives on a scale
rate	raise	views	constructive feedback
express	respond to	objectives	concerns
agree	monitor	annual appraisals	criticism
receive		performance	

5 Match the phrases from **4** to the definitions 1–9.

1 carry out an assessment of how well someone is doing at work

   _____

2 talk about your opinion of something _____
3 decide what to do about a problem/situation _____
4 be told in a useful way how you are doing at work _____
5 give points to measure how well someone has achieved their aims/targets

   _____

6 check regularly how someone is doing at work _____
7 decide with someone else what you hope to achieve at work

   _____

8 reply to negative comments about your performance _____
9 mention and talk about any current points for concern _____

6 Work with a partner. Using six of the phrases in **5**, make questions about appraisals. Then ask and answer the questions with your partner.

7 ▶ 14.1 Listen to a human resources manager describing a system of 360-degree feedback. Then work with a partner and answer questions 1–3.

1 What is the central idea of 360-degree appraisals? How do they work?
2 What do raters comment on?
3 What two things do you need to consider if you use 360-degree feedback?

8 Complete the phrases from **7** with the words from the list.

criteria   appraisal   judgement   tool   management   rating

1 How does 360 degree differ from a more traditional top-down *staff* _____?
2 In what ways is 360 degree a *development* _____?
3 What sort of *assessment* _____ might be used for a 360-degree appraisal?
4 Who would carry out the *peer* _____ in your situation?
5 As a rater, how honest would you be in your *value* _____ of your peers?
6 Do you have a role in *performance* _____ in your company?

9 Work with a partner. Ask and answer the questions from **8**.

10 Match the phrasal verbs in the list to definitions 1–6. Then make a sentence with each of the phrasal verbs.

move on   hand out   end up with   go through   come over   carry on

1 get as a result _____
2 give an impression _____
3 stop doing one thing and start another _____
4 distribute _____
5 look at very carefully _____
6 continue _____

>> For more exercises, go to **Practice file 14** on page 132.

11 Work with a partner. List the job skills required in your job that could be used as assessment criteria. If you used 360-degree appraisals with a person in this job, who would you need to involve in the feedback process?

Business communication | Evaluating performance

Context

Thomas works in the back office of an international car rental company. His team undertakes a range of administrative duties including working with the call centre shift rota. The company's policy is to carry out annual staff appraisals with all its personnel. Its philosophy is that appraisal involves staff in their personal development, allows them to take some responsibility for their work and provides an opportunity for two-way feedback.

1 Read the *Context*. Do you think the company's philosophy for appraisals is true for most businesses?

2 ▶ 14.2 Listen to Thomas having his annual appraisal with his superior, Angelina, and complete this table.

	Appraisee feedback	Appraiser comments	Action to be taken
Positive achievements			
Areas for improvement / development			
Areas of concern			
Resources required			

3 Work with a partner. Read these phrases. Who said them: the appraiser, Angelina (*A*) or the appraisee, Thomas (*T*)?
1 I must say, we're very happy with your overall performance … ___
2 Can I identify that as a personal goal for the coming year? ___
3 You shouldn't have been expected to take on so much. ___
4 Are there any areas you feel you need to improve on? ___
5 If I'd known that … I might have done it. ___
6 You certainly need to focus on gaining some more qualifications. ___
7 Were there any constraints that affected your performance? ___
8 What's the best way to solve this? ___
9 We could do with some training on the new program … ___
10 If there's enough money, I'd also like another software program. ___

4 ▶ 14.2 Listen again and check.

5 Put phrases 1–10 from **3** into categories a–f.
a asking about performance: _____
b giving feedback on performance: _____
c setting goals: _____
d requesting/giving advice to improve performance: _____
e justifying/explaining results: _____
f negotiating time/resources: _____

>> For more exercises, go to **Practice file 14** on page 132.

Tip | *really, certainly, I must say*

Add emphasis to what you are saying by using words such as *really, certainly* and the structure *I must say*.
*You **really** should have done that course.*
*You **certainly** need to focus on gaining some more qualifications.*
I must say we're very happy with your overall performance.

6 Consider your own job over the past year. Think of two or three examples for each of the following (the information you give doesn't have to be true):
- something you've enjoyed or think has worked well
- something you haven't enjoyed or think hasn't worked so well
- something you are concerned about
- something where you've needed more time/resources
- something you would like to achieve/do in the next year at work

7 Work with a partner. Decide what questions from the *Key expressions* you would need to ask to find out the information in **6**. Then take turns to interview each other about your performance at work. Complete the table below with your partner's answers.

	Appraisee feedback	Appraiser comments	Action to be taken
Positive achievements			
Areas for improvement/ development			
Areas of concern			
Resources required			
Future goals			

Practically speaking | Raising difficult issues

1 Work with a partner. Have you ever had to deal with the situations in 1–3? What happened? If you haven't, say how you would deal with them.
1 There has been a complaint about an employee from a colleague in the same office.
2 An employee is going to be made redundant because of restructuring.
3 The feedback on an employee's recent performance has been very poor.

2 ▶ 14.3 Listen to the start of two conversations.
1 Match each conversation to a situation in **1**.
2 How does the employee react in each conversation?

3 ▶ 14.3 Listen again and number the phrases in the order you hear them (1–9).
I'm going to get straight to the point. ___
This is rather delicate, but … ___
I've received a complaint about you. ___
I realize it isn't easy for you to hear this … ___
There's something we need to discuss. ___
I'd like to hear your side of the story. ___
It wasn't an easy decision to make. ___
We don't have much choice. ___
Before we go any further … ___

4 Work with a partner. Practise using the phrases in **3**. Take turns to be the manager meeting an employee and deal with each of the three situations in **1**.

Language at work | Third and mixed conditionals | Perfect modals

1 Read sentences 1–4. What has or hasn't happened in each sentence?

1 If Katy **hadn't left**, I probably **would have done** the course.

2 You **could have thought** a bit more about the call centre rota.

3 If **you'd started** a language course then, **you'd be** quite proficient now.

4 You really **should have done** that course.

2 Answer the questions in the *Language point*.

LANGUAGE POINT

Look at the sentences in **1** again. Write in the correct sentence number (1–4) to complete explanations a–d.

a Sentence ___ is a third conditional and describes an imagined past action and an imagined past result.

b Sentence ___ is a mixed conditional and describes an imagined past action and an imagined present result.

c Sentence ___ expresses irritation and criticism of a past action.

d Sentence ___ suggests a different course of action in the past.

>> For more information, go to **Grammar reference** on page 133.

3 Look at the sentences in **1** again. Which verb forms are used in sentences 1 and 3? Which modal verbs in sentences 2 and 4 could be replaced by *might have* and *ought to have*?

>> For more exercises, go to **Practice file 14** on page 133.

4 Work with a partner. Discuss what you might say in each of the situations. Use the third conditional and at least one mixed conditional.

1 You took the company car without authorization. You drove to the project meeting and arrived on time. There was a possibility of losing the contract. Present result: the company is expanding its business.

2 You ordered some office equipment from your usual supplier who has always delivered on time. A new supplier offered a discount on the same order. The new supplier didn't have a good reputation for delivering on time. Present result: you have enough paper for the current mailshot.

5 Work with a partner. Discuss how you could respond to your colleague in the following situations using *could have* or *should have*.

Your colleague …

1 wrote an angry letter to an important customer.

2 arrives an hour late for an appointment without bothering to phone you.

3 offers a discount to a customer without checking with the manager first.

4 forgot to let you know that a meeting had been changed.

5 made a very costly mistake, but did not get the sack.

6 Work with a partner. Talk briefly about some of the topics below. Say what actually happened to you in the past. Then say what might or would have happened in different circumstances, or how things would be different now.

> ***Example:*** *I decided to become an artist because I loved painting. If I'd followed my father's advice, I would have become an accountant or might have become a banker. I'd be richer, but I'm not sure I'd be any happier.*

• why you chose your current career

• a narrow escape or lucky break

• a good or bad financial decision you made

• a mistake or misjudgement you made

Competition in the workplace

Competition between employees is often considered to be healthy and increase performance. For example, sales teams can receive an award for the 'best annual sales figures' or a fast food chain can nominate its 'employee of the month'. However, competition in the workplace isn't always positive. In the 1970s, Bruce Henderson of the Boston Consulting Group divided his staff into teams called Blue, Red and Green. The teams competed and for a while it improved performance in the company. The Blue team was the most successful but, in the end, this had a negative consequence. The leader of the Blue team resigned and took most of his Blue team members with him to start a rival company. In other words, competition in the workplace can be a dangerous motivational tool and needs to be used wisely. Three important things to bear in mind are:

- **Be fair:** *Your criteria for measuring performance need to be fair. For example, if you are comparing sales figures, then remember that sales figures in an established market will be higher than in a new under-developed market, regardless of who the sales person is.*

- **Make things quantifiable:** *How you plan to measure performance needs to be explained to staff. Using criteria which are subjective and rely on someone else's point of view will probably end in disaster.*

- **Potential problems:** *Competition means having losers as well as winners – the losers could be other staff, your customers, and – in the end – the company. Make sure you monitor closely for any negative impact from not winning.*

Discussion

1   Why do you think competition improved the staff performance, at first, in the Boston Consulting Group? How did it motivate the staff?

2   What was the negative consequence of the competitive workplace at the Boston Consulting Group? Can you think of any other disadvantages of using competition in the workplace?

3   Have you ever experienced competition in the workplace? How could it be effective in your company?

Task

Work in small groups. You are the owners of a small restaurant near a station in the centre of a large capital city. Your main customers are morning commuters who want breakfast and people working in the offices nearby during lunchtimes. You also serve evening meals, but you want to improve sales by attracting tourists and visitors.

1   Have a meeting to discuss how to improve the performance of your staff at different mealtimes through competition. Discuss the following:
- How could you use competition in this workplace?
- How can you be fair? How will your criteria be quantifiable?
- Can you think of any potential problems? How will you monitor these?

2   Present and compare your ideas with the rest of the class.

15008 km NEW YORK   HOBART 1680 km
1401 km CAPE REINGA   SYDNEY 2000 km
6 km

15 Career breaks

Starting point

1 How common are career breaks in your country? What do people use the time for?

2 What problems might a career break cause?

Working with words | Taking a career break

1 Read about three people who took careers breaks in different countries. Which two people …?

1 went to the same part of the world
2 are back working for the same company
3 give similar advice about taking a career break
4 spent time helping other people
5 have changed in similar ways

FREYA
Advertising Manager

STAGE IN CAREER: 'I'd worked in marketing for ten years and had just completed my Advanced Certificate. I resigned.'

MY CAREER BREAK: 'I travelled around the world for 18 months and did voluntary work in Australia. My career break **revitalized** me – it has given me a new **perspective** on life and re-ordered my priorities; quality of life is more important to me now. I'm also more confident. If you're **hesitating** about taking a career break, the best **piece of advice** I'd give is to make sure you've got good relevant career experience before you leave – so it's much easier to get back on the career ladder.'

EFFECT ON CAREER: 'The break acted as a catalyst for me to change career. I **put off** looking for a permanent job for a while, but now I've applied to join a government office.'

ROBERTO
Business Analyst

STAGE IN CAREER: 'I'd worked for the bank for 14 years, so they offered to keep a job open. I **postponed** my planned departure for a year to suit them.'

MY CAREER BREAK: 'I spent a year travelling through South-east Asia and Australia, doing a series of scuba-diving courses. I also learnt to ride a motorbike and fly a helicopter. My **tip** for anyone considering a career break is: take it after you've worked for at least five years. That way you'll really **appreciate** the time off and have enough money to enjoy it. It's the best thing I've ever done.'

EFFECT ON CAREER: 'I came back with my batteries **recharged** and new enthusiasm; and now I am doing a better version of my old job.'

JENNY
Management Consultant

STAGE IN CAREER: 'I was with my company for nine years and having a mid-career crisis. I intended to resign – they said they'd hold my job open.'

MY CAREER BREAK: 'I was in Bangladesh, attached to a **voluntary organization** working with local communities to improve education and healthcare, and to develop new skills and earning potential. It broadened my **outlook** and I experienced a completely different pace of life. I am now less materialistic, and I **feel grateful for** the things I have got. If you're **feeling uncertain** about a career break, just do it – life's too short.'

EFFECT ON CAREER: 'I went back to exactly the same job, but I now do four days a week, spending the fifth volunteering with a children's **charity**.'

2 Work with a partner. Which of the career breaks in **1** would you most like to take and why?

3 Put the words in **bold** in the texts in **1** into pairs that have similar meanings.
Example: revitalized / recharged

4 Complete these sentences using some of the words from **3**.
1 How would you enjoy working for a _____ like the Red Cross or Médecins Sans Frontières?
2 Would you return from a career break feeling _____ and ready to get back to your old job or would you be uninterested in going back to work? Explain why.
3 Have you got any unfulfilled ambitions that you have had to _____ for career reasons?
4 Have you ever done anything that has given you a new _____ on life?
5 Are you constantly seeking new things/opportunities or do you _____ the things that you have?
6 What's the most useful _____ anyone has given you about dealing with boredom or stress at work?

5 Work with a partner. Ask and answer the questions in **4**.

6 ▶ **15.1** Listen to an employer talking about the benefits of career breaks. Work with a partner and answer questions 1–5.
1 Why did the company originally introduce flexiwork?
2 Why was flexiwork particularly suited to this company?
3 What are the current benefits of flexiwork?
4 Why is flexiwork described as a win-win situation?
5 Would the same arguments for flexiwork apply in your company?

7 Choose the correct words in *italics* in each statement.

1 A break might help me head *off* / *round* in a new direction.	1	2	3	4	5
2 I would like the opportunity to develop some *light* / *soft* skills.	1	2	3	4	5
3 I think I would return to work with *renewed* / *improved* enthusiasm.	1	2	3	4	5
4 I would like to *broaden* / *enlarge* my horizons through travel.	1	2	3	4	5
5 My boss would see a break as an important part of my career *development* / *improvement*.	1	2	3	4	5
6 Allowing career breaks will at some stage become our official company *policy* / *doctrine*.	1	2	3	4	5
7 Allowing career breaks would help the *maintenance* / *retention* rate in my company.	1	2	3	4	5

8 For each statement in **7**, circle a number from 1 to 5 using the scoring system below. Compare and discuss your answers with a partner.
1 = agree very much
2 = agree
3 = unsure
4 = disagree
5 = disagree strongly

» For more exercises, go to **Practice file 15** on page 134.

9 Think of a career break that might appeal to you *and* your company. Give a short presentation of your idea, outlining:
• the basic proposition
• what the benefits would be for you
• what the benefits would be for your employer
• what financial arrangements you would propose

Business communication | Putting forward a case

Context

Lena Johnson currently works for an IT company leading a team of technical writers. She has a diploma in photography and has decided to request a nine-month sabbatical to act as photographer for journalists making a documentary in the Antarctic.

1 ▶ 15.2 Read the *Context*. Listen to the meeting between Lena and her manager. Which of the benefits and arguments in the list did she use for taking a sabbatical?

- I've been a loyal employee.
- I'll have to resign if I'm not allowed to take the sabbatical.
- I'll feel more settled and focused after the trip.
- I'll gain experience I can bring to the company.
- It's a lifelong ambition of mine.
- I'm feeling burnt-out!
- If you sponsor my trip, the company will gain advertising opportunities.
- My creativity is being suppressed in my present job.

2 ▶ 15.2 Listen again and number phrases a–i in the order you hear them (1–9).
a It's a once-in-a-lifetime opportunity. ___
b This is a chance I can't afford to miss. ___
c That's hardly fair. I've never refused to take … ___
d It's been a long-term goal of mine. _1_
e I've been inspired by … ___
f I understand your misgivings. ___
g I'd really appreciate it … ___
h It's a win-win situation. ___
i The experience I'd gain would be invaluable … ___

3 Match the <u>underlined</u> words in sentences 1–9 to phrases a–i with the same meaning in **2**.
1 It's <u>something I've wanted to do for a long time</u>. _d_
2 The people I studied with <u>have given me the desire to do this</u>. ___
3 <u>I'll never get this opportunity again in my life</u>. ___
4 <u>It's a situation where we'll both gain something</u>. ___
5 <u>I'd obtain skills that would be very useful</u> for managing the team. ___
6 <u>I know you'll have a lot of worries</u>. ___
7 <u>If I don't take up this opportunity, I'll regret it</u>. ___
8 <u>That's not very reasonable – I've always taken</u> on extra work. ___
9 <u>I'd be very grateful</u> if you could speak to HR. ___

>> For more exercises, go to **Practice file 15** on page 134.

Tip | *valuable* and *invaluable*

Valuable can be used to talk about how much money something is worth.

*It was a **valuable** piece of equipment.*

However, *invaluable* is not the opposite of *valuable* and is not used to talk about monetary value.

An experience can be *valuable*, meaning 'useful'. You can use *invaluable* to emphasize that it was 'very useful'.

*The experience was **invaluable**.*

Key expressions

Stating what you want
It's been a long-term goal of mine to …
I intend to …
I'd really appreciate it if …

Stating motivation
I've been inspired by …
I'd like to do this because …
My motivation for this comes from …

Explaining benefits
It's a win-win situation.
The experience I'd gain would be invaluable for …
The plus points are …

Arguing persuasively
It's a once in a lifetime opportunity.
This is a chance I can't (afford to) miss.
I'll never be satisfied unless I do it.

Dealing with objections
I understand your misgivings, but …
That's hardly fair. I've never refused to …
But there are also (other) benefits for (you / the company).

4 Work with a partner. Read this information.

> You left your college course halfway through for personal reasons. You have performed extremely well in your job, especially since most of your colleagues are better qualified than you. You would now like to go back to college and complete your studies, but the only way to do this is to take a career break for a year.

1 Decide what type of job you have and what type of course you want to complete (use your own job if you like).
2 Discuss how you would present your case for a career break to your manager. Make sure you think of two phrases for:
   • stating what you want
   • stating your motivation
   • explaining the benefits
   • arguing persuasively
3 Think of two objections your boss might have and counter these with appropriate phrases.
4 Work with another pair. Talk them through your case and arguments.

5 Choose one of these things that you would like to do (or an idea of your own) and prepare your case.
   • take paternity leave / extended maternity leave (assuming it isn't a legal option in your country)
   • restructure your department
   • introduce a new procedure in your office
   • apply for a better position internally in your company
   • take a temporary transfer abroad with your company

6 Work with a partner. Take turns to present your case. When you are listening, object to some of the proposals you hear.

Practically speaking | Taking time off

1 ▶ 15.3 Listen to conversations 1–3. How did each speaker spend their time off?
   1 _____
   2 _____
   3 _____

2 ▶ 15.3 Listen again. Match the questions and phrases a–i to the conversations in 1.
   a Did you manage to get away? ___
   b How did you spend the weekend? ___
   c What did you get up to? ___
   d I've always wanted to … ___
   e It needed doing. ___
   f I caught up on … ___
   g It turned out to be … ___
   h We managed to fit in … ___
   i It was a relaxing way to spend … ___

3 Work in groups of four. Think of three examples of recent time off (you can invent the information if you like). Have a different conversation about your time off with each member of the group. Use as many of the questions and phrases from 2 as possible.

Language at work | *-ing* form or infinitive?

1 Work with a partner. Read the pairs of sentences 1–5.
- In which pair of sentences is there little or no change of meaning of the verbs in **bold** before the use of the *-ing* form and infinitive form?
- Discuss the change in meaning of the verbs in **bold** in the other four pairs.

1 a I **remember spending** my year off in Australia. It was so much fun!
  b Did you **remember to book** time off for your next holiday?
2 a They **went on working** for the same company all their life.
  b After they left, they **went on to open** their own business.
3 a Do you **prefer working** for large companies or small businesses?
  b Do you **prefer to take** an early or a late lunchbreak?
4 a Sheila **stopped working** when she injured her back.
  b Sheila **stopped to take** a year off from her job.
5 a I **regret leaving** school at 16 and **not spending** longer at school.
  b I **regret to inform** you that your order has been delayed.

2 Read the *Language point*. Complete the table with the sentences (a or b) in **1**.

LANGUAGE POINT

Some verbs can be followed by either the *-ing* form or the infinitive form with <u>little or no change in meaning</u>. For example, the verbs *like, hate, love, prefer*, etc.: *I prefer working on my own. I prefer to work on my own.*

Some verbs can be followed by either form, but <u>the meaning changes</u>. For example, the verbs *remember, forget, go on, stop* and *regret*.

remember (and forget)	to talk about memories *1a*	to talk about necessary actions ___
go on	to talk about continuing actions ___	to talk about a change in actions ___
stop	to talk about an action which ended ___	to talk about the reason for stopping ___
regret	to express you feel sorry about something you did ___	to introduce bad news ___

» For more information, go to **Grammar reference** on page 135.

3 <u>Underline</u> the correct verb in *italics*.
1 Sorry, I didn't remember *sending / to send* you the job description.
2 I'll never forget *visiting / to visit* Singapore for the first time.
3 After working at our Paris office, I went on *running / to run* the office in Berlin.
4 Stop *doing / to do* everything yourself. Learn to delegate!
5 I'm sure they'll regret *not taking / not to take* a career break later in life.
6 They forgot *bringing / to bring* the contract for your signature.
7 I'm late because I stopped *seeing / to see* a client on the way here.

4 Complete questions 1–4 with the correct form of the verb in brackets.
1 On your CV, it says you stopped _____ (work) for a year. What did you do?
2 Can you remember _____ (deal with) a major problem at work? How did you solve it?
3 After you left school, why didn't you go on _____ (do) a university degree?
4 What is one decision you regret _____ (make) in your career?

» For more exercises, go to **Practice file 15** on page 135.

5 Work with a partner and discuss why a job interviewer might ask the questions in **4**. What answers do you think a successful candidate would give?

Goodbye and see you next year

Career breaks and gap years might sound great, but what if you can't afford to give up your job for a year? Or you don't want to stop working, but you do want to see the world? Remote Year is one solution. The company isn't a job provider because all its participants already have a job. Its role is to set up a 12-month travel programme for remote

workers – people who do their job as long as they have a laptop and an Internet connection.

In its first year, Remote Year received applications from 25,000 people – yes, you have to apply and attend an interview. This number was reduced to a final list of 75 'digital nomads' who want to spend 12 months together in 12 different cities. Remote Year organizes accommodation and workspaces in each new location. It will even provide guidance on how to get your employer on board with the idea.

Of course, there are some difficulties. First, you have to convince your boss that you can still work as effectively on the other side of the world as you can in the office or from home. And what happens if there's no Wi-fi in your hotel or your laptop breaks in the middle of the desert? In reality, these kinds of problems can happen anywhere.

What you learn – according to Remote Year – is that good work doesn't always happen in an office cubicle. 'Your best work happens when you feel inspired. It's hard to find inspiration in routine.'

Discussion

1 What are the advantages of Remote Year compared to taking a career break or gap year?

2 If you went away for 12 months with Remote Year, which 12 cities would you like to visit? Why?

3 Do you think your employer would agree to your plans? What objections might your employer have?

Task

1 Work with a partner. Imagine you work for Remote Year and you are going to interview someone who would like to travel with your organization for 12 months. Think about the types of qualities and skills that a person would need for this way of working and living. Then write a list of around ten interview questions.

2 Change partners with another pair. Take turns to role-play an interview. Ask and answer questions from your list in 1.

3 Work with your partner in 1 again. Report back on your interview and explain if you think the person you interviewed is suitable for the Remote Year program.

Viewpoint 5 | Career perceptions

Focus

Preview

In this lesson, you will watch videos about different perceptions of what a career is. The first interview explores perceptions of career breaks. The second interview looks at the perception of careers for women.

1 **Work in small groups and discuss these questions.**

1 How common are career breaks in your company/country? Are they viewed positively or negatively?
2 Why do you think some people take a career break?
3 What might influence the decision to take a career break?

2 **These words and phrases are from the videos you are going to watch. Match words and phrases 1–8 to their definitions a–h.**

1 soft skills
2 sabbatical
3 perception
4 counterparts
5 lack
6 unconscious bias
7 stake
8 pay gap

a prejudice which you are unaware of ___
b large difference between what one group of people earn compared to another ___
c colleagues working in the same type of business ___
d share of or involvement in something ___
e an extended break from work for study and/or travel ___
f not have enough of something (e.g. confidence) ___
g the way something is viewed ___
h abilities such as leading a team or presenting information ___

Perceptions of career breaks

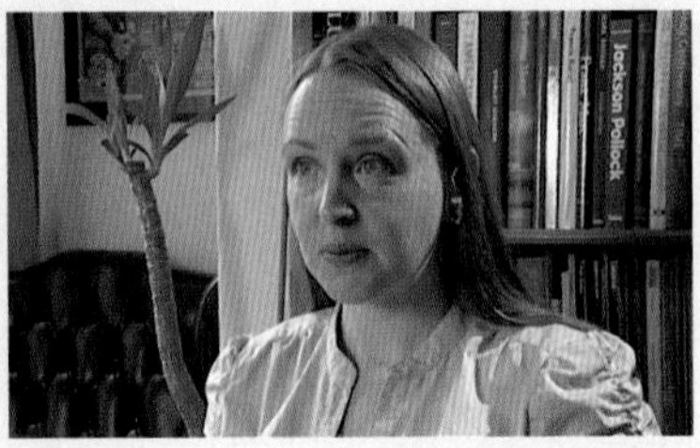

3 ▶ 01 **Watch a video about Rachel Morgan-Trimmer, who set up a company called The Career Break Site. Number topics a–h in the order she mentions them (1–8).**

a the professional benefits ___
b practical advice on what to do with your car, house, etc. ___
c attending a talk ___
d volunteering opportunities ___
e options for taking a career break ___
f the personal benefits ___
g travelling on your own or in groups ___
h company attitudes to career breaks ___

4 ▶ 01 **Watch the video again and answer questions 1–8. Then work with a partner and compare your notes.**

1 Why did Rachel Morgan-Trimmer set the site up?
2 Why do people visit the website?
3 What advice can they also read on the site?
4 What are the main categories for career breaks on the site?
5 What two examples does she give for volunteering opportunities?
6 What personal benefits of a career break does she mention?
7 What professional benefits of a career break does she mention?
8 How might a small company perceive the idea of a sabbatical?

5 **If you took a career break, what would you do and why? Tell the class.**

Glossary
an old saying a commonly known expression or statement with a moral message

career pipeline a way of referring to career history and the natural process of moving up the career ladder

the sky's the limit idiom meaning there is no limit to what you can achieve

Perceptions of careers for women

6 Work in small groups. You are going to watch an interview with Kathy Harvey, Associate Dean at Saïd Business School, about women's careers. Before you watch the video, list some of the possible challenges that you think women might face in terms of their careers and career progression. Afterwards, compare your list with another group.

7 ▶02 Watch the interview with Kathy Harvey. As you watch, number the questions a–d in the order she answers them (1–4).
a How will women overcome these challenges in the future? ___
b What challenges do women in business face today? ___
c How can education help with the challenges that women face? ___
d How much has the position of women changed in business? ___

8 ▶02 Watch the interview again and make notes about what Kathy Harvey says about each of the points below.
- the opportunities for women now compared to 30 years ago
- the pay gap as you go up the career pipeline
- women's own perception of themselves
- people with a stake in encouraging women in business
- three key factors

9 Work with a partner. Read the two quotes from the interview with Kathy Harvey. How much would you agree with the perceptions in both quotes? Are these views mostly true in your country, culture or business? Why/Why not?
'If you educate a man, you educate one person. If you educate a woman, you educate the family.'
'Men and women both want a flexible workplace, where they can take time off … where they can think about different stages in their career.'

Comparing your perceptions

10 Look at the list of different perceptions of careers, 1–7. Score each perception from 1 (I strongly agree with this) to 5 (I don't agree with this at all).
1 Some careers are more suitable for women than for men, and vice versa.
2 People should expect to have three or four different careers in their lifetime.
3 I think most successful professionals dedicate their life to one career only.
4 Career breaks are probably more suitable for women than for men.
5 The idea of flexible working hours and career breaks is fashionable rather than practical.
6 If anyone works hard enough, they will reach the top of their career ladder.
7 Most companies should do more to make sure that all their employees are treated fairly and equally.

11 Work in small groups. Compare your perceptions from **10** and give your reasons. Try to convince other people in the group who have a different perception from you.

Working with words

1 Match 1–8 to a–h.

1 They'll be easy to work with – they certainly have _b_
2 She's quite shy, but sometimes she comes ___
3 As a financial adviser, I have to build ___
4 I thought he was arrogant, so I took ___
5 To attract younger customers, you'll have to project ___
6 If your office is clean and tidy, it creates ___
7 Your company needs to manage ___
8 I'm afraid that these faults might mean our customers start to form a bad ___

a across as being a bit unfriendly.
b a reputation for good communication with clients.
c an impression of efficiency and professionalism.
d an instant dislike to him.
e a more modern image.
f a good relationship with clients so they trust me.
g opinion of us.
h its online profile more carefully.

2 Complete 1–8 with the adjectives from the list.

favourable   trustworthy   simple   ineffective
functional   wary   successful   modest

1 Our new product got good press and _favourable_ reviews.
2 We can speak freely – my assistant is very
___.
3 The advertising campaign was _____ – our sales actually fell slightly.
4 The design is simple and _____ so the product is very easy to use.
5 Fortunately our bid was _____ so we now have funds to develop the new department.
6 It is natural to be _____ of a company that has a poor reputation for customer service.
7 Don't be too _____ about your achievements at the interview. You need to let them know how much you've done.
8 Remember the golden rule when presenting: keep it short and _____.

Business communication

1 Complete the follow-up call from Pierre to Samir with these phrases.

would you like to meet   I wondered if you'd
let's say   can you tell me how   I'll email you a map
let me know where   in from France, won't you
see you   I suggest we meet to   I'm calling about
responding so quickly   whatever's best

Pierre Good morning. This is Pierre Jouet.
1_____ the email I sent you last week in response to your enquiry.
Samir Oh yes. Thanks for 2_____.
Pierre 3_____ had time to look at the brochure I sent you.
Samir Yes – it looks very interesting.
4_____ discuss things further.
Pierre That would be fine. When
5_____?
Samir 6_____ next Wednesday at 10.00.
Pierre Fine. 7_____ for you.
Samir You'll be travelling
8_____?
Pierre That's right. I'm planning to drive and stay overnight in Bilbao. 9_____ I get to your office?
Samir Are you familiar with Bilbao?
Pierre Not really.
Samir 10_____ you're staying and 11_____ and directions from your hotel.
Pierre Thanks. OK. 12_____ next Wednesday at 10.00.
Samir I'll look forward to meeting you. Bye.

2 Put the words in 1–5 in the correct order.

1 and / work / name's / UB / for / my / James Sims / I .

_____

2 given / Jill Sander / your / by / I / details / was .

_____

3 I / interested / offer / in / if / to / our / see / are / you / still / wanted .

_____

4 is / taxi / public / transport / by / best / or / it ?

_____

5 you / later / I'll / my / confirm / call / assistant / to / today / get / to .

_____

GRAMMAR REFERENCE

Present simple

Use the present simple

1 to talk about routines
   *I usually **arrive** at work at about 8.30.*
2 to talk about things we think of as permanent
   *I **work** for IBM.*
3 to talk about states
   *Paris **lies** on the River Seine.*
4 (with future reference) to talk about timetabled events
   *The next train **leaves** at 11.15.*
5 to talk about future time introduced by *when, as soon as, after, if,* etc.
   *When I **see** Margaret tomorrow, I'll give you a ring.*

Common phrases used with the present simple are: *as a rule, generally (speaking), on the whole, once (a week / in a while), every (winter), most of the time.*

Present continuous

Use the present continuous

1 to talk about an action happening at the moment of speaking
   *Mr Takashi **is waiting** for you in Reception.*
2 to talk about a project that is ongoing and unfinished
   *I **am writing** a report on the takeover, and I should finish in a few days.*
3 to talk about things we think of as temporary
   *I **am staying** with my brother while my house is being redecorated.*
4 to talk about a gradual change or development
   *Because of global warming, sea levels **are rising** slowly.*
5 (with future reference) to talk about an appointment or arrangement
   *I **am seeing** Mrs Langer next Tuesday.*

Common phrases used with the present continuous are: *currently, for the moment, at the moment, for the time being, tomorrow (afternoon), right now.*

Stative verbs

Verbs that describe states rather than actions are normally only used in the simple form, i.e. verbs of thinking (e.g. *know, agree*), verbs of appearance (e.g. *look, seem*), feeling (e.g. *prefer, want*), possession (e.g. *own, belong*), the senses (e.g. *taste, sound*). Some stative verbs can sometimes be used in the continuous form, but with a change in meaning.

   simple: *I **see** the Eiffel Tower on my way to work.*
   continuous: *I'm **seeing** Bob on Monday.*
   (= *I am meeting Bob*)

Language at work

1 Complete 1–8 with the present simple or present continuous form of the verbs in brackets.

1 A stockbroker is someone who
   _____ (buy) and
   _____ (sell) shares.
2 The M40 _____ (go) from London to Birmingham.
3 What time _____ (the last flight to New York / leave)?
4 Because of the roadworks, it
   _____ (take) me much longer to get to work.
5 I'm afraid Leon is out at the moment. He
   _____ (have) lunch with a client.
6 I can give Anne your letter. I
   _____ (see) her tomorrow afternoon.
7 Tell Heinrich I'll get in touch when I
   _____ (get back) next week.
8 We _____ (develop) a new anti-malaria drug, and hope to start trials in a couple of years.

2 Write an appropriate question for these answers, using the stative verbs from the list. More than one correct question is possible.

belong   taste   look   own   prefer   ~~sound~~

1 Q: *Does the car sound OK to you?*
   A: I think so – I can't hear anything wrong with it.
2 Q:_____?
   A: He's about 2 m tall, with dark hair and blue eyes.
3 Q:_____?
   A: Tea – I don't like coffee at all.
4 Q:_____?
   A: It's delicious.
5 Q:_____?
   A: It's mine.
6 Q:_____?
   A: No, I rent it.

3 Choose the correct words in *italics*.

1 As a rule, I *catch / 'm catching* the 8 a.m. train.
2 Right now I *design / 'm designing* a new company website.
3 I *stay / 'm staying* with Clare for the time being.
4 On the whole I *complete / 'm completing* most tasks quite quickly.
5 I generally *check / am checking* my emails twice a day.

Working with words

1 Complete 1–10 with the best option a–c.

1 Our perks include subsidized meals, health care and a _____ car.
   a corporate   **b** company   **c** commercial

2 How is company loyalty _____ by senior management in your company?
   a fulfilled   **b** acknowledged   **c** commissioned

3 Does your company offer any kind of non-professional staff _____?
   a development   **b** education   **c** extension

4 We're lucky to have a non-_____ pension plan.
   a contribution   **b** contributing   **c** contributory

5 I work for an airline, so my family gets a really good _____ on flights.
   a discount   **b** decrease   **c** bargain

6 Our company offers free medical _____ so we don't need to worry if we become ill.
   a assurance   **b** insurance   **c** reassurance

7 Non-cash _____ can often be more effective for staff motivation than extra money.
   a repayments   **b** rewards   **c** returns

8 Winning the prize gave me a great sense of _____.
   a realization   **b** completion   **c** achievement

9 I think this person deserves more _____ for her many years of service to the company.
   a recognition   **b** performance   **c** incentive

10 You seem bored most of the time. Maybe you'd get a promotion if you showed a bit more _____ at work.
   a reward   **b** enthusiasm   **c** performance

2 Match the words from the list to statements 1–6.

*appreciation   bonus   commission   feedback
fulfilment   incentive*

1 You've done well this year, overall. There are a few things that need improvement, but you've also had some successes. _____

2 My boss said he would really miss me if I left. It's nice to know he feels that way. _____

3 If I'm one of the top ten salespeople, I'll get a ten-day holiday in Florida. _____

4 The company has had a successful year, so I got an extra €2,000 in November – on top of my salary. _____

5 If I can make six sales this month, that'll be 3% of €24,000 times six, which will be €4,320. _____

6 I work for a charity. The salary isn't very high but the work is interesting and I feel I'm using my skills doing something very worthwhile. _____

Business communication

1 Alain is making small talk with Kirsten at a conference. Number their conversation in the correct order 1–12.

a Kirsten Yeah. See you. ___

b Alain Hello. It's Kirsten, isn't it? _1_

c Kirsten Yes, isn't it? I'm sure you'll enjoy the change in lifestyle. We decided to stay in the city because the house we wanted needed too much work. ___

d Alain How are things? ___

e Kirsten That's right. I thought I might see you here. ___

f Kirsten That's amazing! We considered that line of business, too! ___

g Alain No, not at all. Catch you later. ___

h Alain No? What a coincidence. ___

i Alain Oh dear. Were you disappointed? ___

j Alain Yes, it is. In fact, we've bought a small farm and my wife runs a holiday rental business. ___

k Kirsten No, not really. I don't think our children wanted to move. Well … You don't mind if I go and get myself some food? ___

l Kirsten Very good, thanks. I've heard you've moved into the country – is that true? ___

2 Choose the most appropriate phrases in *italics*.

Jamal Hi, my name's Jamal. [1]*I don't think we've met. / How are things?*

Alicia [2]*No, I don't know you. / Nice to meet you.* I'm Alicia. Is this your first Nordica workshop?

Jamal Yes. My colleague is sick so my manager asked me to come instead. Do you know many people here?

Alicia Not really. I was recently transferred from Purchasing.

Jamal [3]*What a coincidence! / That's lucky!* So was I!

Alicia [4]*By the way / Apparently*, it's our new company policy – transfer rather than hire new people.

Jamal [5]*Really? / Oh dear.* We discussed the idea for our region, too, a few months ago.

Alicia [6]*Well, / By the way*, I'm sure it's a good solution for many companies.

Jamal Yes, you're probably right.

Alicia [7]*So, / In fact*, would you like a drink? I'm going to get a coffee.

Jamal Not at the moment, thanks. [8]*Catch you later. / Is that the time?*

GRAMMAR REFERENCE

Direct and indirect questions

1 In a direct question, the normal word order is verb–subject. In an indirect question, the word order is subject–verb, and the question begins with a phrase like *Do you know* …:
   *When **is Mr Patel** leaving?*
   → ***Do you know** when **Mr Patel is** leaving?*

2 An indirect question does not use the auxiliary *do*:
   ***Where does Mr Elmore** work?*
   → *Could you tell me **where Mr Elmore** works?*

3 For *Wh-/How* questions, we retain the question word:
   ***How much** does it cost?*
   → *Can you tell me **how much** it costs?*

4 When *who* or *what* is the subject of the question, there is no difference in word order:
   ***Who left** this message?*
   → *Do you have any idea **who left** this message?*

5 For *Yes/No* questions, we use *if* or *whether (or not)*:
   Is it going to rain tomorrow?
   → *Do you know **whether** it's going to rain tomorrow?*

Negative questions

1 Negative questions usually begin with the contracted negative form of an auxiliary or modal verb.
   ***Aren't** you based in Milan?*
   ***Didn't** they sell hardware as well as software?*
   ***Can't** you work a bit later tonight?*

2 We often use negative questions to:
   • complain: ***Haven't** you finished yet?*
   • make a suggestion: ***Why don't** you join us?*
   • check information: ***Isn't** this yours?*
   • make a request: ***Can't** we join you at the meeting?*

Question tags

Question tags follow a statement and use the subject and an auxiliary or modal verb in question form.

1 If the statement is positive, the question tag is negative:
   *It's hot, **isn't it**?*

2 If the statement is negative, the question tag is positive:
   *You haven't seen my keys, **have you**?*

3 Statements with auxiliary or modal verbs repeat the auxiliary or modal in the question tag:
   *She **won't** go to China, **will she**?*
   *You **can** swim, **can't you**?*

4 Statements with no auxiliary or modal verb use *do* in the question tag:
   *You **work** for Siemens, **don't you**?*

5 Question tags retain the same tense as the statement:
   *He **left** early yesterday, **didn't he**?*

6 If the subject is *someone, somebody, everyone, everybody, anyone, anybody*, use *they* in the tag:
   ***Anyone** can use the meeting room, **can't they**?*
   If the subject is *nobody* or *no one*, the tag is positive:
   ***Nobody** knew about that, **did they**?*

Language at work

1 Rewrite the direct questions as indirect questions using the words given.
   1 Will he take the job?
     Do you know _____?
   2 When did Amanda send them the catalogue?
     Could you find out _____?
   3 Is this the train for Munich?
     Do you have any idea
     _____?
   4 Where does the bus for Place de la Concorde go from?
     I'd like to know _____.
   5 Have you had anything from the minibar?
     Could you tell me _____?
   6 Who left this package here?
     I was wondering _____.
   7 What time will you be arriving?
     I'd be grateful if you could tell me
     _____.
   8 What day is best for you?
     Please let us know _____.

2 Change 1–5 into negative questions.
   1 Are you in charge of training?
     _____
   2 Have you completed that report yet?
     _____
   3 Should they be here by now?
     _____
   4 Can I have my own team working on this?
     _____
   5 Did you want to say something?
     _____

3 Add a suitable question tag to 1–8.
   1 You're from London, _____?
   2 You couldn't give me a lift to the station, _____?
   3 The bank shuts at 5.00, _____?
   4 You didn't see Anna, _____?
   5 You haven't seen Joe, _____?
   6 You won't tell anyone, _____?
   7 Nobody's called, _____?
   8 That wasn't easy, _____?

Working with words

1 Replace the words in *italics* in 1–8 with the phrases from the list. Change the form if necessary.

miss the deadline   ~~upfront planning~~
fall behind schedule   *an accurate forecast*
stay on track   *budget constraints*
go over budget   *make the launch date*

1 A project like this needs plenty of *preparation beforehand.* _____upfront planning_____

2 The contractors failed to *keep to the agreed schedule* so the new bridge was completed one year late.
_____

3 The whole project has been difficult and we've *lost time* because of unforeseen delays.
_____

4 Can you give me *a detailed prediction*?
_____

5 They didn't *start selling the new product on the agreed date.* _____

6 What *limitations on spending* do we have when it comes to travel costs? _____

7 There are strict penalty clauses, so it'll be expensive if we *are late for that date.* _____

8 I always look at our spending carefully so that we don't *spend more than we have.* _____

2 Complete sentences 1–7. Use the answers to complete the puzzle and find the hidden word.

1 Did you make a detailed _____ before you started.

2 The trains always _____ on time in this country.

3 Their spending on the project went _____ of control!

4 If you don't want to overspend, you need a realistic _____.

5 I hope our next project runs more _____ than this one!

6 Don't use that contractor. They made a real _____ of things last time.

7 We can't afford to _____ the chance of securing the new contract.

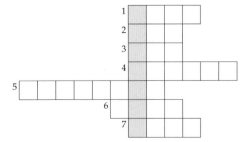

Business communication

1 Sondra is discussing the progress of an HR project with Dimitri. Choose the best answer (a–c) from 1–8 below to complete their conversation.

Sondra OK, Dimitri. What's the current [1]_____ of the staff satisfaction survey?

Dimitri Well, on the whole, we're [2]_____. We've received replies from the questionnaires, but we haven't collated the answers yet.

Sondra You do know the regional HR conference date [3]_____ for next month, don't you?

Dimitri Yes, but we've [4]_____ with IT. They haven't set up the database for us yet, to collate the results.

Sondra So the real problem [5]_____ IT's time management?

Dimitri Partly, yes.

Sondra How about [6]_____ as much of the report as you can?

Dimitri That's [7]_____, but until we have results from the survey, there's nothing to put in the report.

Sondra So what you're really [8]_____ is, without the database you can't continue?

Dimitri Err, yes.

1 a stand   b status   c view
2 a up to scratch   b in the lane   c on track
3 a had set   b had already set
    c has already been set
4 a knocked a problem   b come to a problem
    c hit a problem
5 a lies with   b stands with   c sits with
6 a to prepare   b prepared   c preparing
7 a likely   b possible   c probable
8 a saying   b telling   c talking

2 Match 1–8 to a–h.
1 How far are you ___
2 Things aren't running ___
3 We finalized the draft ___
4 So what do you ___
5 If you ask me, ___
6 I'm not ___
7 That's not ___
8 Up to now ___

a the launch dates have been set for …
b we should scrap the idea.
c as smoothly as I'd hoped.
d with the new packaging?
e an ideal solution.
f mean exactly?
g three weeks ago.
h convinced.

GRAMMAR REFERENCE

Present perfect

Use the present perfect

1 to link a present situation with something that took place at an unspecified time in the past

*Ana **has sent** the new brochure to all our clients.*

The present situation is that all the clients have the new brochure. The past event is that Ana sent the new brochure (we don't know when).

2 with *yet* and *already* to talk about tasks expected to be done or which are done earlier than expected

A ***Have** you **finished** that report **yet**?*

B *Yes. And **I've already done** most of the next one as well.*

3 with *how long, for* and *since* to talk about duration of states and activities

4 with *just* to talk about things that have happened very recently

***I've just seen** Tom in the cafeteria.*

5 with unfinished time periods: *since, so far this week, up to now, recently, this month, today.*

*You've **been late** three times this month – please be on time for the rest of the month.*

Past simple

Use the past simple

1 when referring to (or thinking of) a finished time period like *yesterday, last week, at 5.30, on 11 May, at Christmas, in 2002,* etc.

*I **went** to the sales conference last week.*

2 for questions with *When? What time? How long ago?* etc. because the expected answer is a finished time period

A *When **did** you **see** Mr Li?*
(NOT: *When have you seen Mr Li?*)

B *I **saw** him yesterday.*
(NOT: *I have seen him yesterday.*)

3 with many present time expressions usually used with the present perfect, like *this week, today, just,* if they refer to a time period that is about to finish or has just finished

*We've **made** a lot of progress this week.* (said on Wednesday – the time period is still in progress)

*We **made** a lot of progress this week.* (said at 4.30 p.m. on Friday – the time period is about to finish)

Language at work

1 Complete the two dialogues with the past simple or present perfect form of the verbs in brackets.

A I need to ask David if he
¹_____ (decide) to set up the focus group.

B Don't worry. I ²_____ (already / speak) to him about it.

A Really? When ³_____ (you / see) him?

B I ⁴_____ (call) him first thing today.

A What ⁵_____ (he / say)?

B He ⁶_____ (not / make) up his mind yet. He needs some documents from head office, and they still ⁷_____ (not / arrive).

C ⁸_____ (you / finalize) all the arrangements for Mr Eng's visit yet?

D I'm dealing with it now. I
⁹_____ (fix) a date for him to come and visit – the 19th.

C What about Bob? I think he needs to be there.

D That's fine. I ¹⁰_____ (speak) to Anna a couple of days ago, and the 19th is fine for him, too.

C ¹¹_____ (you / arrange) the visit to the warehouse yet?

D Yes, I ¹²_____ (just / organize) that – for the afternoon.

C What about dinner that evening?

D I ¹³_____ (book) a table yesterday – at The Mill – I hope that's OK.

C Fine. That all sounds excellent. You
¹⁴_____ (be) very efficient.

2 Match 1–6 to contexts a–f.

1 Has our bid for the contract been successful? ___
2 Was our bid for the contract successful? ___
3 Have you spoken to the caterers this week? ___
4 Did you speak to the caterers this week? ___
5 I've just cancelled the order. ___
6 I just cancelled the order. ___

a The result of the contract bids was announced last week.

b I only cancelled the order. I didn't reorder or complain.

c They're announcing the results of the contract bids now.

d I am expecting you to speak to the caterers some time this week. (It is Wednesday.)

e I was expecting you to speak to the caterers this week. (It is 5 p.m. on Friday. I am about to leave the office.)

f I cancelled the order a couple of minutes ago.

Working with words

1 Complete the phrases in **bold** in the text with a suitable word from the list.

benefits   concept   innovative   practical
proposition   technology

> The Cell Zone™ is an ¹_____ **idea** from Salemi Industries. The **key** ²_____ behind this sound-resistant cell phone booth is that it lets you make and receive cell phone calls without disturbing anyone. It's a ³_____ **solution** to the increasing problem of making calls in noisy public spaces where you need somewhere quiet and private to talk.
>
> With its ergonomic cylindrical shape, the Cell Zone™ is a product where **cutting-edge** ⁴_____ is combined with a stylish design. It's made from two steel cylinders fitted inside each other. The space between is filled with a soft, sound-absorbing material that acts as an additional sound barrier.
>
> One of the **major** ⁵_____ of the Cell Zone™ is that it can be located almost anywhere – airports, nightclubs, restaurants, libraries, sports stadiums, hotels, shopping malls or even on the street. The exterior of the booth can also be used for advertising, making it a **commercially-viable** ⁶_____.

2 Replace the verbs in *italics* in 1–9 with a phrasal verb from the list. Change the tense if necessary.

get round   bring about   come up with   take forward
pay off   carry out   bring down   take up   set up

1 I'm thinking of leaving the company to *start* _____ my own business.

2 We're over budget on this project – we need to do something to *reduce* _____ the costs.

3 That's a great idea – I knew you would *create* _____ a plan to solve the problem.

4 I'm really pleased the company has *responded to* _____ the challenge of recruiting across the EU.

5 We *performed* _____ a lot of tests before we launched this product.

6 Concern about global warming has *caused* _____ a number of changes to environmental guidelines.

7 We put a lot of money into this idea – hopefully the investment will *have a good result* _____.

8 We *avoided* _____ the problem of relocating extra staff by recruiting locally.

9 The first stage of the project went well, and we're now *developing* _____ our plans for the next stage.

Business communication

1 Number the extracts from a presentation about a new product in the most appropriate order 1–10.

a First, I'll give you a brief overview of the product. ____

b Basically, Minute Monitor consolidates a department's time schedules. It … ____

c Does that sound OK? ____

d Now I'd like to move on to some of its features. I'd like to demonstrate this by using the tool itself. ____

e Then I'll talk about its benefits. After that I'd like to show you some of its features. ____

f Good. The greatest benefit of this is that all your staff's appointments are logged in one main diary so everyone can see who's in the office and when. ____

g What I'd like to do in this presentation is demonstrate a new scheduling tool. _1_

h Have a look at the screen – with your current system you can't link everyone's calendars. However, with Minute Monitor, you'll all be able to access this central one. ____

i Is everything clear so far? ____

j OK. We call the product Minute Monitor, and it's a pretty simple concept. ____

2 Complete the rest of the presentation with the words and phrases from the list.

this means   the biggest potential benefit of
in the future   the other major advantage   whereas
at the moment   is another great thing about

Minute Monitor scheduling tool can be set up with your current system immediately, ¹_____ similar tools on the market require much higher investment to make them compatible. ²_____ is that the program is very user-friendly and doesn't require a lot of previous knowledge or training. A drop-down user-guide assists you every step of the way, which ³_____ Minute Monitor. ⁴_____, your system is able to schedule 25 employees' appointments, but with Minute Monitor you can increase this to 50. ⁵_____ that project leaders and department heads can have a better overview of the activities taking place. ⁶_____ Minute Monitor is that physical project scheduling can be delegated to admin staff ⁷_____, giving the team leader more time on the project.

GRAMMAR REFERENCE

Use *can* or *(be) able to* to talk about ability. *Can* has only two forms: *can* (present) and *could* (past). Use *be able to* when an infinitive is needed.

Present ability

1 Use *can* to talk about general or present ability.
   *I **can** speak French, but I **can't** speak German.*
   *Could you speak louder – I **can't** hear you.*

2 *Is/are able to* is possible instead of *can* but *can* is more common.
   *Are you **able to** hear me at the back of the room?*

Past ability

1 Use *could* to talk about general ability in the past and with verbs of perception (*feel, see, hear*, etc.).
   *Anna **could** speak four languages when she was six.*
   *I **could** see that she was upset.*

2 For a single specific action in the past (as opposed to general ability), to mean 'tried and succeeded', use *was able to*.
   *I **was able to** run fast enough to catch the bus.*
   *I **could** run fast when I was young.*
   However, if the specific action is negative, use *couldn't* or *wasn't able to*.
   *I called customer services again and again, but I **couldn't** / **wasn't able to** get through.*

3 To talk about a specific action in the past, especially when we succeed in doing something difficult after trying hard, use *managed to*. It can be used in the positive or negative.
   *They didn't want to give us the discount at first, but we **managed to** persuade them.*

4 To refer to past ability with a connection to the present, use the present perfect form of *be able to*.
   *I **have** always **been able to** learn languages quite easily.*

Future ability

Since *can* has no infinitive form, use *be able to* to talk about future ability

1 after *will* and *going to*
   *Perhaps Jane **will be able to** help you.*
   *I'm afraid I'm not **going to be able to** do anything for you.*

2 after modals
   *I **may/might be able to** help you.*

3 after verbs like *would like to* and *want to*
   *I **would like to be able to** help you.*

Language at work

1 Complete 1–10 with the correct form of *can* or *be able to*. Sometimes more than one answer is possible.

1 Do you think you _____ come to the launch party next week?

2 We may _____ offer you a slightly better discount – I'll try my best.

3 So far I _____ (not) get in touch with her, but I'll keep trying.

4 As far as I _____ see, you have a valid complaint.

5 Do you know if Amanda _____ speak Spanish?

6 Do you think you will _____ finish on time, or will you need a few more days?

7 I'm afraid I _____ (not) come to the meeting next week.

8 We'll need an interpreter because I _____ (not) speak Chinese.

9 _____ (she) finish that report yet?

10 I _____ understand your worries, but I think we should take the risk.

2 Choose the correct words in *italics*.

1 A Did the hotel have a good view of the mountains?
   B Yes, I *could / was able to* see Mont Blanc from my room.

2 A When I got to the office, I was locked out.
   B How *could you / were you able to* get in?

3 A So what happened when you missed the plane?
   B Luckily I *could / was able to* take another flight.

4 A Did she complain to you, too?
   B Yes she did, but I *couldn't / wasn't able to* understand what the problem was.

5 A If the safe was locked, how *could you / were you able to* get the documents out?
   B One of the managers had a spare key.

6 A What did you think when you heard Jan had been promoted?
   B Well, at first I *couldn't / wasn't able to* believe it.

7 A Did you renegotiate the contract?
   B Yes, we *could / were able to* obtain a slightly better deal.

8 A *Could you / Were you able to* contact Katie?
   B No, not yet, but I'll call again later.

Working with words

1 Match 1–7 to a–g.
1 We work with local communities and take ___
2 We have strongly held beliefs about equality and intend to stay ___
3 We need to do more to reduce ___
4 Environmental groups share ___
5 We work hard to ensure that our subsidiaries all act ___
6 Trading standards officers make sure that companies comply with ___
7 As a fund-raising manager, I encourage companies to donate ___

a regulations and follow official guidelines.
b money to our charity.
c the impact our factories have on air pollution in the local area.
d an active part in managing health and education projects.
e a strong commitment to caring for the environment.
f true to our principles.
g responsibly and follow our environmental policies.

2 Complete the text with the correct form of the words in brackets.

Choosing investments carefully

¹_____ (ethics) investments are having an increasing impact on the financial services sector. These investments, also known as socially ²_____ (responsibility) investments, are beginning to have more ³_____ (credible) than they did when they started 30 or 40 years ago.

Investing in one of these funds is meant to be a sound investment choice rather than an act of ⁴_____ (generous). Fund managers invest in companies with a good reputation which treat their workers with ⁵_____ (fair) and avoid all forms of ⁶_____ (discriminate) or ⁷_____ (prejudiced). In theory, this should lead to better industrial relations and greater long-term profitability.

Fund managers also tend to avoid unstable and undemocratic regimes where there is evidence of ⁸_____ (bribe) and ⁹_____ (corrupt), as well as companies who do things by ¹⁰_____ (deceptive).

Business communication

1 Jana at Events4U has been asked to organize an information day at RCI for key clients. She is meeting with Xavier from RCI. Number their conversation in the correct order (1–10).

a **Jana** Oh, speaking of staff … We aim to have the reps available to the clients as long as possible. They're welcome to attend the whole day and the evening gala dinner, too. ___

b **Jana** Well, the idea is to focus on the different products you offer and to provide interactive stands. The clients can then try out your new products and speak to you – the reps – directly. ___

c **Jana** I've called this meeting to tell you about the key account event you asked us to organize. We're planning to hold it at the Lichtenstein Palace. _1_

d **Jana** Finally, we'd like to offer you two possible 'performances' during the day, too. I'll email you the details next week. ___

e **Jana** Yes, I thought that might be a problem. We recommend you arrange a shift system throughout the day, so reps attend either the afternoon or the evening. ___

f **Xavier** That's a great idea. I'm glad you're involving the staff. ___

g **Xavier** That makes sense. The reps can decide which shift they prefer. ___

h **Xavier** I'm not sure many reps will stay in the evening if they've been at the event all day. ___

i **Xavier** Thanks, you've done a great job so far. It's exactly what we're looking for. ___

j **Xavier** That sounds great – a lovely venue. How are you going to organize the event? ___

2 Put the words in *italics* in the correct order to complete 1–7.
1 *We / you / going / provide / are / to* _____ with free transport.
2 *You'll / to / opportunity / get / the / sample* _____ our products.
3 The Acto Museum *is / visit / worth / well / a* _____.
4 *It / a / would / good / to / be / idea* _____ buy a ticket in advance.
5 *We'd / to / to / like / you / invite* _____ an information evening.
6 *It's / thing / need / the / just / kind / we / of* _____ for our clients.
7 *Alternatively, / show / be / you / delighted / we'd / to* _____ our facility in Prague.

GRAMMAR REFERENCE

will

Use *will* + infinitive

1 to make predictions or talk about future facts

*It looks as if the economy **will slow** down next year.*

2 to make decisions at the moment of speaking

A *I'm sorry – I'm really busy at the moment.*

B *Don't worry – I'll call back later.*

For decisions made earlier, when you mean 'I've decided to', use *going to*, not *will*.

*I should be back in an hour. I'm **going to get** my hair cut.* (NOT: *I will get …*)

be going to

Use *be going to* + infinitive

1 to talk about a plan or intention where the decision has already been made

A *I've asked the contractors to meet with us.*

B *I see. What **are you going to say** to them?*

2 to make a very definite prediction based on evidence that you can see or know about

*My manager likes to start meetings on time, so he's **going to be annoyed** when I arrive late.*

Often either *will* or *going to* can be used to make predictions.

*When interest rates go up, people **will / are going to** start spending less.*

Present continuous

Use the present continuous to talk about arrangements, appointments, social events and anything you would put in a diary, particularly when the time, place or purpose is mentioned.

*I'm **seeing** Bill in Paris tomorrow to discuss the project.*

Going to can almost always be used in these situations, but use of the present continuous is very common in everyday spoken English.

Present simple

Use the present simple to refer to future events that are in a timetable.

*Do you know when the last train **leaves**?*

The verb *be* is often used in the present simple when talking about personal schedules.

*I'm **in Madrid** on Friday and I'm **away** for a couple of days next week as well.*

Language at work

1 Read the situations and the responses 1–7. ~~Cross out~~ one option in *italics* that is incorrect.

1 You come to an office to see either Mr Peters or Miss Winston. The receptionist tells you that Mr Peters is away for the day.

That's OK. *I'll see / I see / I am seeing* Miss Winston.

2 A colleague asks you if you are free this afternoon. You have arranged to take Ben to the airport.

No, *I'm taking / I will take / I'm going to take* Ben to the airport.

3 A colleague asks if you have any plans for the weekend.

Yes, *I'm meeting / I will meet / I'm going to meet* Jack for a meal this evening.

4 A friend asks you what the future holds for property prices.

Most people seem to think *they are falling / they are going to fall / they will fall* next year.

5 You are at a football match. Your team is 3–0 down and there are only 2 minutes to go. A friend asks why the manager doesn't bring on some new players.

It's too late. *We will lose / We are going to lose.*

6 A colleague wants to arrange a meeting for Tuesday.

Sorry, that's no good – *I'm / I'm being / I'll be* in Paris on Tuesday.

7 A colleague tells you that she can't give you a lift to the station as originally planned and she apologizes.

Don't worry – *I'll get / I'm going to get* a taxi.

2 Complete these dialogues with the best form of the verbs in brackets (sometimes more than one form is possible).

A Where are you going?

B I ¹_____ (pick up) the new catalogues from Amanda today.

A Do you think Bill ²_____ (be) there?

B Yes, I ³_____ (see) him after Amanda – why?

A I've got a new price list for him …

B OK, I ⁴_____ (take) it with me if you like. I ⁵_____ (make sure) he gets it.

C Have you decided on your holiday yet?

D Yes – we ⁶_____ (go back) to Spain. I booked everything a few weeks ago.

C ⁷_____ (you / stay) in the same place as last year?

D Yes, it's much easier. But we ⁸_____ (not / fly) this time.

C How ⁹_____ (you / get) there?

D Ferry and car. There's a ferry that ¹⁰_____ (leave) at 8 p.m. every night. The whole journey ¹¹_____ (only / take) 24 hours, and it means we ¹²_____ (have) our own transport when we're there.

Working with words

1 Someone is talking about their colleagues. Match the adjectives from the list to statements 1–8.

conventional   creative   determined   impulsive
indecisive   methodical   outgoing   thoughtful

1 First Su Li said she was going to apply for the job; then she said she would stay where she was; then she had second thoughts. So I don't know what she's planning. _____

2 Tony isn't exactly boring, but he always wears a suit and tie. He wants to get married and have two children, work from nine to five and retire at 65. _____

3 Everyone loves Bob – he's always in a good mood, and he likes chatting to new people and making friends. _____

4 I asked Bill what he was doing at the weekend and he said 'nothing'. Then, on the way home, he decided to go skiing. So he went to the airport, got a ticket and off he went! _____

5 The thing about Jane is that when she's made her mind up, nothing will stop her. So, if she says she wants to become Sales Director, then that's what she'll be. _____

6 I couldn't find the mistake in the figures, so I asked Arturo to look. He started at the beginning, read every sheet, and finally worked out what the problem was. _____

7 She'll be a great art editor – she's very talented. She's a musician *and* a painter. She's got good fashion sense and she's always full of bright ideas. _____

8 If you ask Jonas something, he doesn't suggest a solution straightaway. He goes away and considers it quietly, but when he does come up with an answer, it's usually right. _____

2 Choose the correct words in *italics*.

1 I need to show this to my line manager to get a different *perspective / attitude* on the project.

2 Let's not reject anything – we need to *think / consider* all the options and then make a choice.

3 I need time to *balance / weigh up* the information and work out what to do.

4 It's hard when you have to decide *about / between* two extremely good candidates.

5 In business you have to be rational and logical. It's no good *relying / trusting* on feelings.

6 You're very experienced and you should have more *assurance / confidence* in your own judgement.

7 If I don't have enough information, I usually *wait / delay* my decision until I've done more research.

Business communication

1 Put the words in 1–7 in the correct order.

1 white / black / here / they're / in / and

_____

2 think / be / it / to / crazy / I / would …

_____

3 me / should / if / we / ask / you …

_____

4 us / detail / you / please / could / some / give ?

_____

5 Clare / to / let's / what / on / has / hear / hang / say

_____

6 right / says / is / John / what

_____

7 facts / look / the / if / we / at / we'll / see …

_____

2 Abigail, John and Bettina are discussing language training at their company. Complete their discussion with the phrases from the list.

let's draw up some action points   in other words
I don't want to spend too long   I don't think we
what you're getting at is   it'll mean we
as far as I'm concerned   that's my view
what's your position   today, I'd like to
I'm not convinced   the fact is

A ¹_____ discuss the three offers for Spanish training. John, ²_____ on this?

J ³_____ there are two very fair offers and one that looks quite expensive.

B ⁴_____ should only consider price. ⁵_____, the more expensive course includes all materials plus holding the training here.

A So ⁶_____ the more expensive option also includes more?

B Exactly.

J ⁷_____. We don't know the quality of these courses – have we received any recommendations?

A The more expensive course is offered by an established institute, but the cheaper options have good marketing.

B But if we take an all-inclusive package, ⁸_____ won't have any unforeseen costs.

J True, but we should meet with the three companies first. ⁹_____.

B ¹⁰_____ we need to discuss the offers in detail with the language provider before a decision is made?

J Yes. ¹¹_____ on what we've discussed so far.

A OK, but ¹²_____ on this point. We have other items still to discuss.

GRAMMAR REFERENCE

Countable nouns

1 A countable noun (e.g. *chair, cat*) can be singular or plural: *a chair, three cats*
2 Single countable nouns have a singular verb.
   *My office **is** in Manhattan.*
3 Plural countable nouns have a plural verb.
   *The managers **are** unhappy about the new proposal.*
4 Some nouns are always plural (e.g. *scissors, clothes*).
   *The scissors **are** on Jamie's desk.*

Uncountable nouns

An uncountable noun (e.g. *advice, equipment*) has a singular verb and has no plural form.
   *Your advice **was** very useful.*

Countable and uncountable nouns

1 Some nouns can be both countable and uncountable, but there is a change in meaning.
   coffee – the drink or the crop
   two coffees – two cups of coffee
   time – minutes and hours passing
   four times – four occasions
2 Additional words can also be used to refer to parts of a whole: *a piece of information, an item of furniture*

Expressions of quantity

1 To talk about something in general, use a plural countable noun and no quantifier
   Computers are getting cheaper all the time.
   or an uncountable noun and no quantifier.
   Cash is less secure than a cheque.
2 When talking about quantities, use the following quantifiers with these classes of nouns:
   singular, countable: *a, an, the, one* (You must have a quantifier of some kind.)
   plural, countable: *how many, (too) many, (not) many, more/fewer, (a) few, very few* and numbers (1, 2, 3)
   uncountable: *how much, (too/not) much, more/less, (a) little, very little*
   uncountable or plural countable nouns: *lots of, plenty of, masses of, most, most of the, some, some of the, all of the, all my, (not) enough, hardly any, (not) any, no, none of the*

Language at work

1 Complete the table with matching pairs of countable and uncountable nouns.

~~traffic~~   correspondence   training   furniture
hotel room   equipment   ~~car~~   letter   money
accommodation   software   time   table   euro
photocopier   lesson   week   computer program

countable	uncountable
car	traffic

2 Choose the correct verb forms in *italics*.
   1 The equipment you need for the presentation *is / are* at Reception.
   2 The people I met at the conference *was / were* very friendly.
   3 The sales statistics *don't / doesn't* show a rise in demand for the product.
   4 Could you turn on the TV? The news *is / are* going to be on soon?
   5 Progress at the site *has / have* been very slow recently.
   6 My clothes *isn't / aren't* smart enough for the interview.
   7 When I was in the UK, the weather *was / were* very varied.
   8 The new software *is / are* being developed in-house.

3 Choose the correct words in *italics*.
   1 I need *many / more* time to make a decision.
   2 She's managed to get *a / some* job with an insurance company.
   3 There *is very little / are very few* information about this on the website.
   4 I had *too much / too many* emails to reply to before the end of the day.
   5 I think there are *very little / very few* people who understand the theory fully.
   6 I'm sure we can find you *a / some* suitable accommodation.
   7 If we agree to that clause, we'll have *very little / very few* room for manoeuvre.
   8 Would you like *morning paper / a morning paper* delivered with your breakfast?

Working with words

1 Complete 1–7 with the words from the list.

process   home   activities   facility
growth   location   workers

1 If we outsource the administrative tasks, our European centres can focus on their core _____.

2 If the business _____ outsourcing goes ahead, all our filing, etc. will be done in China.

3 In the next few years, we plan to move many of our operations closer to _____.

4 R-IT is a new training _____ for students, focusing on all aspects of information technology.

5 Karnataka has 77 engineering colleges producing more than 29,000 graduates a year so there is a large group of skilled _____.

6 We are selling more and more of our products abroad, so our export _____ is rising steadily.

7 We decided to outsource software development to an offshore _____ rather than to one in our own country.

2 Rewrite the words in *italics* in 1–7 using the phrases from the list. Change the form if necessary.

take cost-cutting measures   lead to job losses
improve the quality of life for
create new jobs   streamline our operation
free up resources   gain a competitive edge

1 Some politicians argue that BPO *results in a substantial reduction in employment* _____ at home.

2 Outsourcing has led to the building of new roads and housing in Bangalore and has subsequently *increased personal satisfaction in life experienced by* _____ many local people.

3 Our budget deficit has increased again this year so we need to *do something to make savings* _____ and reduce our office costs.

4 RGM's help desk outsourcing services have helped us to *make the way we work simpler and more efficient* _____.

5 We decided to outsource our back office work in order to *make money and personnel more available* _____ for our core activities.

6 Thirty new offices were opened in the area last year – this *generated 980 additional positions* _____ in the IT industry.

7 We want to *achieve an advantage* _____ over our competitors so we aim to increase production by 10%.

Business communication

1 Complete the extracts from a presentation about outsourcing with the phrases from the list.

due   data   have a   move on   looked at
notice on   look at   the facts   has resulted in
leave   a result   turn our attention to

Recent [1]_____ shows that outsourcing of office cleaning, catering for the staff restaurant and the customer helpline [2]_____ financial benefits for the company.

Let's have a [3]_____ this slide. On the left you can see our expenditure five years ago …

I'd like to [4]_____ to give you some background about each sector we've outsourced. Firstly, cleaning. [5]_____ to increasing personnel costs, outsourcing seemed to be our only option. You will [6]_____ this chart savings other companies achieved. We analysed these carefully and as [7]_____ decided to do the same.

OK, we've [8]_____ cleaning, so let's [9]_____ the staff restaurant. After careful research, [10]_____ were clear: employing staff to run a restaurant was too expensive and not cost-effective. [11]_____ look at these figures …

Finally, I'd like to [12]_____ you with some interesting statistics regarding the customer helpline …

2 Choose the correct prepositions in *italics*.

1 Due *for / to / from* the recent large increase …

2 A knock-on effect *of / to / on* this was …

3 This relates back *for / at / to* the point I made earlier.

4 To illustrate this, let's have a look *on / at / to* this chart.

5 This resulted *to / for / in* huge financial losses.

6 You will notice *on / to / by* this chart how big our market share has become.

7 Let's turn our attention *from / to / on* the drawbacks involved.

8 As a result *from / to / of* public criticism, we stopped our ad campaign.

9 Let's consider financing the project, which I referred *to / about / of* earlier.

10 To conclude, I'd like to leave you with some food *for / to / in* thought …

GRAMMAR REFERENCE

The passive

Form

1 Verbs in sentences can either be active or passive. To make the passive, use the verb *be* in the appropriate tense and a past participle.

Tense	Active	Passive
Present simple	*We do the job.*	*The job is done.*
Present continuous	*We are doing the job.*	*The job is being done.*
Past simple	*We did the job.*	*The job was done.*
Past continuous	*We were doing the job.*	*The job was being done.*
Present perfect	*We have done the job.*	*The job has been done.*
Past perfect	*We had done the job.*	*The job had been done.*
Future and other modals	*We will do the job.*	*The job will be done.*
Infinitives	*We need to do the job.*	*The job needs to be done.*
-ing forms	*We object to someone doing the job.*	*We object to the job being done.*

2 Make questions and negatives in the same way as in active sentences.
   Was the email **sent** to Mr Jordan?
   *The email **wasn't sent** this morning.*

Use

1 To change the focus of a sentence from who does something to what happens to something.
   *My assistant **has prepared** the contract.* (The focus is on my assistant, the subject of the active sentence.)
   *The contract **has been prepared**.* (The focus is on the contract and what has happened to it.)

2 To describe processes or how something is done.
   *When the grapes **have been picked**, they are taken to the factory.*

3 When the person who does the action is unimportant, unknown or we want to avoid saying who it is.
   *My secretary **has lost** the order form.*
   *The order form **has been lost**.*
   Use *by* after the passive verb to say who does the action.
   *The decision **has been made** by the CEO.*

4 To talk about reputation and with phrases like *is said to be*, *is believed to be*. These phrases are used in news reports and make the information more impersonal.
   *California is **said to be** warm and sunny.*
   *The Prime Minister **is believed to be** in talks with …*

Language at work

1 Change the phrases in *italics* to the passive.

1 *Somebody has lost all my important files.*
   _____

2 When I returned from holiday, I found that *somebody had broken into my flat.*
   _____

3 My colleague is expecting *somebody to promote her.*
   _____

4 I don't like *people telling me* what to do.
   _____

5 *Somebody must have hacked into our computer system.*
   _____

6 I feel that *somebody is not telling us* the whole story.
   _____

7 *They are sending me* to Shanghai for three months.
   _____

8 When I finally arrived at the conference, *someone was putting away the chairs.*
   _____

9 *Somebody unveiled Microsoft's latest operating system* last month.
   _____

10 After the Games, *they will close the Olympic Village.*
   _____

2 Complete the article with the active or passive form of the verbs in brackets. Use these tenses for each paragraph A–D:

A present simple   C present perfect
B past simple   D *will* future

A A report today [1]_____ (accuse) leading stores of exploiting workers in Bangladesh: 'Workers in factories there [2]_____ (pay) low wages; the employers [3]_____ (not / recognize) unions, and workers [4]_____ (often / force) to work seven days a week.'

B The author of the report [5]_____ (visit) several factories: 'On one occasion, the owner [6]_____ (tell) in advance of our visit. That time, there [7]_____ (be) 30 workers in the factory and they [8]_____ (give) regular breaks. When we [9]_____ (make) a surprise visit a few days later, the same room [10]_____ (pack) with over 100 workers.'

C A spokesperson for one of the stores said: 'We [11]_____ (have) factories in Bangladesh for years and are proud of the real improvements in working conditions that [12]_____ (make). The factories [13]_____ (always / produce) high-quality goods, and customers in Europe [14]_____ (benefit) from low prices.

D The report says: 'We expect this issue [15]_____ (raise) in boardrooms over the next few weeks, and we [16]_____ (get) lots of promises. But we need more than this – so we [17]_____ (keep up) the pressure. We hope that something [18]_____ (finally / do).'

Working with words

1 Match 1–8 to a–h.
1 Many women feel there is a glass ceiling which ___
2 There isn't much opportunity for advancement ___
3 I could take early retirement which ___
4 He felt the new job was a sideways move ___
5 When the factory closed down ___
6 With the current recession, the career prospects ___
7 To save costs, the company made ___
8 I can't move house because of the children's schools, so ___

a would mean stopping work at 55 rather than 65.
b relocation is not an option.
c in an industry like mine don't look great.
d rather than a promotion.
e a lot of the staff redundant.
f so I need to start looking elsewhere if I want to move up the career ladder.
g a third of the workers were laid off.
h stops them from getting top jobs.

2 Complete 1–8 with the correct form of the word in brackets.
1 He was fired from his last job for stealing. As a result he's virtually _____ now. (employ)
2 Instead of going to university, I did an _____ with a local engineering firm and it gave me a job for life. (apprentice)
3 The government keeps raising the pensionable age, so I don't know when I'll reach the age of _____. (retire)
4 In the last few years, our core business has become _____ so we either need to diversify or close down. (profit)
5 The two _____ have decided to sell their share of the business to a large multinational. (own)
6 Every employee has a share of the business, but we have an _____ board who make the day-to-day decisions. (operate)
7 The _____ and union leaders have not come to an agreement so now we have to vote on whether to take strike action. (manage)
8 Money is important, but job _____ also includes things like opportunities for advancement and training. (satisfy)

Business communication

1 Anton and Carolina are meeting with Bob from HR to negotiate the annual staff trip. Complete 1–10 in this extract from their meeting with the correct words a–d.

Anton What we need to ^{1}_____ on today is what to do for the staff trip this year. Let's look at what our ^{2}_____ are.

Carolina ^{3}_____ about we charter a plane to Morocco for a weekend?

Anton We do have that on our list of options, but ^{4}_____ need to stretch the budget if we did that.

Carolina Yes, you're right. Bob, how does HR view things? What can you ^{5}_____ us?

Bob Well, the worker's council always offers an outing to employees – so we can't stop this – but what we ^{6}_____ is that it should be educational as well as entertaining.

Anton You mean, ^{7}_____ we include something cultural we can choose any of our suggestions?

Bob Yes. Let's say you take the Morocco option. ^{8}_____ you offer excursions to places of interest as part of the package, HR might veto the whole trip.

Carolina OK. We can ^{9}_____ with that and would organize the trip to conform to HR's wishes.

Anton So, a quick ^{10}_____ – if …

1 a talk   b meet   c decide   d discuss
2 a opportunities   b options   c opinions   d opponents
3 a What's   b Who   c Why   d How
4 a we'll   b we   c we'd   d we've
5 a lend   b help   c proposed   d offer
6 a plan   b propose   c aim   d intend
7 a provided   b would   c were   d supposing
8 a Until   b Providing   c Unless   d If
9 a be   b remain   c stay   d live
10 a review   b recap   c repeat   d outline

2 Put the words in *italics* in the correct order to complete 1–5.
1 *discuss / the / areas / we / to / need / are*
_____ the weekend rota and overtime.
2 *to / one / would / option / be*
_____ cancel the event.
3 *we / don't / on / why / take*
_____ two temporary staff for our busy period?
4 *far / what / so / got / we / so / have* ?
_____
5 *sounds / a / plan / like / that*
_____ – could you let Jan know the details?

GRAMMAR REFERENCE

First conditional

In the *if* clause of first conditional sentences, we talk about a present or future situation that is quite likely to happen; in the other clause, we talk about the result.

If clause (likely situation)	Result
If + present tense	*will* + infinitive
If you order 20 units,	*we'll give you a 15% discount.*
If I'm not promoted,	*I'll leave the company.*

Variations:

1 You can use the present continuous or present perfect in the *if* clause.
  *If anyone **is waiting** for you there, I'll let you know.*
  *If he **hasn't emailed**, I'll call instead.*
2 You can use other modals instead of *will* in the result clause.
  *If we hurry, we **may** / **might** / **can** get there in time.*

Second conditional

In the *if* clause of second conditional sentences, we talk about an imaginary present or future situation that is less likely; in the other clause, we talk about the result.

If clause (likely situation)	Result
If + past tense	*would* + infinitive
If we accepted the takeover bid,	*we would be out of a job.*

Variations:

1 You can use the past continuous in the *if* clause.
  *If you **were applying** for a job, what would you put on your CV?*
2 You can use *could* instead of *would* in the result clause.
  *If we got a bit more help, we **could** finish on time.*

Linking words

1 A number of expressions mean 'if and only if', and emphasize the condition: *provided (that)*, *providing* (less formal), *as long as* and *on the condition that*.
  *I'll help you today **providing** you do my shift on Friday.*
2 *Supposing* means 'just imagine', so it is normally used with second conditionals.
  ***Supposing** they offered you the job, would you take it?*
3 *Unless* is similar in meaning to 'if not'.
  *I'll be home by 5.30 **unless** the meeting finishes late.*
4 We use *in case* to talk about action taken to avoid something happening.
  *I'll take a spare battery **in case** the main one runs out.*

Language at work

1 Choose the most appropriate words in *italics* to complete 1–8.

  1 Daniela's application to move to your team has been approved, so if you *want / wanted* her to start this month, then you *will / would* have to let HR know by tomorrow.
  2 We could easily fulfil orders for a few hundred metres of cable. However, if you *want / wanted* 50,000 metres, for example, that *will / would* take a lot longer.
  3 I think you're being very rash. If I *am / were* you, I *will / would* reconsider your decision.
  4 I *will / would* agree on the deal now if I *have / had* the authority, but I have to check with the directors first.
  5 Can you leave this with me until tomorrow? I think I *will / would* be able to work something out if you *give / gave* me a little more time.
  6 I *will / would* apply for the Madrid job if I *speak / spoke* good Spanish, but unfortunately I don't.
  7 If you *are / were* applying for only a couple of days off, I *will / would* agree to it, but I'm afraid I can't agree to two weeks holiday at this point in the project.
  8 Let me know if you *want / wanted* to read the contract again before signing and we *can / could* resume our meeting in half an hour.

2 Which of the situations in 1 are …?
  1 first conditional _____
  2 second conditional _____

3 Complete 1–5 with the words from the list.
  if   unless   provided   as long   in case
  1 I'm organizing some insurance _____ I get ill.
  2 I'm very busy, so please don't disturb me _____ it's an emergency.
  3 _____ that sales don't start falling, we'll reach our targets this year.
  4 I should be able to get there by 10.30, but I'll let you know _____ there's a problem.
  5 _____ as we get the funding, we can go ahead with the project in October.

4 Complete 1–4 with your own ideas, using first or second conditionals.
  1 If I ever had the chance, _____
  _____
  2 I wouldn't take time off work unless _____
  _____
  3 If it's a nice weekend, I think _____
  _____
  4 If he hasn't arrived in the next five minutes, _____
  _____

Working with words

1 Complete 1–10 with the best option a–c.

1 It was obvious there was a ___ in the market for more affordable lenses.

   a space   b break   c gap

2 Unless we can secure more financial ___, we won't be able to go ahead with our expansion plans.

   a approval   b backing   c aid

3 How much start-up ___ do we need for equipment, rent and supplies for the first year of operation?

   a capital   b assets   c wealth

4 Investors will want to look at your business ___ in detail to assess the potential of your idea.

   a map   b chart   c plan

5 We need investment to start the business so we're going to approach a ___ capitalist.

   a business   b project   c venture

6 Most investors want to be confident they'll receive a good return on ___.

   a asset   b investment   c speculation

7 We're initially renting this temporary ___ and then we'll think about finding somewhere permanent.

   a fund   b outlet   c backing

8 Many ___ entrepreneurs fail in their first year of business.

   a can-be   b will-be   c would-be

9 Our business ___ is based on using pop-up stalls at public events like music festivals.

   a model   b return   c diagram

10 We turned ___ our first million this year so I feel like we've reached the next stage in our growth.

   a up   b over   c around

2 Choose the correct words in *italics*.

1 This proposition is *hugely / totally* ridiculous – there's no way we can agree to it.

2 So far we've had an *extremely / absolutely* successful year.

3 The demands they have been making are *extremely / absolutely* outrageous.

4 The prices you've been quoted seem *completely / incredibly* high.

5 The concept is extremely *brilliant / clever* – there's no way it could possibly fail.

6 The sales conference was incredibly *helpful / fantastic*. You should have gone.

7 I think it would be absolutely *impossible / difficult* to cut costs any further.

8 Developing a good business model is *totally / very* important before approaching people for funding.

9 The weather has been absolutely *bad / terrible* recently.

10 Your business plan is *incredibly / completely* useless, so it will be hard to attract investors.

Business communication

1 Two business acquaintances meet up at a trade fair. Correct the mistakes in the phrases in *italics* in their conversation.

Barbara Is that you Josef? [1]*What you do here?*

_____

Josef Hello, Barbara [2]*I don't see you for ages.*

_____

Barbara [3]*How does life treat you?*

_____

Josef I've been working on a big project for Avrim. [4]*How's you with business?*

_____

Barbara Well, I've moved house, changed jobs and I'm about to set up on my own. Actually, with that in mind, [5]*could you make me a favour?*

_____

Josef If I can – what do you need?

Barbara [6]*The things is, I look for someone* to come into partnership with me. Would you be interested?

_____

Josef Me? [7]*That not something I can deciding on right now.*

_____

Barbara OK. I'll email you more details and maybe we could discuss it over lunch.

Josef Well, [8]*I'll surely think about it.*

_____

2 Match 1–10 to a–j.

1 That's actually ___

2 Let's chat ___

3 By the way, could ___

4 The thing is, we're looking ___

5 It's been a long time since ___

6 With that in mind, maybe ___

7 What have you ___

8 Are you still working ___

9 I haven't seen you ___

10 We're looking for an investor and ___

   a for SFL?

   b I could ask you for a favour.

   c for someone to help us out.

   d we've been in contact.

   e about that over dinner.

   f I wondered if you were interested.

   g for ages.

   h been up to?

   i you do me a favour?

   j the reason why I'm calling.

GRAMMAR REFERENCE

Present perfect simple and continuous

Talking about duration

1 Use the present perfect continuous with *How long …?*, *for* and *since* to talk about continuous activities or repeated actions that started in the past and are still going on now.
*How long **have you been learning** English?*
*I've **been learning** for three years / since I joined ILS.*

2 Use *for* to talk about amounts of time (*for three weeks*, *for two months*). Use *since* to talk about points in time (*since 10.30, since Monday, since the end of May*).

3 When talking about a state, use the present perfect simple, because stative verbs are not used in the continuous form.
*How long **have you known** Pia?*
*I've **known** her for five years.* (NOT: *'ve been knowing*)

Unfinished time periods

1 Use the present perfect continuous or simple with unfinished time periods like *recently*, *this week*.
*I've **been trying** to call her all day.*
*We've **had** six offers so far this week.*

2 Use the present perfect continuous when talking about activities that are temporary or unfinished.
*Temporary activity: I've **been staying** with my brother this week. (I usually live in my own flat.)*
*Unfinished activity: I've **been talking** to my accountant this week. (The discussions are continuing.)*

3 Use the present perfect simple for stative verbs.
*My boss **has been** away in London this week. (It is Thursday and he is still not back.)*

4 Use the present perfect simple when talking about completed actions and to give details of quantities.
*I have seen my accountant **three times** this week. (Those three occasions are in the past.)*

No time period

When no time period at all is mentioned, the difference between the present perfect simple and continuous depends on whether the action is finished (and we stress the result) or unfinished (and we stress the action).
*Sam's **read** your report. (He's finished it.)*
*Sam's **been reading** your report. (He hasn't finished it and the activity is continuing.)*

BUT the present perfect continuous can be used to talk about recent activities that are finished if there is some evidence of the recent activity.
*It's stopped now, but it's **been snowing** and the roads are still very dangerous.*

Language at work

1 Complete 1–10 with the present perfect simple or the present perfect continuous form of the verbs in brackets.

1 I can certainly recommend Mr Hiro to you – I _____ (know) him for a long time.

2 The Finance Director is in Hong Kong – he _____ (stay) at the Excelsior for the last two weeks.

3 Someone _____ (use) my printer – feel how hot it is – and half the paper's gone!

4 We _____ (negotiate) the new contracts since May, but there are still areas of disagreement.

5 I _____ (read) the report, but I haven't got to the final recommendations yet.

6 I _____ (go sailing) for five or six years now – I go most weekends.

7 So far we _____ (have) over 400 complaints about the software, so we've definitely got a problem.

8 I'm really sorry to have kept you – _____ (you / wait) long?

9 I _____ (try) to get in touch with customer service for days but the line is always busy.

10 It _____ (rain) for days and days – when is it ever going to stop?

2 Match 1–10 to the most likely context in a–j.

1 I've written the report. ____
2 I've been writing the report. ____
3 I've talked to Mr Holmes. ____
4 I've been talking to Mr Holmes. ____
5 What have you done? ____
6 What have you been doing? ____
7 The weather has got better. ____
8 The weather has been getting better. ____
9 Jack's been skiing. ____
10 Jack's gone skiing. ____

a I'm asking about your life in general since we last met.
b I have finished my discussions with Mr Holmes.
c It's summer now and it's warm every day.
d The report is not finished.
e It's warmer than it was, but it's not warm every day.
f I am still in discussions with Mr Holmes.
g I'm asking what tasks you've completed on your 'to do' list.
h Jack is an expert skier. Ask him about Austria.
i The report is finished. Here it is.
j Jack is on holiday in Austria at the moment.

Working with words

1 Choose the correct words in *italics*.

1 Were you able to integrate the new database *into / at / by* the old one or did you have to start from the beginning?

2 With Internet banking, you can have access *for / to / in* your account at any time.

3 The new tax laws will have a dramatic impact *on / for / to* company profits.

4 What's the company policy *in / for / on* personal use of the Internet?

5 We need to focus *into / over / on* our core business and the activities we do best.

6 We don't put limits *in / on / at* the number of calls you make home during the working week.

7 The restructuring brought *with / for / about* a huge change in the company culture.

8 On this project we'll be collaborating *with / by / in* colleagues in Frankfurt and Milan.

9 The whole team needs to communicate *with / into / over* each other on a weekly basis.

2 Complete 1–10 with the correct form of the words from the list. Use each base word twice.

analyse   communicate   consult   develop   economy

1 A systems _____ is an IT expert who looks at needs and designs software.

2 To solve the problem you need a clear, logical, _____ approach.

3 My colleague's not very _____ – he rarely talks to the rest of us.

4 Modern forms of _____ make it very easy to stay in touch.

5 With the fall in turnover this year, we need to find ways to _____ next year.

6 There are a group of _____ who are interested in buying the land and building new houses on it.

7 An outside agency has prepared a _____ document to suggest solutions to our current communication problems.

8 The charity Mercy Ships often uses _____, like Dr Arras, who specialize in trauma surgery.

9 Most _____ don't seem very optimistic about this recession ending anytime soon.

10 Recent _____ in broadband speeds have made online meetings the norm.

Business communication

1 A customer is calling TNC about a banking problem. Complete the dialogue with the phrases from the list.

by tomorrow   in time for the   you mean
how can I help you   could you give me
once I've looked into it I'll call you back
let me get this straight
could you explain exactly what the problem is

A TNC, Customer Service.
   1 _____?

B Hello. I'm calling about my online bank account. I'm having problems completing a transaction.

A 2 _____?

B Well, I've entered the payment details to pay an invoice for my holiday and the computer won't let me send it.

A Hmm. 3 _____ – you want to transfer some money but you can't?

B That's right. I'm trying to pay an invoice. I've left it a bit late and need to pay it 4 _____.

A 5 _____ your user number and the name of the account. 6 _____.

B Thanks.
   (5 minutes later)

A Hello. This is TNC. The account you're trying to access is a savings account and you can't use your online facility with that.

B 7 _____ I can't pay my invoice online with that account?

A That's correct. You can transfer money into your current account and then pay the invoice.

B If I do that, will the invoice be paid 8 _____ deadline tomorrow?

2 Correct the one mistake in each sentence.

1 What can I do you for?

_____

2 If I understand you right, you received the wrong items.

_____

3 I'll look under it straightaway.

_____

4 We need the goods in time to the training day.

_____

5 Once I've found your order, I'll get you back.

_____

6 It should be by Friday by the latest.

_____

GRAMMAR REFERENCE

Phrasal verb word order

A phrasal verb is a verb + a particle (a preposition or an adverb). You can use the same verb with different particles which changes the meaning.

*Can you **look up** his number?* (= research/find)

***Look out**! That box is going to fall on your head.*
(= beware / be careful)

*Please **look after** the visitors.* (= take care of)

Intransitive phrasal verbs

Some phrasal verbs are intransitive, meaning they are not followed by an object:

*What time do you normally **get up**?*

*Please **speak up**. I can't hear you.*

*We probably **eat out** about twice a month.*

Transitive phrasal verbs

Most phrasal verbs are transitive, meaning they are followed by <u>an object</u>:

*I **deal with** <u>clients</u> from all over the world.*

*Can you **read** <u>the number</u> **back** to me?*

*Let me **write down** <u>your contact details</u>.*

Separable phrasal verbs

1   For transitive separable phrasal verbs, <u>the object</u> can go before or after the particle, with no change in meaning:

*Let's **put off** <u>the decision</u> for a month*

*Let's **put** <u>the decision</u> **off** for a month.*

2   For some separable phrasal verbs, <u>the object</u> can only go between the main verb and the particle:

*After three hours, we finally **talked** <u>the client</u> **round** to signing the deal.*
(NOT: … *we finally talked round the client* …)

3   When the object is a pronoun, <u>the object</u> can only go between the main verb and the particle.

*Let's **put** <u>it</u> **off** for a month.*
(NOT: *Let's put off it for a month*)

Inseparable phrasal verbs

With transitive inseparable phrasal verbs, <u>the object</u> can only go after the particle:

*Don't **count on** <u>Michael</u> for any help.*
(NOT: *Don't count Michael on for any help.*)

Language at work

1   Rewrite 1–10 with the particle in brackets in the correct position. In three sentences, there are two possible positions.

1   Please call him straightaway. (back)
   <u>Please call him back straightaway.</u>

2   Can you look this report for me? (over)
   _____

3   Please drop the package before lunchtime. (off)
   _____

4   She called me for a quick chat. (over)
   _____

5   I'm just showing these people the factory. (round)
   _____

6   Have you given smoking yet? (up)
   _____

7   He's out of the office, but I can put you to his voicemail. (through)
   _____

8   I don't think we managed to get our main message. (across)
   _____

9   They've looked the spreadsheet in detail. (through)
   _____

10   I wouldn't count them agreeing to that price. (on)
   _____

2   Replace the phrases in *italics* in 1–9 with a phrasal verb from the list. Change the form of the verb or add any extra words if necessary.

count on   read back   set up   lay off   come across as
put off   carry out   hang up   weigh up

1   Could you *repeat* your telephone number?
   _____

2   At the interview he *gave the impression of* someone who has a problem with authority.
   _____

3   They've *postponed it* for another week.
   _____

4   *Put the phone down* and try calling again.
   _____

5   They've *made 300 people redundant*.
   _____

6   The two brothers *started* the family business in 1959.
   _____

7   We should *compare* both sides of the argument at this point of the meeting.
   _____

8   Is there a good reason why you didn't *follow* my instructions?
   _____

9   I wouldn't *rely on* them for any help if I were you.
   _____

Working with words

1 Read definitions 1–8 and complete the puzzle.

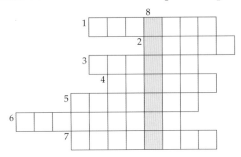

1 Show you agree with something.
2 Respond to something someone says or does.
3 Produce a change in someone or something.
4 Do something in the way you used to do it.
5 Succeed in doing something.
6 Make something start to happen.
7 Keep something going at the same level.
8 Stop something from happening.

2 Match the adjectives from the list to statements 1–8 describing how each person is feeling about a proposed change at work.

ambivalent   critical   anxious   receptive   concerned
enthusiastic   optimistic   hostile

1 'It's very worrying. How will it affect me? I felt much safer with the old system.' He is _anxious_ about the change.
2 'This is the most ridiculous idea I've ever heard, and I will not tolerate it.' She is _____ to the idea.
3 'I think there are some problems with the idea. The finances haven't been worked out properly, and the implications for the staff haven't been examined fully.' He is _____ of the idea.
4 'I like the idea of the extra free time at weekends, but I don't like the idea of starting earlier in the morning.' She is _____ about the idea.
5 'This sounds like quite an interesting idea – I'd like to hear more about it.' He is _____ to the idea.
6 'I think that it will work out well and will improve our working conditions.' She is _____ about the change.
7 'Some of these proposals worry me – I'm not sure they've been properly thought through.' He is _____ about the proposals.
8 'This is going to be absolutely fantastic – I just can't wait.' She is _____ about the change.

Business communication

1 Dermot is explaining the proposed changes in production to worker representatives. Complete his presentation with the phrases from the list.

we're calling on you to   you may be wondering
as you all know   starting from February next year
let's digress for a moment and
we are fairly certain everyone
I'd like to pass this point over to   we'd like to assure you

Dermot ...¹_____ BRT is going to diversify into manufacturing energy drinks. ²_____ we'll be producing our new brand called Boost. ³_____ that sufficient training will be given to everyone involved in this new product and ⁴_____ look at this as a positive move. Training will take place for everyone from October onwards and ⁵_____ will have trained by the end of the year. ⁶_____ why we're moving into energy drinks. There are several reasons so ⁷_____ Xavier from Sales and Marketing. He can show you some interesting statistics.

Xavier Thanks, Dermot. I have a market survey here which compares the sales of soft drinks across Europe. The figures are quite revealing, so ⁸_____ look at these in detail. Over the last five years …

2 One of the worker representatives presents the changes from the presentation in **1** to production staff. Put the words in *italics* in the correct order to complete 1–6.

1 *from / starting / learning / month / we'll / next / be*

_____
how the new drink will be produced.

2 *aware / well / your / regarding / we're / of / concerns*

_____
new technology.

3 *next / weeks / the / few / over / be / we'll / nominating*

_____
some of you to become trainers.

4 *also / introduce / proposing / we're / to*

_____
shift work.

5 *Veronika / now / will / deal / with*

_____
remuneration …

6 *be / this / we'll / month / later / recruiting*

_____
five new workers.

GRAMMAR REFERENCE

Future continuous

Use the future continuous (*will be + -ing*) to talk about

1 activities that will be in progress (and unfinished) at a certain time in the future

I can't see you at 11.00 on Monday because I'll be visiting the factory.

2 repeated or continuous activities over a period of time, often with the prepositions *for* and *until*

I'll be meeting Matthew regularly until the project is finished. (repeated many times in the future)
We'll be living in Osaka for 6 months. (continuous over a period of time)

3 activities that are part of a future programme

Welcome to the course. Over the next few weeks, we'll be looking at methods for making marketing more effective, and we'll be discussing new ways of reaching customers.

Future perfect

1 Use the future perfect (*will have* + past participle) to talk about an action that will be completed before a point of time in the future.

A How's the report?
B It's going well. I'll have finished it by Friday.

2 The prepositions *by* or *before* are normally used with the future perfect. The negative future perfect + *until* is also common.

I won't have finished the report until Friday.

Probability

1 Use *may* and *might* to suggest some uncertainty.

I may come to the party. Then again, I might not. It depends on how I'm feeling.

2 Adverbs like *probably* and *definitely* give a clear indication of how probable we think something is.

I'll definitely come to the meeting. (certain)
I'll probably come to the meeting. (very likely)

In positive sentences, the adverb usually comes after *will* (*I'll definitely be there*). In negative sentences, the adverb usually comes before *won't* (*I definitely won't be late*).

3 Adjective structures like *is certain to, is sure to, is bound to, is (pretty) likely to, is (highly) unlikely to* + infinitive can also be used to indicate degrees of probability.

We won't wait for John. He's bound to be late.
I think out application is unlikely to be successful.

Language at work

1 Complete A and B with the future continuous or future perfect form of the verbs in brackets.

A We're starting our consultation process today, and over the next few weeks, we ¹_____ (talk) to you individually about how you feel about the changes. We ²_____ (finish) our research by the end of March. During the first two weeks in April, we ³_____ (analyse) the findings. We ⁴_____ (publish) a report with the main conclusions by May at the latest. During the consultation period, we ⁵_____ (also / hold) a series of meetings to debate the issues, and senior managers ⁶_____ (give) a range of presentations on the key topics.

B It's proving very hard to arrange a meeting with Mr Sanchez next week. You can't do Monday because you ⁷_____ (not / agree) a price with Jenny by then – you need this for your meeting with Mr Sanchez. He can't do Tuesday because he ⁸_____ (visit) his suppliers. Wednesday's no good because you ⁹_____ (attend) that exhibition in Paris. Thursday's out because you ¹⁰_____ (not / get back) from Paris by 12.00 – the only time he's free.

2 Rewrite 1–8 using the words in brackets.

1 She'll definitely be unhappy about these proposals. (bound)
   She's bound to be unhappy about these proposals.

2 To be honest, I'm unlikely to get the job. (probably)
   _____

3 They may very well cancel the whole order. (quite likely)
   _____

4 There will almost certainly be some changes in the final design. (certain)
   _____

5 They probably won't accept these terms. (unlikely)
   _____

6 I think there's a chance I'll be offered a promotion. (might)
   _____

7 There's a chance we will face some opposition to these changes. (may)
   _____

8 If this goes ahead, there are bound to be some job losses. (definitely)
   _____

Working with words

1 Complete the text with the words from the list.

*gather   behaviour   age   driven
demographics   analytics   history*

Since the beginning of the information ¹_____,
many successful business operations have become
data-²_____. As a result, many new jobs have
emerged including that of the data scientist. These are
people who specialize in data ³_____. They are
highly trained professionals who love to ⁴_____
customer data and discover things about our
⁵_____ as consumers. This can include everything
from studying our transactional ⁶_____ when
we buy things online through to looking at the
⁷_____ of customers spread across the world. So if
you have a love for big data, this is the job for you.

2 Match 1–8 to a–h.

1 I'd like to make ___
2 We monitor the ___
3 There's been an overnight data ___
4 The company mustn't abuse the ___
5 Click this box if you agree to the privacy ___
6 Do not disclose your ___
7 This advertising campaign targets ___
8 Online shopping sites have to encrypt ___

a trust of its customers when they give permission to
   use their data.
b the users in our European markets.
c some recommendations based on this data.
d breach and some credit card numbers were stolen.
e policy on data use.
f online behaviour of staff using this software.
g password details to anyone.
h the credit card numbers of all customers.

Business communication

1 Choose the correct word in *italics* in 1–7.

1 Roughly *spoken / speak / speaking*, by 2020 it will be
   up by 25%.
2 *Accord / According / Accorded* to a recent
   study, there has been a big increase in podcast
   advertising.
3 So what are the facts and *numbers / amounts /
   figures*?
4 The *final / bottom / end* line is that user-generated
   media will continue …
5 So how should we *interpret / analyse / describe* this
   drop?
6 Can you give us the *run-down / downturn / low-
   down* on the types of advertising available?
7 In *generally / general / generality*, traditional forms
   of advertising …

2 Regina asks the project manager, Ursula, to explain
the spending on a project. Complete 1–8 in their
conversation with the phrases from the list.

*what's that in terms of   Stani assured us that
can we look at the figures   according to
apparently, figures from   in general
overall, things are looking   show*

Regina ¹_____ for the project so
far?
Ursula ²_____ we are within
budget.
Regina Are you sure? ³_____
Stani, you're spending a lot on external staff.
Ursula He's right. We do have a lot of contractors
working for us but the fact is, we can't make the
deadline date without them.
Regina I see. ⁴_____ overall
expenditure then?
Ursula ⁵_____ the overspend
now will be balanced out when we reach the test
phase of the project.
Regina What do you mean?
Ursula ⁶_____ a similar project
in our Polish office ⁷_____ that
they came in under budget because they took on
specialist contractors to do the programming. This
meant they saved money in the testing phase.
Regina OK, so ⁸_____ positive,
despite the over-spend?
Ursula That's right.

GRAMMAR REFERENCE

Reporting

1 You can report what something or someone says by using either direct speech or reported speech.

Direct: *She said, 'I buy vinyl records.'*
Reported: *She said (that) she bought vinyl records.*

2 To report what someone said, thought or asked we use reporting verbs: *say, tell (someone), explain, complain, think, wonder, ask, want to know,* etc.

3 The main verb usually moves back a tense if the reporting verb is in the past:

*'Sales **are** rising.'* → *He **said** sales **were** rising.*

When the reporting verb is in the past tense, the table shows the tense changes in reported speech:

Direct speech	Reported speech
Present simple	Past simple
Present continuous	Past continuous
Simple Past	Past perfect
Past continuous	Past perfect continuous
Present perfect	Past perfect
Pres perf continuous	Past perf continuous
Past perfect	No change
Past perf continuous	No change
am / is / are going to	*was / were going to*
will future	*would* future

4 Modal verbs change as follows:

Direct speech	Reported speech
can	*could*
may	*might*
must	*had to*
need	*needed*
will	*would*

5 If the reporting verb is in the present tense and the situation is still current, the tense doesn't change.

*'I really **like** working here.'*

→ *He **says** he really **likes** working here.*

6 To report *Wh-* questions: retain the question word, but change the tense (as above) and change the subject-verb word order:

*When **is Jane** going?*

→ *He asked me when **Jane was** going.*

7 To report a yes/no question, use *if* or *whether*.

__Has__ Bill spoken to you?

→ *He asked me **if / whether** Bill had spoken to me.*

Time references

For reported speech, the time references change:

'I'll speak to him this week.' → *He said he'd speak to him last week.* (reported the week after)

Common changes include: *now* → *then*, *today* → *that day*, *yesterday* → *the day before*, *this morning* → *that morning*, *next year* → *the following year*.

Language at work

1 Rewrite 1–10 as reported speech, using the words given.

1 'The plan will not work', I said.

I said _____.

2 'I don't believe in working at weekends', my boss always says.

My boss always says _____.

3 'Can you send this letter?' he asked me.

He asked me _____.

4 'How long have you been waiting?' she asked me.

She asked me _____.

5 'We had a great time on holiday', they said.

They said _____.

6 'What do you think about the proposal?' he asked her.

He asked her _____.

7 'A lot of people are unhappy about these changes', she says.

She says _____.

8 'I haven't shown anyone these plans yet', he told me.

He told me _____.

9 'Have you ever been skiing?' she asked her.

She asked her _____.

10 'I'll be back on Friday', he said.

He tells me _____.

2 Report the information given by a project manager about a meeting using reported speech.

'The project is progressing well and we will probably finish stage one by the end of this week. The three construction firms are going to begin work on the stadium next week.'

'We had originally budgeted for two construction firms, but the timing of the project has meant that we needed to contract another so we can finish on time.'

The project manager ...

1 said _____

2 ... and explained _____.

3 He reported _____.

4 He also told the project team

_____

5 ... but pointed out _____

6 ... so _____.

Working with words

1 Match the adjectives from the list with statements 1–10.

hierarchical   strict   cautious   individualistic   egalitarian   formal   liberal   collectivist   open   accepting

1 'I like to make my own choices about the way I live my life.' _____

2 'My parents allowed me a lot of freedom when I was young.' _____

3 'We are all the same here – there's no separation between bosses and workers.' _____

4 'My boss is a Level 1 worker, and I'm a Level 4. You're only Level 7, but you'll climb the ladder over time.' _____

5 'If they introduce a shift system, I'll take part – I won't complain.' _____

6 'I'm not going to invest the money in shares. It's going into a bank account where I know it'll be safe.' _____

7 'I would be grateful if you would call me Mr Jones rather than Barry.' _____

8 'My organization has a lot of rules that we have to obey.' _____

9 'I'm always willing to listen to new ideas and suggestions.' _____

10 'Team effort is more important than individual achievement in my company.' _____

2 Complete 1–8 with the correct prepositions.

1 My last boss was sensitive _____ people's needs and treated everyone very well.

2 The company I work for isn't very tolerant _____ individualists.

3 I've just read an article about Finland, so I'm informed _____ business etiquette there.

4 I'm not familiar _____ your customs, so could you explain what I'm meant to do?

5 In some cultures, it's important to be respectful _____ tradition.

6 If you do business in this part of the world, you need to be used _____ dealing with bureaucracy.

7 When I moved to the USA I found it hard to adjust _____ the directness of the people there.

8 What customs do I need to be aware _____ when I visit South Korea?

Business communication

1 Jorge and Lana are talking about doing business in Ukraine. Put the words in *italics* in 1–8 in the correct order.

Jorge I had an interesting time in Ukraine and [1]*the / in / end* _____ a deal was done.

Lana Was doing business there different to Greece?

Jorge Yes, very. We had a lot of misunderstanding at first. [2]*it / because / about / came / of* _____ our lack of knowledge about negotiating in Ukraine.

Lana So what happened?

Jorge We met our Ukrainian colleagues and expected to get down to business. But it seemed a long time before we even spoke about the negotiation. [3]*that / problem / the / was / first* _____.

Lana [4]*so / did / do / you / what* _____?

Jorge We made small talk – about our journey, our families and so on. Eventually we spoke about the real business. [5]*seems / it / that* _____ relationship-building before business is very important to them.

Lana [6]*what / next / happened* _____?

Jorge The Ukrainian team looked at the deal as a whole. They told us exactly what they required from the contract and [7]*when / that / was / uncomfortable / I / felt / really*. _____ I mean, we don't negotiate like that here. We do it bit by bit.

Lana And then?

Jorge [8]*time / by / went / as* _____, we became more aware of each other's culture and how business is done and …

2 Jorge continues his story from **1**. Choose the correct words in *italics* in 1–6.

Jorge [1]*At last / At first* it seemed that the Ukrainians were very direct and abrupt, but this was just their style. [2]*What's most / What's more*, they said 'no' to us quite frequently, which was difficult to get used to. [3]*It wasn't until / It wasn't since* I read up about the Ukrainian negotiating style that I found out they say 'no' about nine times more often than Western negotiators! [4]*In spite / Despite* this we became quite good friends. There were a few times when it was tough and we thought we'd lost the deal. [5]*Luckily / Happily* my colleague knew that hospitality is also very important to business relationships and he invited the Ukrainian team to dinner. The idea was that it would get our relationship back on track. [6]*It really shocked me, but it functioned / It really surprised me, but it worked*. I've certainly learnt from the experience.

GRAMMAR REFERENCE

Past continuous

1 The past continuous (*was doing, were doing*) is often used to set the scene and give background information at the beginning of a narrative.

> *When I got to the trade fair, it was still early. Some of the exhibitors **were setting up** their stands and others **were unpacking** their publicity materials.*

BUT the past continuous is not used with stative verbs or when describing permanent features.

> *Our stand **looked** very professional and it **was** ideally placed because it **was** on the aisle that led to the main restaurant.*

2 The past continuous is also used for an action in progress that is interrupted by another shorter action. (Use the past simple for the action that interrupts.)

> *I **was unpacking** one of the boxes for our stand when my mobile **rang**.*

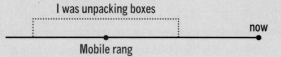

Past simple

The past simple (*did*) is used for the main actions and events in a story that happen one after the other.

> *He **said** I was wanted back at the office immediately and **ended** the call. I **tried** to call back, but there **was** no reply.*
>
> *In the end, I **packed** everything up, **locked** it away and **left** the hall.*

Past perfect

The past perfect (*had done*) is used when we are already talking about the past and want to refer to an earlier action, event or state.

> *When I **got** to the station, I realized I'**d left** my briefcase at the exhibition.*

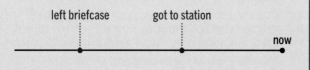

Language at work

1 Complete 1–8 with the past continuous, past simple or past perfect form of the verbs in brackets.

1 I _____ (not recognize) him because he _____ (change) so much.

2 While I _____ (wait) for the train, I quickly _____ (call) the office to leave a message for Joe.

3 On my way to work this morning, the sky _____ (be) grey and it _____ (rain) lightly.

4 I first _____ (meet) Harry while I _____ (work) for Morgan Stanley in New York.

5 When I _____ (get) to the checkout, I realized that I _____ (leave) my credit card at the office.

6 When they _____ (arrive) back from their holiday, they were shocked to see that their apartment _____ (break) into.

7 I _____ (jump) up, _____ (run) across the room and quickly _____ (smash) the glass to set off the fire alarm.

8 I _____ (notice) a couple of small mistakes while I _____ (read) your report.

2 Complete this story about a boat trip with the past simple, past continuous or past perfect form of the verb in brackets.

A few years ago, while I [1]_____ (do) a training course in Borneo, I [2]_____ (go) on a boat trip with some colleagues to an island that was an animal sanctuary – with lots of wild monkeys. We [3]_____ (arrive) at about lunchtime, and I [4]_____ (decide) to have a look at the jungle. I [5]_____ (walk) along a path when I [6]_____ (see) a very large and mean-looking monkey sitting on a branch in front of me, making a rather menacing noise. I [7]_____ (stop) because I [8]_____ (never / come) across wild monkeys before, and I [9]_____ (not know) what to do. Suddenly, the monkey [10]_____ (jump) down from the tree and [11]_____ (come) towards me very aggressively. I [12]_____ (turn) and [13]_____ (run) as fast as I could, shouting loudly as I got to the beach. When my colleagues [14]_____ (look) up, I [15]_____ (race) towards the water and the monkey [16]_____ (chase) after me. I finally [17]_____ (reach) the safety of sea and [18]_____ (dive) in. When I [19]_____ (look) round, I [20]_____ (be) pleased to see that the animal [21]_____ (disappear), but my colleagues [22]_____ (laugh) uncontrollably.

Working with words

1 Put the letters in the correct order to make words relating to appraisals. Then complete sentences 1–7 with the words.

sadders   corucstetivn   sarie   espxrse
ccdnotu   tjebicoev   imnoort

1 If you don't _____ performance, you may overlook important areas where change is essential.
2 Always allow yourself enough time to _____ an appraisal – don't rush things.
3 Could we set up a meeting to _____ these issues with the new filing procedure?
4 During the appraisal we rate each _____ on a scale of one to five.
5 The weekly meeting gives us an opportunity to _____ our views to the manager.
6 It's important to give _____ feedback rather than criticizing things that haven't been done properly.
7 You should _____ the issue of equal pay at tomorrow's meeting with HR.

2 Complete the text with the words from the list.

peer   value   performance   tool
appraisals   criteria   form

¹_____ management is not just about carrying out top-down *staff* ²_____; it's about encouraging change and making sure everybody gets the chance to perform to the best of their abilities. In this respect, a 360-degree appraisal system is a really useful *development* ³_____. In our department, we spend a lot of time working out the *assessment* ⁴_____ we are going to use so that the *feedback* ⁵_____ we end up with is as comprehensive as possible. And people enjoy taking part in the process – they quite like having the chance to make ⁶_____ *judgements* on their colleagues' performance; and if they are being assessed, they take it very seriously, because ⁷_____ *rating* is somehow much more honest than anything a boss might say.

3 Complete 1–6 with the correct preposition.
1 My manager handed _____ a feedback form to all my colleagues.
2 We go _____ the form during the appraisal.
3 My manager plans to carry _____ doing 360-degree appraisals every year.
4 I usually come _____ as very confident at work.
5 I've decided to move _____ from learning French to learning Spanish.
6 I think I will end up _____ a good score at the end of my appraisal.

Business communication

1 Sylvie is conducting an appraisal with Julio. Complete the words 1–7 in their conversation.

Sylvie So, Julio, what do you consider were your ¹s_____ and ²f_____ this year?

Julio I think I've performed quite well and reached my sales targets. And if I'd secured the Zipco contract, I'd ³h_____ b_____ salesperson of the month.

Sylvie Yes. I must say, we're very ⁴h_____ with your achievements. Are there any areas you feel you need to ⁵i_____ on?

Julio Yes. I sometimes have difficulty closing a sale. I know my performance has been good, but I would like some help. What's the ⁶b_____ w_____ to deal with apprehensive clients?

Sylvie There are quite a few approaches you could take. You ⁷o_____ to observe some of your colleagues and see what they do.

Julio That sounds like a good idea.

2 Complete the rest of their conversation by correcting the mistakes in the phrases in *italics*.

Sylvie Yes, you need to focus on encouraging more teamwork. ¹*Throwback from the sales force* _____ has been rather poor.

Julio ²*How I should this do* _____? Perhaps I could arrange the observation as a team-building activity.

Sylvie Good idea. ³*Can we identification that as* _____ a personal goal for next year?

Julio Yeah. But ⁴*we could help with some support* _____ from our managers, so we're given enough time for teambuilding.

Sylvie OK. Now, ⁵*you delegated good* _____ interpersonal skills when working with clients, and we'd like to involve you in training new graduates in customer care.

Sylvie Sounds great. But if I'd known about this earlier, ⁶*I would may not have organized* _____ so many business trips in the next few months.

Sylvie Oh. We'll talk about dates later then. Let's turn to the issue of remuneration.

Julio Good. ⁷*While we're talking to money* _____ can we discuss travel expenses, too?

Sylvie Hmm, I suppose so.

GRAMMAR REFERENCE

Third conditional

1 Use the third conditional to talk about things that did not happen in the past (imagining what would have happened if things had been different). It is often used to criticize past actions or to express regrets. In the *if* clause we talk about the imagined past situation; in the other clause we talk about the imagined past result.

Past situation	Past result
If + past perfect	*would(n't) have* + past participle
If you'd concentrated,	*you wouldn't have made the error.*
If I'd studied harder,	*I would have passed my exam.*

2 Notice how negative changes to positive and positive changes to negative.

> Real past: **You didn't give** me the information. (negative)
> Imagined past: **If you'd given** me the information. (positive)
> Real result: **I made** the error. (positive)
> Imagined result: **I wouldn't have made** the error. (negative)

3 In the result clause, use *might have* or *could have* to talk about a less certain result.

> *If you'd helped me, we **could have** finished on time.*

Mixed conditional

Change the verb forms in conditional sentences to talk about an imagined past situation and present result.

Past situation	Present result
If + past perfect	*would(n't)* + present infinitive
If you'd done what I advised,	*we wouldn't be in trouble now.*
If I hadn't won the money,	*I would still be working in a supermarket.*

Perfect modals

1 Use *could have*, *might have* and *would have* to talk about something that was possible in the past but didn't happen.

> *It's a good thing you didn't invest in that company – you **could / might / would have** lost everything.*

2 *Could have* and occasionally *might have* can be used to express irritation and criticism.

> *I was expecting you at the meeting – you really **could / might have** told me you weren't going to come.*

3 Use *should have* to criticize what people have or haven't done.

> *You **should have** asked me for authorization – you **shouldn't have** made the decision yourself.*

Language at work

1 Complete 1–8 with the correct form of the verbs in brackets. Sometimes more than one answer is possible in the result clause.

1 That was a missed opportunity. If we _____ (buy) the shares in April, we _____ (make) a lot of money.

2 It's just as well we took the train to the airport. We _____ (miss) the flight if we _____ (drive), because there was an accident on the motorway.

3 If I _____ (study) English when I was at school, I _____ (not need) to go to language classes now.

4 They called the strike off because if it _____ (go on) for any longer, the company _____ (shut down) the factory.

5 Of course I've got my mobile. If I _____ (not bring) it with me, I _____ (not / talk) to you now!

6 This is all your fault. If you _____ (pack) the items more carefully, none of this _____ (happen).

7 If we _____ (leave) an hour earlier, we _____ (be) there by now, instead of being stuck here in this traffic jam.

8 I understand why you made that decision – if I _____ (be) in your position, I think I _____ (do) the same thing.

2 Rewrite the phrases in *italics* in 1–7 using *could have*, *should have* or *might have*. More than one correct answer is sometimes possible.

1 That wasn't a very sensible decision. *You ran the risk of being dismissed.*

_____

2 What a pity you didn't come five minutes earlier. *You have missed the chance of seeing Anne.*

_____

3 *You were wrong to speak* to her like that.

_____

4 *I'm irritated you didn't let me know* you were coming.

_____

5 *It was a mistake not to send* the price list with the catalogue.

_____

6 *We're very lucky we didn't lose* the contract.

_____

7 *I'm irritated that you didn't call* to say the meeting had been cancelled.

_____

Working with words

1 Complete 1–7 with the words from the list.

appreciate   charity   hesitate   perspective
put off   tip   revitalized

1 Going away for a year gave me a whole new _____ on life.

2 I really _____ what you've done for me, so thanks.

3 If you _____ any longer, the opportunity is going to slip by.

4 That was a very useful _____ you gave me.

5 I had to _____ my trip for a couple of months for family reasons.

6 I've applied for a job as a fundraiser for a _____.

7 I feel really _____ after my six-month break from the office.

2 Put the letters in the correct order to answer clues 1–7. Then complete the puzzle with the answers to find the hidden word.

retnetnio   nthsmiseua   cilypo   sfto
oetdlvempne   ehad fof   bnroade

1 After a break, people often return to work with renewed _____.

2 _____ skills are just as important as technical qualifications.

3 Learning a new language would help my personal _____.

4 We have a very high _____ rate, which shows that our staff are happy.

5 Seeing other countries gave me the chance to _____ my horizons.

6 Time away from work can sometimes help people _____ in a new direction in their career.

7 Car-sharing is now official company _____.

Business communication

1 Marion is talking to her boss about taking six months off to travel. Complete 1–8 in the conversation with the correct options a–d.

M It's been a long-term [1]_____ of mine to travel to Australia.

B But what about your job here?

M Well, I'd like to take six months off. And I'd really [2]_____ it if you could consider keeping my job open for me.

B I'm not sure that's fair on your colleagues.

M I understand your [3]_____, but none of my colleagues have shown interest in doing something similar.

B Maybe not, but I need to know more about your plans.

M Well, I've been offered a work placement for four months and then I'd like to travel.

B Go on.

M The fact that I can travel and gain experience is unique. It's a once in a [4]_____ opportunity.

B OK. But what are the [5]_____ for the company?

M I intend [6]_____ apply for a project manager position and the experience I'd gain would be [7]_____.

B It sounds interesting and you're showing promise with project work. I'll need to discuss this with HR.

M Great. Do tell them it's a [8]_____ situation for us all!

1 a goal   b target   c point   d task
2 a depreciate   b enjoy   c appreciate   d pleasure
3 a warning   b suspicions   c misgivings   d mistrust
4 a life   b lifetime   c century   d blue moon
5 a wins   b uses   c profits   d benefits
6 a towards   b to   c for   d on
7 a priceless   b valueless   c precious   d invaluable
8 a win-lose   b win-win   c benefiting   d profit

2 Put the words in 1–5 in the correct order.

1 finish / a / of / long-term / been / mine / to / goal / it's / my university course

_____

2 and / points / more leadership experience / are / the / plus / skills development

_____

3 my / this / for / from / motivation / comes / my volunteer work / with the Red Cross

_____

4 I'll / satisfied / be / never / unless / do / I / it

_____

5 fair / – I've / do / hardly / never / to / overtime / that's / refused

_____

GRAMMAR REFERENCE

Verb + *-ing* form

1 A number of verbs are followed by the *-ing* form rather than the infinitive including *dislike, enjoy, can't stand, look forward to, avoid, miss*.

> I really **enjoyed seeing** Martha again.

2 When a verb follows a preposition it is connected with, it always takes the *-ing* form rather than the infinitive.

> I'm **keen on travelling**, but I'd be **worried about taking** a whole year off.

Verb + infinitive form

1 A number of verbs are followed by the infinitive rather than the *-ing* form such as *agree, arrange, expect, hope, manage, offer, plan, prepare, promise, refuse, afford, want, would like*.

> We **arranged to meet** the following week.

2 The infinitive is also used to express purpose.

> I'm **taking** a year off **to travel** round the world.

Verb + *-ing* form or infinitive

Some verbs can be followed by the *-ing* form or the infinitive. Sometimes there is little or no change in meaning and sometimes there is a change in meaning.

1 Little or no change in meaning with verbs such as *like, love, hate* and *prefer*:

> I **like travelling**. / I **like to travel**.
> They **love playing** golf. / They **love to play** golf.

2 Changes in meaning with verbs such as *stop, remember, forget, go on,* and *regret*:

> I **stopped going** to the gym on my way home. (I used to go to the gym on my way home, but I gave up the activity.)
> I **stopped to go** to the gym on my way home. (I was driving home and stopped in order to go to the gym.)
> I **remember seeing** Ken at the party. (I saw him, and I have a clear memory of it.)
> I **remembered to see** Ken at the party. (I knew he wanted to speak to me, so I went over to him.)

Language at work

1 Complete this email with the correct form of the verbs in brackets.

Dear Hanno

I'm writing [1]_____ (tell) you about what I'm planning [2]_____ (do) next year because it will affect you, and you may want [3]_____ (think) about [4]_____ (find) a replacement for me.

As you know, Ingrid has arranged for me [5]_____ (send*) to the Seoul office [6]_____ (oversee) the new branch out there. I originally expected [7]_____ (be) away for six months. However, I would like [8]_____ (explore) that part of the world. I asked Ingrid if she would consider [9]_____ (let) me have an extended break, and she has agreed [10]_____ (give) me an additional six months' unpaid leave.

This means I'll be away for a year, which I appreciate is not ideal for you. However, it is very important for us [11]_____ (keep) you as a client, so Ingrid has suggested [12]_____ (take) over the day-to-day running of your account herself. I'm sure you'd enjoy [13]_____ (work) with her, but I thought it was important [14]_____ (check) that you would be happy about [15]_____ (collaborate) with her.

Please let me know your feelings about this, and contact me if there is anything you want [16]_____ (discuss).

I look forward to [17]_____ (hear) from you.

Dan

* TIP: active or passive?

2 Match 1–8 to a–h.

1 I stopped to have a coffee ___
2 I stopped having coffee ___
3 I regret to say ___
4 I regret saying ___
5 I don't remember signing the cheque ___
6 I didn't remember to sign the cheque ___
7 I'll never forget sending you a birthday card ___
8 I'll never forget to send you a birthday card ___

a because I didn't want to fall asleep at the wheel.
b because it's in my computer's calendar.
c that your application for secondment to Brussels hasn't been successful.
d but I must have done, because the bill was paid.
e and that's why the bank sent it back.
f because I couldn't sleep if I drank it at night.
g because I was stuck in the post office for hours.
h I'd apply for the post in Brussels.

Communication activities

Unit 3 | Language at work, Exercise 4

Student A

1 Your colleague is in a project team which is converting an old building to provide new company premises. Ask how the project is going. As your colleague is speaking, comment on what he/she says and ask additional questions.

2 Your company is building a new warehouse and office complex. Update your colleague, using these prompts and/or your own ideas. Use *already* and *yet* and appropriate time expressions.
   - finish the main building work
   - have problems with some of the suppliers
   - not install the IT system
   - not complete electrical wiring
   - reschedule the opening date

Unit 3 | Business communication, Exercise 5

Student A

1 Read the 'To do' list you sent to Ian and the notes you have written under your tasks (M).

2 Begin by calling Ian. Ask Ian to update you on his tasks (I).

3 Answer his questions about your tasks.

4 Make and respond to suggestions as necessary.

Launch date 'To do' list

- Bring Anvikon merchandise to venue (I)
- Finalize timetable of day with sound engineers (M)
    Meeting with them later today.
    Suggestion: sound check night before?
- Brief Anvikon staff about handset demonstration (I)
- Check replies from the press – who's coming? (M)
    Behind schedule! Some invitations sent only 2 days ago!
    Suggestion: we plan for more people than expected?
- Send Anvikon PR manager's speech to MMT-Tec (I)
- Make sure Sarah's briefed on everything (I / M)
    Suggestion: Wait till last minute – want to give her positive information!
    Make good impression!

Unit 5 | Working with words, Exercise 10

Company X

- donated 100,000 trees to Nairobi, Kenya, to aid reforestation
- provides funds for a project that gives loans to farmers and fishermen
- established fund to promote research into conservation of drinking water
- sponsors disabled sports in Germany
- committed to offering equal entrance requirements and development opportunities to male and female employees

Company Y

- failure to perform routine inspections led to corroded pipelines and oil leaks
- oil spill has polluted large area of coastline
- lack of attention to safety led to oil refinery explosion – injuries to employees
- currently an investigation into whether company manipulated oil markets – staff bought large quantities of company's product
- committed to renewable energy: invested heavily in solar and wind power; runs a project to generate electricity from petroleum coke

Unit 5 | Business communication, Exercise 8

Kokua Likeabike – based in Germany

Core business: selling wooden children's bikes – various models and styles

- made from various types of wood – environmentally-friendly, sustainable product, sourced from well-managed forests
- specially designed without pedals for young children to learn to balance before moving on to a 'real' bike
- distributors and sales partners are worldwide

Possible open day ideas:

- demo of new models
- tour of the factory
- trip to wood source for forest management presentation
- Likeabike races – challenge country against country in a race on the bikes
- ideas exchange – distributors share marketing ideas/strategies from each country
- gala dinner

Unit 8 | Business communication, Exercise 7

Pair A: Managers

Your company is finding it difficult to keep staff – apparently your competitor has better working conditions. Two members of staff have recently told you that they are thinking of leaving. Hold a meeting with them to discuss working conditions. Find out what they want. Then decide what you can offer them and what you are willing to compromise on. Likely areas of discussion are:

- flexible hours / home working
- better travel expenses
- more perks: fitness club membership, lunch vouchers, new computer
- increased salary (this should be no higher than 1% more than inflation)
- less bureaucracy in the job
- more training for future promotion

You will lead the discussion. Make sure that you outline the situation, put forward proposals, state the consequences of these, bargain as necessary, and summarize your progress.

Unit 8 | Language at work, Exercise 6

Student A

You are the manager in a small country office. Student B wants a temporary secondment for six months in a department in a large city office – to get wider experience (and to fill in for someone on maternity leave). Say 'no' to the request at first, but see if you can come to an agreement.

Student B

You work for Student A in a small country office. You have the chance of a temporary secondment for six months in a large city office. This will help you get wider experience while filling in for someone on maternity leave. You are prepared to make a lot of compromises to get Student A's agreement.

Talk about:

- A: the negative effects on the day-to-day running of office
  B: the positive effects in terms of learning new skills, etc.
- A: the staffing difficulties this would cause
  B: the solutions for the staffing problems
- A: the negative effects on B's ability to do the job when B returns
  B: the positive effects of the secondment in terms of personal development and experience
- A: the impracticality of a long transfer as opposed to a two-week secondment
  B: the impracticality of a two-week secondment as opposed to a long transfer
- A: the possibility of a salary reduction after the secondment
  B: the possibility of a salary increase after the secondment
- A: other outcomes if the secondment was approved
  B: other outcomes if the secondment was not approved

Unit 9 | Language at work, Exercise 5

Student A

1 Use the information in the table to answer your partner's questions. Say what you have been doing this week and what tasks you have/haven't done.

Ongoing this week	Done	Not done
• Telephone insurance companies to get quotes.	• Write business plan.	• Contact solicitor about drawing up legal documents.
• Research possible accounting systems.	• Check availability of our proposed company name.	
• Discuss website with local IT company.		

2 Use these prompts to ask questions about the progress your partner has made. What two tasks has your partner actually completed?

- contact business adviser
- think about business locations
- make list of estate agents
- find information about premises
- look into transport
- visit any locations

Unit 3 | Language at work, Exercise 4

Student B

1 You are in a project team which is converting an old building to provide new company premises. Update your colleague, using these prompts and/or your own ideas. Use *already* and *yet* and appropriate time expressions.

- finish the first floor building work
- have delays caused by plumbing contractors
- not complete the second floor adaptations
- postpone date for roofing work
- find good decorating firm

2 Your colleague is involved in the building of a new warehouse and office complex. Ask how the project is going. As your colleague is speaking, comment on what he/she says and ask additional questions.

Unit 12 | Business communication, Exercise 5

Student A

	Facts and figures	Comments
No. people surveyed	Just over 4,500	
Type of people	1 _____	2 _____

Survey results		
read blogs	80%	ads will reach a lot of people
read blogs once a week	3 ___% (approx. 4 _____)	
read blogs weekly for business information	5 _____	6 _____
read weekly on technology topics	57%	
pass on information or content from blogs	70% (approx. 3,150)	word-of-mouth advertising will be useful
indicate that blogs influence their purchase decisions	7 _____	8 _____
are thinking of starting their own blogs	32%	growing market!

Unit 10 | Business communication, Exercise 4

Student A

1 You are the Departmental Administrator and receive a call from the Sales Department.
   Action to promise: look into problem / call back tomorrow
2 You work in the Customer Services Department and phone the Travel and Logistics Department.
   Problem: a customer needs its goods earlier than expected.
   Further information: a loyal customer has asked if their goods can be sent a week earlier – is this possible?
   Deadline: need to let the customer know by tomorrow afternoon at the latest

Unit 3 | Language at work, Exercise 5

1
Student A

You were unexpectedly called away from the office and left a list of tasks for your colleague to do. It is now 4 p.m. and you are back in the office. Ask your colleague about the tasks on the 'To do' list.

Student B

Decide which two tasks you have done on the 'To do' list, when they were done and what exactly you did. Decide which two tasks you haven't done and think of an explanation why.

2
Student B

Your colleague has asked you to attend a conference in Madrid on his/her behalf. This morning you gave your PA a list of things to organize for the trip. It is now 4 p.m. Ask your PA about the tasks on the 'To do' list.

Student A

Decide which two tasks you have done on the 'To do' list, when they were done and what exactly you did. Decide which two tasks you haven't done and think of an explanation why.

Unit 8 | Business communication, Exercise 7

Pair B: Employees

Your company is finding it difficult to keep staff – its competitor has better working conditions. You have spoken to your managers about leaving to join the competition. You don't really want to change jobs, but the offer is very attractive. Your managers have invited you to a meeting to discuss whether they can improve working conditions. The areas that the competitor has made attractive to you are:

- flexible hours / home working
- better travel expenses
- more perks: fitness club membership, lunch vouchers, new computer
- increased salary
- less bureaucracy in the job
- more training for future promotion

Discuss these with your managers and see if they can improve your working conditions. Decide which points are important to you and what you want the company to offer. Be ready with some proposals and be prepared to bargain.

Unit 6 | Working with words, Exercise 6

You will have four letters: E or I, S or N, T or F, J or P. Find your corresponding four-letter combination in the alphabetical list:

ENFJs care about people and seek peaceful relationships. They are expressive, warm and intuitive, and enjoy helping others develop their potential. They like to organize the world around them, and get things done.

ENFPs are excited by anything new – ideas, people, or activities. They have a deep concern for people, being especially interested in possibilities for people. They are energetic, enthusiastic, and lead spontaneous and adaptable lives.

ENTJs need to analyse and bring into logical order the outer world of events, people and things. They are natural leaders who like to plan. They are intuitive and can think in abstract terms.

ENTPs are excited by anything new – ideas, people or activities. They look for patterns and need to analyse, understand and know the nature of things. They are energetic, enthusiastic, and lead spontaneous and adaptable lives.

ESFJs care about people and seek peaceful relationships. They like to organize the world around them and get things done. They are pragmatic, take their work seriously and believe others should as well.

ESFPs are enthusiastic, and are excited by new activities and new relationships. They care about people and like to give practical help. They are energetic and adaptable, preferring to experience and accept life rather than judge or organize it.

ESTJs need to analyse and order the world of events, people and things. They work hard to complete tasks so they can move on to the next. They are pragmatic, take their work seriously and believe others should as well.

ESTPs are enthusiastic, and are excited by new activities and challenges. They are logical and analytical, with an innate sense of how things work. They are energetic and adaptable, preferring to experience and accept life rather than judge or organize it.

INFJs are interested in their inner world of possibilities. Insight is very important, and they care for people and relationships. They are interested in creative expression, spirituality and human development, and like to use their ideas to help people resolve things.

INFPs are caring and idealistic, both in relationships with people and in projects they see as important. They are skilled communicators, and like ideas that can develop human potential. They are adaptable and have concern for possibilities.

INTJs are interested in their inner world of possibilities. They think systemically and logically, and need to demonstrate competence in their areas of interest. They are insightful and will work hard to make their visions into realities.

INTPs want to make sense of the world and are creative. They are logical, analytical, and detached; they naturally question ideas. They don't need to control or order the outer world, and are very flexible and adaptable.

ISFJs feel responsible for doing what needs to be done. They are pragmatic. They are realistic and organized, and thorough in completing tasks. They are warm, caring and dependable; they take their work seriously and believe others should as well.

ISFPs care deeply for living things, and can be playful and adventurous. They are practical and prefer action to words. Their warmth and concern are generally not expressed openly. They are adaptable, realistic and spontaneous.

ISTJs feel responsible for doing what needs to be done. They are realistic, well-organized and thorough. Being logical pragmatists, they make decisions based on experience. They are committed to people and the organizations they work for; they take their work seriously and believe others should as well.

ISTPs are logical and realistic, and natural trouble-shooters. They are quiet, analytical, and can appear detached and pragmatic. However, they like variety and excitement, and have a spontaneous, playful side.

Audio scripts

Unit 1

1.1

Presenter So is most of your work to do with translating websites from English?

Zhifu No, not really, although we do get a lot of Western companies who want to break into Asian markets. The problem is … they think they can just come along and translate their website, just like that … But really that's a very expensive and ineffective way of doing things.

Presenter There's more to it than that?

Zhifu Yes. And to be honest, it's quite arrogant to think you can create a favourable impression and attract a lot of customers without really trying. To start with, customers are still wary …

Presenter What … of newcomers? Or of the technology?

Zhifu Both. You have to work hard to show that you are trustworthy and to make customers feel confident in your company.

Presenter Yes, but that's not a particularly Asian phenomenon, is it? I mean, if you have a website with spelling mistakes, people are bound to be suspicious, aren't they?

Zhifu That's right, but just like in traditional advertising, some things are more effective in some cultures than others.

Presenter So you're saying a localized website would need to be genuinely different in some way?

Zhifu Yes. In the West, the websites have a lot of words – lots of facts and figures, they're often quite complex. But here, the websites that work best are simple and functional … in the same way that many Asian cultures prefer offices that are modest rather than ostentatious.

Presenter A case of less is more?

Zhifu Yes, exactly. And you have to understand the local culture. For example, here in China, when people go shopping online, they like sites where they can bargain and make a deal, because that's what they like to do in real life.

Presenter So a website like that would need a lot more than just translating. You might have to rebuild the whole site.

Zhifu That's right. For really successful website localization, you have to start the process from the beginning, taking all these cultural things into account … not just translate the words and hope for the best.

1.2

Ivan Ivan Formanek. How can I help you?

Sean Hello, Ivan. This is Sean McFee. I'm calling about the email I sent you regarding your new website.

Ivan Oh, hello. Yes, I remember. Thanks for responding so quickly.

Sean No problem. I wondered if you'd had time to look through the portfolio I sent.

Ivan Yes, I have. Your work looks very interesting.

Sean What exactly do you want to do? Do you want to change the whole site or just update parts of it?

Ivan Well, we're currently updating our corporate image, which means redesigning the logo, the brochures and the website. We've already done some of this in-house, but we need help with the website in particular.

Sean Well, I could certainly help you with that.

Ivan Great. I suggest we meet to discuss things further. I have to be honest, though. You aren't the only designer we're talking to.

Sean I understand. When would you like to meet?

Ivan Well … I go to Berlin once a month to interpret for a client of ours – I'm covering for a colleague who's on maternity leave. In fact, I'm leaving the day after tomorrow, but we can meet when I get back.

Sean Fine, whatever's best for you.

Ivan Let's say, provisionally, Tuesday the 13th at eleven o'clock and I'll get my assistant to call you later today to confirm. You'll be travelling in from Krakow, won't you?

Sean That's right.

Ivan It might be best to discuss travel arrangements with my assistant then. Her name is Catherine, by the way.

Sean Fine. Well, thanks for your time.

Ivan You're welcome. See you in a couple of weeks.

1.3

Sean Hello, Sean McFee.

Catherine Hello, this is Catherine, Ivan Formanek's assistant. I'm calling about the meeting on Tuesday the 13th.

Sean Oh, right. Thanks. I wanted to speak to you about that. I'm actually going to be in Prague already as I've arranged to meet some other clients on the Monday.

Catherine OK.

Sean Can you tell me how I get to Simply Speaking? Is it best by taxi or public transport?

Catherine Public transport's fine. Let me know where you're staying and I'll email you a map and directions from your hotel.

Sean Thanks. Another thing I wanted to check … How long are you scheduling the meeting for? There's a train that leaves at three o'clock. Will I have time to catch that one or should I take a later one?

Catherine We'll be finished by 2.00 at the latest … It only takes 20 minutes to get to the station, so you'll have plenty of time.

Sean Thanks. I'll probably take a taxi to the station to be sure.

Catherine OK. When you arrive at the company, give your name to Reception and they'll send you up to us on the fifth floor. And let me know if you need a taxi and I'll book one for you.

Sean That's very kind. Thanks a lot.

1.4

1

A Let me take your name and number and I'll let you know when we're having another exhibition.

B That's great. Thanks. Here's my card.

2

A Can I have Suzy's number and email address? I want to invite her to the next training day.

B Sure. They're in my phone, so I'll send you her contact details by text. Is that OK?

A Yeah, fine. That way I'll have your new mobile number, too.

3

A It was great meeting you again. Let's get together again next month. I have an email address for you but I'm not sure if it's current.

B No, you've probably got my old one. But I've got yours so it's probably easiest if I email you when I get back to the office.

A OK, great.

Unit 2

2.1

1

Claudia My job involves visiting different hotels to sell various ranges of soap, shampoo and other toiletries for their guests. My sales territory covers the whole of Germany and Austria. I love my job. I get a lot of fulfilment from meeting new people, and from the travel – I can't imagine being stuck in the same place all the time. I also value the autonomy the job gives me – I have to report to my manager once a week, but apart from that, I'm responsible for all day-to-day decisions and organization. Because I'm on the road so much of the time, I'm provided with the essential benefits like a BlackBerry® and a laptop, and a company car, of course. I get quite a good basic salary, but what is also very important for me is the amount I can earn in commission – I get 15% of everything I sell and there's no upper limit – and that's a big incentive for me because I'm one of the top-selling sales people. My company are very generous with rewards, too … you know, merchandise, vouchers, social events. I do think these help me to do my job better – it's nice to be acknowledged and recognized for my achievements.

2

Peter Every month, we have a sales competition with lots of prizes, and each dealership has to send in figures for the month to Head Office – you know, to show them how well we're doing – and then, if you've met your targets, you get reward vouchers for things like … I don't know, a hot-air balloon trip or a spa treatment, or something … and I usually give these to someone on my sales team, whoever deserves them. I think it works well – it motivates them – but the real value of prizes is that it helps to make people feel appreciated. Positive feedback and praise are very important, they do a lot for job satisfaction. Managers like myself don't get monthly prizes. The real incentive for us is that, if we make the grade, we get invited on a special trip once a year. It really makes you feel positive about working for the company, you feel valued … like an important member of the team. Last year, it was a week in Africa and a chance to climb Mount Kilimanjaro, and that's something I'll never forget. The company also thinks that development is important for staff morale, so there are lots of opportunities for training, not just staff development but non-professional training like horticulture or painting. That's a popular benefit of the job, but one of the biggest perks is the very generous staff discount we get on all our models – and when you're talking about a new car, you're talking about a lot of money.

3

Macie There are a lot of popular misconceptions about this job … you know? I mean, people seem to think you get to travel all over the place and see different countries every week. But that's only true on long-haul flights … most of the time it's a fast turnaround, and back to checking seat belts and serving drinks. So, on a regular basis, the travel really isn't that exciting. But one of the main benefits is the staff discount. Me, my husband, my kids … even my parents … we get hugely reduced fares when we use the airline – and that's when we can really travel and … see the world. The salary's OK, a little below average maybe, but the compensation plan is good. Let's see … it includes a profit-sharing scheme, a non-contributory pension plan … we have private medical insurance and there are incentives like attendance rewards and on-time bonuses – so, all in all, yeah, it's a pretty good deal. One of the good things about the company is that we do get appreciation when we do our jobs well. Senior management actually comes round and thanks us personally when we've met our targets … and that certainly gives me a sense of achievement.

2.2

Conversation 1

Harry Hello, I saw you sitting on my table at dinner, but I didn't have a chance to speak to you. I'm Harry.

Alessandro Hi. I'm Alessandro.

Harry Who did you come with? Is this your first company event?

Alessandro Yes.

Harry Well, I'm sure you'll have a great weekend. Have you seen the programme?

Alessandro No, not yet.

Harry Oh. Well, it looks very entertaining. I think there are some left at the information desk. Are you, um, here with colleagues?

Alessandro No.

Harry Well, you'll soon get to know people. So, um, would you like another drink?

Alessandro No, I'm fine, thanks.

Harry Well, it's been nice talking to you … erm … Alessandro. You don't mind if I go and get myself a coffee? See you later.

Conversation 2

Paolo Hi, I don't think we've met. I'm Paolo from Napoli – I work for one of the company's suppliers.

Sonia Hi, nice to meet you. I'm Sonia … from France.

Paolo Nice to meet you.

Sonia So … I've heard that Naples is becoming very popular for foreign investors – is that true?

Paolo Well, Sonia, it's interesting that you say that because …

Conversation 3

Sumitra Hi, I'm Sumitra, based in the UK.

Krishnan Hello, I'm Krishnan. Sorry, where are you from originally?

Sumitra Well, my parents live in Calcutta. I was born there, but I've moved around a lot.

Krishnan You are from Calcutta? No! That's amazing! My parents are from India – in fact, they are there now visiting relatives.

Sumitra What a coincidence! Where do they come from?

Krishnan From Bhiwandi – near Mumbai.

Sumitra Bhiwandi … Isn't it famous for its textile industry?

Krishnan That's right, yes … So have you spent much time in India recently …?

Conversation 4

Adam Good evening, Adriana. I thought I might see you. Back for another company event?

Adriana Oh, Adam – how lovely to see you here. I heard you weren't coming.

Adam Really? Who told you?

Adriana Um, I can't remember – but anyway, how are things?

Adam Oh, Adriana – where should I begin? I injured my leg in January in a skiing accident. The doctor told me to take it easy. But how could I rest, with my job? Then I got flu, but we were organizing a huge trade fair at the time so I had to keep going …

Adriana Oh, oh dear …

Adam … then I had problems at home with my daughter, she's fifteen, you know, and …

Adriana Oh, I'm so sorry to hear that. Look, I have to go, Adam. Catch you later.

2.3

Harry Hello. It's Adriana, isn't it? We met before dinner.

Adriana That's right. You're Harry. Dinner was fantastic, wasn't it?

Harry Yeah, it was, yeah.

Adriana How are you enjoying the event?

Harry Very much. It, you know, it's good to meet people from different parts of the group. Have you been before?

Adriana Yes, I have. About three years ago, in Egypt. Were you there?

Harry No, I wasn't, unfortunately. I heard it was good fun. Where are you from, by the way?

Adriana I'm from Spain originally, but I'm working in Switzerland. I have a two-year posting in Head Office in Geneva.

Harry I see. Who are you working with?

Adriana With the European HR team. I work with Ulrika Thomson.

Harry No! What a coincidence! I know her very well. We joined the company on the same day. It's a shame she couldn't be here. Say hello to her for me, won't you?

Adriana Of course I will.

Harry So … um … what are you working on?

Adriana Er … right now, we're trying to harmonize remuneration packages across the group. I'm working on pension plans and other savings schemes. What about you? Don't you live in Italy?

Harry Yes, I do. In Milan. I work in R&D, but I'm thinking of moving.

Adriana Really? Can I ask where?

Harry Well, I'd like to stay in Italy but maybe move within the group. I'm thinking of talking to HR, actually. Apparently they're interested in people who've worked in different divisions …

Adriana That sounds interesting. In fact, I'm coming to Milan in a couple of weeks. Would you like to meet up and talk some more?

Harry Yes, I would. Thanks very much. Do you know Milan?

Adriana No, not really. I've just been there for meetings.

Harry Well, I'd be delighted to show you around.

Adriana Thank you. That would be very nice.

Harry Good. So do you actually live in Geneva …?

2.4

1

Oh, no! Is that the time? My parking ticket runs out in five minutes. Can we continue talking later?

2

Sorry, but I promised to meet someone in ten minutes. But I'll come back when I've seen them. Catch you later.

3

I'm going to get some food. I missed lunch because of a conference call. So see you later.

4

Is that James over there? Excuse me, I really must go and speak to him.

5

Look, I have a meeting now. But it ends at five, so perhaps we can continue our conversation then?

Unit 3

3.1

Part 1

Sarah … OK, I sent you a proposed agenda yesterday. Have you had a chance to look at it?

Ian Yes, it looks fine.

Sarah So, the purpose of today is to update each other on progress and consider anything that might affect our schedule.

Ian OK.

Sarah So, Michelle, why don't you start? How are things with the marketing department?

Michelle Up to now, the launch date has been set for the 15th of November, to capture the Christmas trade – this means we must meet our deadlines.

Sarah Good point. So how's the advertising campaign coming along?

Michelle That's fine. We've set a realistic schedule and planned in a bit of extra time in case the printing takes longer than expected.

Sarah Great. And how far are you with preparations for the launch party?

Michelle Our events manager says we're on track. He booked the venue two weeks ago and I've already received offers from various catering companies. I haven't made a final choice yet, but most of them are well within our budget.

Sarah That sounds good, Michelle, thanks. So, how does your side of things look, Ian?

Ian Well, actually, things aren't running as smoothly as I'd hoped. We've hit a problem with the handset battery life.

Sarah OK … so what do you mean exactly?

Ian Well, in some cases, the battery can run out in six hours if its key features are in permanent use.

Michelle So what you're saying is we're about to launch a new revolutionary low cost mobile phone and its battery only lasts six hours!?

Ian Well, obviously, that's an extreme case, but the engineers *have* identified that there is a basic design problem with the battery.

Sarah So the *real* problem lies with the battery manufacturers?

Ian Yes.

Michelle But, Ian, what about our deadlines? Can this problem be resolved?

Ian Well, our engineers are looking into it and if it's fixable, they'll do it, but they'll need time. We may have to reschedule.

Michelle But we can't postpone the launch at this stage! There must be something you can do.

Sarah Are there any alternatives?

Ian Well, I've got some suggestions, but you may not like them.

Sarah Ian, you've put us in a difficult position – why don't we get another coffee and then we'll look at our options?

3.2

Part 2

Sarah The battery problem has to be resolved; otherwise the whole project is in trouble – that's how I see it.

Michelle Is that really the case? How about finding another battery supplier?

Ian I don't think that would help us meet our current deadlines. We could keep the same battery but not mention its lifespan.

Sarah That's possible, but our reputation is at stake here.

Michelle Yes, and if the project fails we have no chance of becoming market leader!

Ian OK. Why don't we wait and see what the technicians suggest and in the meantime move the launch date?

Michelle That's not an ideal solution. It means cancelling the printers, the caterers, the advertising …

Sarah Do we have any other options?

Ian Well, using a different phone for the launch would be my proposal. We could use the VP20: it's new, cheap, but not as hi-tech.

Michelle I'm not convinced. The whole idea of this project was to offer a hi-tech phone and services at an attractive price.

Sarah Yes. If you ask me, we should look at what we can reschedule.

Michelle Oh, I suppose so.

3.3

1

A And I think you'll need one more person on your team as it's quite a big job. I think we can divide Peter's time between his current work on the Lansdown contract and working with you. And when Lansdown finishes, he can work with you full-time.

B Are you sure that's the best way forward? They still have another three months left on that project. To meet these deadlines I'll need someone who is 100% dedicated from now on.

2

A Well, we are about a month behind, but we've been unlucky for various reasons. I'm sure we can make up the time with a bit of overtime here and there.

B Is that really the case? According to these dates you are more like six weeks behind. And we're already paying a lot of overtime on this project.

3

A So you can see from these forecasts that the final costs would in fact be lower than we previously predicted.

B Sorry, but I'm not sure I agree. The previous figures allowed for changes in the exchange rate. Given that we're buying the steel from China we need to be realistic.

Unit 4

4.1

Bridges to Prosperity is an organization which works on projects in regions of the developing world where walking is the main form of transportation. Surprisingly, many people in these parts of the world don't have access to healthcare, education and markets simply because they can't get across rivers. So Bridges to Prosperity has come up with the practical solution of not only building bridges, but also setting up educational programmes that teach people how to build their own footbridges. The key concept behind every new project is that it doesn't require cutting-edge technology with a large carbon footprint, but instead it only uses low cost locally-sourced materials. Projects like this bring about real improvements for everyone. The bridges mean people can buy and sell locally-produced goods, children can go to school, and doctors and nurses can travel to every part of the region – on foot.

Many of us take lighting for granted, but in some parts of the world lighting is a luxury. So a few years ago, Greenlight Planet came up with the innovative idea of bringing affordable and safe lighting to developing countries. It got round the problem of no access to electricity by developing a solar-powered lamp which was safe and reliable. Since then it has sold 5 million lighting products across 54 countries and provided electric light to millions of people for the first time. As well as revolutionizing access to lighting, Greenlight Planet has also taken an innovative approach to selling the lamp. On the one hand, it has to be a commercially-viable proposition, but on the other, the lamps must be affordable. In order to achieve this, the company has brought the cost down as low as possible and also allows local communities to pay off the cost in small monthly instalments.

4.2

Part 1

Shireen First of all, I'd like to thank you for inviting me here today. We really appreciate this opportunity to work with you. What I'd like to do in this presentation is three things. First, I'll give you a brief overview of the new DiScan product. Then I'll talk about some of the advantages for your company. After that, I'd like to show you a short video so that you can see the system in operation. And after that, you can ask me any questions. Does that sound OK?

… OK. We call this new system the DiScan2. Basically, DiScan2 is a state-of-the-art security system based on iris recognition. Iris recognition is part of the next generation in security and is already used in government security. Now Securikey is able to make this technology available to commercial businesses and organizations.

How does it work? Well, it's a pretty simple concept. Employees are identified by the unique patterns in the iris of their eye. So that when you look at a camera, the system scans your iris and matches it to a central database …

4.3

Part 2

Shireen OK, let's look at what DiScan2 has to offer. There are two main benefits of using DiScan2 – enhanced security, and increased flexibility.

Why enhanced security? Well, the biggest potential benefit of iris recognition is that no two people have the same iris – everyone is unique.

This means that DiScan2 is extremely secure in comparison to your current system where a code is needed. You can find out someone else's code, whereas you can't copy the patterns of their iris. Currently, if someone gets hold of a security code, they can go anywhere they want in your company. However, with the DiScan2 iris recognition system they won't be able to do that.

The other major advantage of DiScan2 is its flexibility. Although it may sound radical, it's up to you how far reaching you want the security to be. You can decide exactly which employees have access to which parts of the building – so you have complete control over who goes where. And here is another great thing about the DiScan2 – you can not only control entry to all parts of the building, but also control access to your computer system.

Now I'd like to move on to the question of personal safety, because the most common question I'm asked is about how it scans your eye …

4.4

Audience member 1 Thanks for your presentation. I think this is a very interesting area. I've also heard of retinal scanning. Can you say something about the difference?

Shireen Sure. Thanks for the question. With retinal scanning you use the back of the eye to check a person's identity. So it's the same idea as iris recognition and they are both reliable. However, for a retinal scan, you need to put your eye very close to the camera, whereas with an iris scan, the camera can read your eye at a distance of about twenty centimetres. And academic studies show that we feel more comfortable with iris scans than retinal scans. Does that answer your question?

Audience member 1 Yes, thank you.

Shireen Yes, another question?

Audience member 2 Hi. I know you said it's safe, but over time is it really? Surely if the scanner looks in your eye every time you enter the building or log onto your computer, isn't it bad for you?

Shireen I understand your point, but the technology was first invented in 1994 and since then all the medical evidence suggests that it's safe for the human eye. As I say, iris recognition is already being used in government security, which demonstrates how effective it is.

4.5

Richard So to sum up, Boatnet is a specialist Internet service provider that provides wireless Internet access at all the major marinas in the country. From the start, I could see that there was definitely a market. Boat owners want to be able to access the Internet to get information about the weather and sea conditions, as well as sending and receiving email. In the past, they could only do this on land because the technology wasn't in place. At the moment, in most parts of the world, you still can't access the Internet from your boat without the right technology. From now on, our subscribers will be able to access the Internet from their boats for a basic monthly fee. We set up a very successful pilot project in three marinas last year, so we were able to test the system extensively and we know it works. We've done a lot of research and we can offer the service for £25 a month – that's less than €40. We'd like to be able to increase this in the future.

Jason My name's Jason Black. It's an interesting idea. Have you been able to get any sort of protection for it?

Richard Well, of course, we couldn't get a patent or anything like that because it's not new technology, but we have been able to get exclusive contracts in all the major marinas in the country.

Jason And how long are these contracts?

Richard Seven years.

Jason So other companies won't be able to compete with you for the next seven years?

Richard That's right.

Unit 5

5.1

Interviewer … and now on to business. And we have with us in the studio Shamsul Aziz from Carno Oil and Gas Exploration who will be telling us about their latest initiatives in social responsibility. Mr Aziz, isn't it dishonest to pretend that you're anything other than a big multinational, motivated by greed, with a reputation for ruining the environment and exploiting local people?

Shamsul Not at all. We take corporate social responsibility very seriously, because as a leading gas and oil exploration company, we know that we can have a dramatic effect on people's lives …

Interviewer Not necessarily a good one.

Shamsul If I may answer the question … We are proud of our business ethics. Looking after our staff isn't just something we have suddenly discovered – it's one of our core values. We've always had a strong commitment to our workforce and an ethical approach to the environment … and the communities we work in. We have a reputation for fairness, we work hard to combat discrimination and prejudice within our organization, and we are constantly improving working conditions for our staff. Safety has always been at the top of our agenda, but we have schemes in place for education, health and training. We do take care of our people.

Interviewer Leaving that aside for a minute … How can an oil company have any credibility when it claims to be environmentally friendly? Surely that's deception … Your industry is probably the greatest contributor to pollution that there is.

Shamsul No. Not at all. As regards the environment, we can't say how people should or shouldn't use oil, but what we can do – and what we have done – is to reduce our own methane and hydrocarbon emissions … and we've made good progress. We also support a range of local projects – to take just one example, we provide financial support for turtle conservation in Bangladesh, and have done for several years.

Interviewer Apart from a few turtles, what do you actually do to help the people who are affected by your operations?

Shamsul One of our guiding principles is to give back to the communities where we are carrying out our operations. So, in Sangu, for example, we have established a community project to provide skills training for unemployed youths, and in Rajasthan we have undertaken health initiatives and other schemes to encourage sustainable livelihoods.

Interviewer Some people might see that as a form of bribery rather than generosity.

Shamsul I don't agree. It could be seen as corruption if all the money went to just one individual. But the support we provide, the health clinics, assistance to the air ambulance and so on, now these are things that benefit everyone, not just the people who work for us directly.

Interviewer OK, well, if I can now turn to the question of …

5.2

Part 1

Reporter 1 … Will we get our itinerary in writing after this meeting or should we take notes?

Clare We'll email you the final itinerary once you've decided what you'd like to see. And if you have any other questions, you can ask our Travel Coordinator, Janet Lawson – she's coming in later on this morning to speak with you.

Reporter 1 Thanks.

Clare So, we're planning to show you how Hummingbird's operation works in China and some of the projects it's involved in.

Reporter 2 That sounds good.

Clare The idea is to spend four days at one of the sites where the tea is grown. This will give you the opportunity to talk to the locals who supply the company.

Reporter 2 So, can we interview them?

Clare Yes, but we advise you to set this up directly with them and ask their permission first. And of course, do be discreet and respect their privacy.

Reporter 2 Of course.

Clare While you're there, you'll get the opportunity to accompany the workers in their daily work. This will give you a real insight into their lives and how Hummingbird's teas are produced.

Reporter 1 That sounds really interesting.

Clare OK, now, the schedules. We've looked at all the options, and we're going to arrange two dates – one in February and one in May. The February flight leaves on the 15th so we need fixed bookings from you by January the 10th.

Reporter 3 Can I just ask – are we returning on the 19th or 20th of February?

Clare The 20th. The trip will involve a lot of road travel and one internal flight …

5.3

Part 2

Clare … So that was the timetable. Now, I'd like to tell you a bit about your stay. Feel free to ask any questions you may have. We'd like to invite you to watch the tea being prepared and spend a day sampling the local specialities which are produced by the cooperative in the village.

Reporter 1 That would be great. Er … Does anyone there speak English?

Clare On the whole, English isn't spoken so we strongly recommend you stay with our guide who can interpret for you.

Reporter 1 Good idea.

Clare On the subject of language – you're also welcome to visit a project set up to help build a new school.

Reporter 2 That sounds really interesting. I'd like to take you up on that.

Clare Good … but I should warn you it's quite a long trip. Let me know how many of you would like to do this as it would be a good idea to travel with our interpreter.

Reporter 2 That makes sense. We'll speak to our colleagues and let you know.

Reporter 3 What about environmental projects?

Clare The company is supporting a charity called Tree 2000 Foundation and there's a reforestation scheme in one of the regions where it does business. As Hummingbird Teas is just a financial backer, it doesn't actively work in this field, but a visit to the site is highly recommended.

Reporter 3 What will we see?

Clare The project managers who work on site are all professional environmentalists. They'll explain what's happening to the area and show you what the charity is doing to improve the management of the forests. I was there for the first time last month and found it fascinating. It's well worth a visit.

Reporter 2 Mmm … That's not really what I'm looking for. The feature I want to write should focus more on the people.

Clare Well, alternatively, we'd be delighted to introduce you to the team who work for Hummingbird in China. They aren't tea makers – they're employed to coordinate the business. I'm sure they have some interesting experiences they'd like to share.

Reporter 2 That would be great – it's just the kind of thing I need.

Clare OK, so let's just run through …

5.4

1

A How about joining us for a coffee after work?

B That would be nice, but can I let you know later?

2

A Do you feel like coming to the cinema with us?

B Sorry – I'm heading straight home tonight – it's my partner's birthday.

3

A Would you like to go to that new pizza place for lunch?

B Why not? Sounds good.

4

A I've got two tickets for the theatre next Thursday evening and was wondering if you'd like to come with me.

B That's very nice of you, but I'm fairly sure I've got something on that night. I'll have to check my calendar.

5

A Some of us are playing golf this weekend. Are you interested in coming along?

B Thanks for the invitation, but I'm not sure I can. I'm waiting to see if I have to work this weekend. I'm meeting my boss at three today to find out what's happening.

Unit 6

6.1

1

The most important factor in making and implementing decisions is listening. I like to ask everybody I know to give me an opinion. I get different perspectives – and I listen to them. I also listen to my own intuition. I really do believe that using your intuition is the best way of processing and weighing up information. If I have to make a big decision, I'm never impulsive. I think about it, and I listen to what other people think. But ultimately, I listen to my intuition. I delay my decision until I wake up one morning and know what I'm going to do.

2

I used to think that decision-making was something you could do logically … but for me, this didn't always work and I made some bad decisions. So I thought I'd try a new approach – one that takes feelings more into account. So now … particularly for the big decisions in life – what job to take, where to live – I let my inner wisdom emerge and trust my instincts. We don't always make strictly logical deductions. Instead, we rely on patterns – and on feelings associated with those patterns. So for those big decisions, you need to let patterns develop in your mind. Once you realize that your intuition is reliable, making a decision is quite easy.

3

If you have to make a decision, don't listen to your intuition. Intuition is for people who don't want to think. OK … it's fine for the small decisions in life, like what kind of ice cream to buy. But for the big decisions, you need a more systematic way of thinking. Let's say you have to decide between two things – two applicants for a key position, two properties you're thinking about buying. You check the facts, check the figures, and your analysis says to pick A over B. But your intuition says to choose B. What do you do? Most people stick with their intuition – which is wrong. You need to delay your decision until you can work out why your intuition is telling you something different. That's the whole point of analysis: to make you consider all the options – so you don't make the wrong decision.

4

To make good decisions, you need to have confidence in your own judgement. We all make bad decisions, but the important thing is not to worry about them. As a judge, I often have to decide between the evidence of two people standing in front of me. I don't know which one is being honest, but I know one of them is lying. That's when making decisions becomes very difficult. Even so, I never base my courtroom decisions on my feelings or my instinct. I do it by the evidence, and by what the law tells me.

6.2

Sinead Today, I'd like to establish where we think we can cut costs. We can discuss actual figures when we've considered what's possible. Jens, could you start us off, please?

Jens Yes, well, if we look at the facts, we'll see that our costs for personnel are very high …

Anna Yes, but we've discussed lay-offs before.

Sinead Hang on, let's hear what Jens has to say about personnel before we reject the topic.

Jens You're right, Anna, but I'm not talking about reducing the number of employees. Look at the overtime figures. They're here in black and white, and they're costing us a lot of money. The fact is we need to keep these to a minimum to save money.

Sinead Matt, what's your position on this?

Matt What Jens says is right. The thing is, we need to look at why we have so much overtime and if it's realistic to try to reduce it.

Anna If we do reduce it, it'll mean dramatic savings. We could set up a programme …

Sinead … That all sounds pretty positive. Let's look into it at a country level and discuss it again at our next meeting. Can we move on to office resources? Anna, this was your point. Could you give us some detail, please?

Anna Yes, what I mean is paper, office supplies, that sort of thing. I think if we look closely at what we actually use, we'll find there's a lot of waste. A classic example is printing emails out on expensive copy paper.

Matt So what you're getting at is monitoring the office supplies and making sure we're not using too many or wasting too much?

Anna Exactly.

Jens I'm not convinced. As far as I'm concerned, we'd make hardly any savings compared to the personnel costs.

Matt The drawback is, it's quite labour intensive to keep a check on this. … But it could be a project for one of our work experience students.

Anna Yes, we're actually in a position …

Sinead … I don't want to spend too long on this point. We should set up the project Matt mentioned with the student – and see how it goes. There are plenty of other areas we could consider. Let's turn to the next item, customer expenditure.

Matt If you ask me, we should look carefully at client travel expenses and entertainment costs.

Jens Absolutely. We spend far too much money on clients. The expense accounts aren't taken seriously enough … that's my view.

Sinead Anna, you've been very quiet.

Anna Yes, I was just doing some calculations … Matt is right. But I think it would be crazy to cut expense accounts. In my opinion, we should introduce tighter guidelines.

Sinead Good, we seem to be getting somewhere. Let's draw up some action points on what we've discussed so far.

6.3

1
A What've you got on this weekend, Alex?
B Well, I'm supposed to be helping a friend move house.
A Oh, poor you.

2
A What are you up to tonight?
B We'll probably catch a movie.
A Sounds good.

3
A Are you taking any time off in the summer?
B Mmm – it depends on my colleagues and their vacations.
A I see.

4
A What are you doing this weekend?
B We're off to Paris!
A Lucky you!

5
A Anything nice planned for the weekend?
B Nothing special. What about you?

Unit 7

7.1

1

Paula Every day, EU companies are outsourcing business process tasks to emerging economies where labour costs are lower – in areas like call centres, airlines, legal processing, finance, and IT of course. The UK jobs are going to India, French jobs to North Africa, Spanish jobs are going to Latin America. Germany is outsourcing to Central European countries like Poland and Hungary, and Scandinavia is outsourcing to the Baltic States and India. Of course outsourcing benefits these countries – by injecting money into their economies and driving the development of a modern communications infrastructure. But it also leads to significant job losses in the home countries. I believe that member states of the EU need to do much more to respond to such losses, which can have a big impact on communities. This is not about protectionism. But we need to develop strategies to cope with serious job losses, and to create more high-quality jobs in the EU.

2

Christian I work for a Swiss financial services company. We first started outsourcing some of our back-office work to India a couple of years ago – at a time when we were considering what cost-cutting measures we could take. Labour costs out there were actually 70% lower than in Switzerland. It's been very successful. We've been able to streamline our operation and free up resources for our core activities. We've now moved two thirds of our IT work to India. We have an IP-based VPN, a Virtual Private Network, which simplifies the operation and improves efficiency. But it's not just about savings, or gaining a competitive edge. If you look at countries like Brazil, Russia, India and China – they're obviously very important for outsourcing, but they are also important potential markets in their own right. They're growing very very fast, and with hundreds of millions of customers, you can't afford to ignore them.

3

Chitra I am working in Bangalore as a customer adviser for a UK company. There are many companies coming over here nowadays, and it's not just because they can achieve lower overheads. There are a lot of advantages for the companies – they have 24/7 productivity, and with the extra staff, they can be much more flexible and responsive, and they can get through a higher volume of work. Personally, there are a lot of benefits for me. It's a dream job and it has certainly improved my quality of life. In the past, it was really difficult to get a well-paid job here in southern India, especially for a woman. It's not a rich part of the world. But the pay I get now is absolutely fantastic. Call centres are a growth industry in India – and working for a western company is a high-status job for Indian people. So if you perform well, you stand to make a lot of money, about the same as a junior doctor.

7.2

Part 1

Director Thank you all for coming this morning. As you know, we are looking into the possibility of outsourcing our IT department overseas. This is being done in order to cut costs and improve efficiency. I'd like to introduce you to Sanjit Kundu, from Business Initiatives Bangalore, who is here to tell us about Bangalore as a possible location for outsourcing. Sanjit …

Sanjit Good morning, and thank you for inviting me to your headquarters. Today, I'd like to give you an overview of the business potential and possibilities of Bangalore as a location for outsourcing. As you probably know, Bangalore is situated in central southern India – it's the capital of the state of Karnataka. So, to begin with, let's look at some general facts about the area. What does Bangalore have to offer in business terms? Well, statistics show that 10,000 companies are based in the region, and a population of nearly seven million people ensures that there is a buoyant labour market. How well qualified is the workforce? Recent data illustrates the fact that Bangalore's educational institutions have been awarded international recognition as a result of the quality of graduates being produced – from the Indian Institute of Science, for example. In fact, due to the dominance of a highly-educated workforce, Bangalore is becoming the fastest growing city in Asia and has earned the nickname 'India's Silicon Valley' …

7.3

Part 2

Sanjit … I've briefly looked at the background, so let's move on to some business facts. You will notice on this chart the breakdown of traditional industries, such as engineering, in relation to the emergence of IT companies. Bangalore has a strong tradition of attracting engineering companies to the region as a result of its engineering colleges. A knock-on effect of this has been the establishment not only of government-run companies such as Hindustan Machine Tools, but also companies from the private sector. A subsidiary of the German Robert Bosch group has been present in this region for several years. What's more important and exciting for our potential investors is the new emerging economy focusing on IT. As I mentioned earlier, this has earned us the name 'India's Silicon Valley' and it is easy to see why. IT is booming. Let's turn our attention to some specific facts on the IT sector. Looking at this slide, we can see it is expected that Indian IT services will continue to grow by 25–28% annually, and Bangalore accounts for about one-third of India's software exports. And have a look at these figures: more than 1,500 software and outsourcing companies – 512 of them multinationals – have offices in Bangalore, employing over 170,000 workers. In the first four months of this year alone, 64 new offices were opened in the city. Subsequently, nearly 1,000 new staff are being taken on every month. The job market is being fuelled by the tens of thousands of students in the area, many of them graduating from the Institute of Science, which I referred to earlier – and many of them specializing in IT-related subjects. A further point to mention is that a new sector of the job market is being opened up, offering opportunities for women employees – 25% of the workforce in software companies here is now female. The effect of this is more financial independence and greater freedom for them to pursue a career … Before I go today, I'd like to leave you with some … er … some food for thought. Investment in Bangalore has resulted in dramatic, positive lifestyle changes for its people. Their futures are being secured and their quality of life has been improved threefold. By investing in our region, you will not only have the advantage of obtaining highly-skilled employees with a strong work ethic, but you will also ensure that our skilled workforce remains within India. Surely a win–win situation for us all.

7.4

1

I'd like to pick up on a point you made about the language skills of your employees. How do you test their level of …?

2

First of all, I'd like to thank you for giving us such an interesting presentation. I think everyone found it useful. One question I have is this: How long do you estimate it takes to transfer …?

3

Can I ask you to show us the slide again with the overhead estimates, and could you talk us through them in a bit more detail?

4

I'd like to make a comment, if that's OK. Clearly there are lots of benefits to what you're proposing, but the time scales involved are very long. And the forecasts don't seem to take into account the costs at our end. I was wondering if you'd like to comment on that?

Unit 8

8.1

1

I left school at 16 without any qualifications so my career prospects weren't particularly good, but I got on an apprenticeship scheme with the local car factory. I learnt a lot at first, but after a while it was a bit monotonous. But after I completed the apprenticeship I got full-time employment, so I had job security and a decent wage. I'd worked there for almost 30 years when I was suddenly made redundant – the company got taken over, and just like that they decided to downsize and shut our factory down. You can imagine, in a small town like ours, when you get that many people laid off all at once, there are no job opportunities. I'd lived there all my life so relocation was out of the question. I had some redundancy money, and I went for retraining; first on a short computer course to update my skills and increase my employability, then a two-year course in programming, and because of my background, I ended up as an IT consultant to manufacturing companies – so it was a complete change of direction, but I don't regret a minute of it, and it was a lot better than being unemployed or just taking early retirement.

2

I had worked for the recruitment company in Lausanne for six or seven years. The salary was good, but after a while I started to feel there wasn't a lot of opportunity for advancement. I started to look for a change of direction, but then they announced their plans to open a new office in Geneva, so I thought about making a sideways move and relocating. I put in my request to move there, and to my surprise they replied by saying they wanted to redeploy me to the new office as its operational manager. Well, of course I said 'yes'. And to think I'd been considering changing jobs! Since then the office has grown, and based on my experience and working with clients, I think I've come to understand what motivates employees to either stay with their employer or to change jobs – and it's hardly ever about money. Often it's just about ambition and job satisfaction. Sometimes they leave because of some sort of issue with their boss. And we also work with very successful women who feel there's a glass ceiling at their company, and they know they can only get on if they move elsewhere. For others, it's all about growth opportunities – they're looking for training and personal development, but it's just not on offer in their company.

8.2

Johanna Right, Dermot, this is quite a challenge! What we need to decide on today is how to put together this new team.

Dermot Yeah – it's not going to be easy. The areas we need to discuss are: the makeup of the new team, who would be most suitable for it, and how our current teams can manage without them.

Johanna OK. So, let's look at what our options are. What I propose is we simply identify who our most capable workers are and send them.

Dermot Yeah … If we did that, we'd end up with two weaker teams back here doing all the work, and I'm not sure they'd cope.

Johanna It wouldn't be for very long, but maybe you're right. We can't send all our best people in case we need them here.

Dermot How about we look at our team members' individual strengths and then each select three people based on this?

Johanna You mean we build a team from the good workers who have other skills we need as well?

Dermot Exactly. They're going to be working together for six months so they've got to be team players.

Johanna Right. I can see we'd at least have a strong team if we did that. But I've got another idea. Supposing we stretch the budget a little, why don't we take on two contract workers and use just four internals? That'll solve the problem – if we only have four experienced staff in the new team, we won't lose our best workers.

Dermot No way! It just wouldn't work if we took on contract workers. We all know they get paid more, and that would be bad for team spirit. No. Let's try my idea of choosing our team from our existing staff – based on their strengths.

Johanna OK, I'm happy with that …

8.3

Dermot … So let's just summarize the situation. Taking on contract workers is a no-no. And if we chose our best workers and sent them, it would be damaging to our departments because the knowledge base would be gone. So, what we've decided to do is propose staff based on their personal strengths as well as their professional capabilities.

Johanna Exactly.

Dermot Now I've identified four possible candidates from your team who look ideal.

Johanna Wait a minute, four from my team? We can't do that. If I transferred four people, I'd only have three left! I could offer you three, but I'd expect three from your team, too.

Dermot Well, yeah, I suppose that's only fair. If you guaranteed Brett, I'd let you have Jamie, Pascale and Timo from my team.

Johanna But both Jamie and Timo are straight out of school! You can't expect Brett to work with two trainees on something as important as this. He'd end up doing the work of three people.

Dermot But it'd be a great experience for them.

Johanna I don't care. It's not fair. I'll be happy for Brett to be on the team, provided you replace one of the trainees with someone experienced.

Dermot OK. I didn't think you'd agree. I'll send Sabrina instead of Timo. She's had international experience and she's good with people, too.

Johanna Good. So who have we got so far? Brett, Sabrina, Jamie and Pascale. That just leaves two more from my team. How long do I have?

Dermot Unless we get this list to HR before Friday, we won't be sending anyone – it all needs discussing again with them before contracts are drawn up.

Johanna Right. Let's get this done now. I need to find two more people.

Dermot Provided one of them has got some experience, the other one could be a trainee.

Johanna Well, in that case, I'd like to send Lena and Marlon.

Dermot Great. I know them both – good choice!

Johanna So, a quick recap: if I send Brett, Lena and Marlon, you'll send Sabrina, Jamie and Pascale.

Dermot Yeah, I can live with that.

Johanna Great. That sounds like a plan!

8.4

1
A Do you have a minute? I'm doing a survey about the use of our Intranet.
B Yeah, sure … I never use it!
A Oh … thanks a lot.

2
A Could you just have a quick look at my computer? The screen's gone blank.
B Sorry, I'm a bit busy right now.
A Oh, well, never mind.

3
A Would you mind checking my English in this email before I send it?
B Sorry, I'm just on my way to a client's. I'll be back around three.
A OK, it's not that urgent.

4
A Excuse me, am I disturbing you? I need some help with the photocopier.
B Give me two minutes and I'll be right with you.
A Thanks.

5
A Excuse me, could you spare a few minutes?
B Certainly. Take a seat.
A Thanks. Er, I'm not sure about these figures and I was hoping you could tell me …

6
A Can you give me a hand with the holiday roster?
B Sorry, no time! Email it to me and I'll look at it later.
A OK.

8.5

1
I'll work over the weekend, provided you pay me overtime.

2
Unless you fix this fault by the end of today, we won't pay the balance.

3
Supposing we included a five-year lease instead of two, would you sign the agreement today?

4
I'll need some kind of money-back guarantee this time in case the response rate to the advert is as low as this again.

Unit 9

9.1

James I run Glasses Direct. We sell glasses and contact lenses online, at a fraction of the price you pay if you go to a high street optician. I got the idea when I discovered the size of the mark-up on glasses. Did you know that a pair of glasses that cost, say, 15 euros to make can sell for as much as 150 euros? It's completely outrageous.

So, I researched the optical market – good market research is very important when you're starting out. I learnt about optometric testing, how the frames are made and the lenses are cut, and it was clear there was a gap in the market. I worked out a business plan for selling discounted glasses online; it seemed like a viable idea that I could turn into a profitable business.

My parents were absolutely fantastic – they gave me a loan to get started, which meant I didn't have to raise finance by getting a bank loan or bringing in an outside investor who would want a share of the profits. The other people who were extremely helpful were some of my fellow students, who designed and set up the website for me – I couldn't have done it without them.

The only real problem we had was getting the manufacturers to work with us – they didn't want to damage their relationship with the big retailers. It was incredibly difficult to persuade them, but in the end we managed to get them on board.

The other challenge was marketing. We're an online business so it's really hard to compete with everyone else out there. One way to reach new customers was to hold some pop-up events in cities around the country. We looked at renting empty shops on high streets, but the rents in most places were totally ridiculous. So we set up stalls in markets and those worked well. You can't underestimate the amount of time you need to spend on this kind of marketing, but it generated interest and an initial client list.

Anyway, my advice to anyone starting out would be, if you've got a sound business model and you see a gap in the market, go for it.

9.2

1
Did you know that a pair of glasses that cost, say, 15 euros to make can sell for as much as 150 euros? It's completely outrageous.

2
I researched the optical market – good market research is very important when you're starting out.

3
My parents were absolutely fantastic – they gave me a loan to get started.

4
The other people who were extremely helpful were some of my fellow students, who designed and set up the website for me.

5
It was incredibly difficult to persuade them, but in the end we managed to get them on board.

6
We looked at renting empty shops on high streets, but the rents in most places were totally ridiculous.

9.3

Conversation 1

Erik … Hello.

Nicole Is that Erik Lundberg?

Erik Yes, speaking.

Nicole Erik, this is Nicole Dupont from GBF Electronics – I'm not sure if you remember me.

Erik Nicole! Hello – of course I remember you. I haven't seen you for ages, though.

Nicole That's right – about three years, I think. Since you left GBF, life's been extremely hectic.

Erik So … What have you been doing? How's work? It's good to hear from you.

Nicole Well, GBF have been keeping me very busy – I was promoted shortly after you left and for the last three months I've been commuting between France and Belgium.

Erik Congratulations – that sounds a bit tough, though.

Nicole Yes, it is and, er, that's actually the reason why I'm calling. The thing is, I'm looking for someone to work with us in our business in Belgium – someone local so I don't have to commute. Have you made any contacts in that region?

Erik Well, no names come immediately to mind, but I'll certainly think about it. Ah, just a minute. What about Natalie Hemery? She's lived in Brussels for years – I'm sure she'd be able to help …

Conversation 2

Xavier José? Hey, what are you doing here?

José Xavier! I don't believe it! Are you getting the flight to Lisbon, too?

Xavier Yeah, I've got a meeting there. What about you?

José I live there now – with my wife and kids.

Xavier I didn't know you were married! When was the last time we saw each other?

José I'm not sure … it must have been at that college reunion … but that was seven years ago.

Xavier Really? Yes, I suppose so … Anyway, what have you been up to? Are you still working in the car industry?

José Where should I start!? So much has happened. After the exchange programme at Birmingham University, I stayed another year and worked for Nissan, in their finance department. That job took me all over Europe and on one of my trips I met my wife, Isabella, in Lisbon. After that, I got a transfer and, well, I've never looked back since! What about you?

Xavier Nothing much has changed for me, but I've worked my way up in my present company. Things are going well, but I'm looking to … you know, branch out, maybe move on. Actually, I've been doing some freelance consulting recently, which is partly why I'm going to Lisbon.

José That sounds interesting …

Xavier Well, it's all about making contacts. Hey, by the way, could you do me a favour? Could you put me in touch with a reputable consultancy, since you live in Lisbon now? I'm looking to collaborate with an established firm.

José Let's chat about that over dinner. How long are you staying?

Conversation 3

Stanislav Good morning, Nadia. Thank you for finding the time to meet.

Nadia No problem. It's been a long time since we've been in contact, Stanislav. How's life treating you?

Stanislav Well, there have been a lot of changes in the company since we last met, but I'm fine. How's business with you?

Nadia Well, pretty good, actually. Our company has secured a huge contract with Mobelitec. We've also been talking to Strauz & Co. They've just gone public, so there should be money in that one. Anyway, you mentioned changes. What's been happening?

Stanislav Oh, things have been tough in the insurance field. We've been directing our attention to the online market recently … they've taken a serious number of our customers.

Nadia Oh, dear, I'm afraid that's the way things are going.

Stanislav Exactly. And with that in mind, maybe I could ask you for a favour. We are looking for a collaboration with some direct insurers – you have a lot of contacts and I wondered if …

Nadia Oh … I'm not sure.

Stanislav I'd really appreciate your help.

Nadia Well, it sounds an interesting proposal. Send me the details – here's my card – and I'll see who I know in the field. I can't promise anything, though!

Stanislav No, I understand that, but thank you anyway.

9.4

1

A Oh, I'm glad I saw you before you left. Could you do the on-call shift this weekend?

B Err, I'd love to help, but I think I'm away visiting family. Any other weekend would have been OK, but this one …

2

A I know you're busy, but can I ask a favour? There's a customer with a complaint about …

B Sorry. You know I'd normally help, but at the moment I'm so busy. Can you ask someone else?

3

A I was wondering if you'd be interested in coming in on a consultancy basis to oversee a new project we have starting next month. I realize it's short notice, but a full-time member of staff has just handed in his notice.

B Well, you know I never like to say 'no' when it comes to work, but I'm afraid I don't have any spare time at present. Maybe, try me again in a few months' time …

9.5

So take a look at this next slide. It shows a business model called 'The Long Tail', which was an idea created by Chris Anderson in his book of the same name. So this end of the chart shows the 'head' and it represents mass-market products – you know, the kind of profitable brands you see on the shelves of a bricks-and-mortar shop that sell in high volumes over short periods of time. Most business entrepreneurs dream of producing something that will sell like this. However, with the arrival of the Internet and the online business model, there's an alternative approach, and that's the 'long tail' shown here on this side. The idea is that you can offer a much wider range of products over long periods of time to a niche market. Take online movies for example. You might sell the latest movies on DVD from a supermarket, but online movie sites like Netflix can offer films made years ago to many individual customers. Similarly, a company like Amazon allows customers to find specialist products that wouldn't normally be stored at a high street shop. As the demand grows for online businesses selling niche and individualized products, it's even likely that the turnover from the long tail could overtake the 'head'.

Unit 10

10.1

The Internet and mobile technology have been integrated into every part of the modern workplace and digital technology has brought about huge change. It's had a huge impact on the most sophisticated scientific enterprise to the smallest corner shop; life on the job means you have to have access to the Internet. In recent surveys focussing on adult Internet users and the role of digital technology on their work lives, 94% of workers now use the Internet. Key findings include the fact that email remains the number one form of communication when it comes to communicating with clients on a daily basis. That's despite predictions in the past that social media and texting might take over from email as the main form of communication. Video communication tools such as Skype have also increased in popularity because they allow us to collaborate with colleagues in other parts of the world on shared projects. Furthermore, the belief that being online provides too many workplace distractions and can have a negative effect on productivity was not supported by the survey. 46% of workers felt more productive and only 7% felt that their productivity had fallen. Attitudes also seem to be changing with regard to workplace policies on Internet use. Well below 50% of the respondents said their bosses put limits on Internet usage, such as blocking access to certain websites or controlling what employees can say or post online. That figure seems to be lower than previous results in similar surveys.

10.2

Conversation 1

Boris Hello, Procurement, Boris speaking.

Paola Hi, Boris. This is Paola, from Sales in the Milan office. I have a question about an order we placed.

Boris What seems to be the problem?

Paola It's the approval for our training course – the course should begin next week, but the training company hasn't received the signed contract from us.

Boris OK. Could you give me the order number and I'll look into it?

Paola Uhuh. It's 02/584.

Boris Right. Can you tell me when you sent it to us?

Paola At least a month ago. Training Direct needs the contract before the course can begin. That's by Friday at the latest.

Boris OK, let me get this straight. What you're saying is we still have the contract and you need it back, signed by us?

Paola Well, yes.

Boris OK. These things do take time, I'm afraid. Ah … I have the contract here. What I'll do is check the figures and see if Angela can sign it by tomorrow. If you give me the fax number of Training Direct I'll fax it straight to them and post you a copy.

Paola Will it be ready in time for the deadline?

Boris I'll do my best.

Conversation 2

Chris IT Help Desk. Chris speaking. How can I help you?

Johann Hi, Chris. It's Johann here from Copenhagen.

Chris Ah, hello, Johann. I haven't heard from you for a few days! Have you worked out our new customer database yet?

Johann Yes, just about. This isn't a problem about that. My computer keeps going black.

Chris You mean the screen goes blank?

Johann Er, yes – but the hard drive light is still on.

Chris If I understand you correctly, this is a hardware problem, so I'm afraid I can't help. Ask one of your IT guys in house.

Johann I tried. They told me to call you.

Chris OK. Could you explain exactly what the problem is? Talk me through it.

Johann Well, firstly, when I open the customer transactions program …

Chris … Good. OK, I've noted all that down. I'm going to have to look into this. I'll get back to you shortly.

Johann Do you know why it's doing this?

Chris Give me time to check the system. Say, by lunchtime? Don't open the program for the next couple of hours and I might be able to sort out the problem.

Conversation 3

Marcel Hello, Marcel LeGrand speaking.

Donna Hello. This is Donna Fitzpatrick from AS Consulting.

Marcel Good morning. What can I do for you today?

Donna Well, we received a paper delivery from your company, but it arrived out of office hours and was just left in front of our door.

Marcel Could you tell me when this happened?

Donna A couple of hours ago.

Marcel OK. And can you tell me if you've got an order number?

Donna Umm … 560H. We specifically requested that our paper delivery arrive between 9.30 a.m. and 4 p.m. We now have twenty heavy boxes that need carrying up to the third floor. You're normally so reliable.

Marcel Right … Could I just clarify what you're saying? You ordered paper and informed us of the required delivery date and time?

Donna Yes. I have it here in black and white. Oh, and even more importantly – the order was wrong, too! There's too much paper and no printed envelopes.

Marcel OK. Once I've checked the details, I'll call you back.

Donna Could you let me know how long it will take? We need the missing envelopes for a mailing tomorrow.

Marcel As soon as I've looked into it, I'll call you back.

10.3

1

A … So as I was saying, any chance of getting it to me by tomorrow?

B You're breaking up. I'm afraid I didn't catch that last bit.

A I said, any chance of getting it to me by tomorrow?

B Sorry Veronica, it's a really bad signal.

A OK. I'll hang up and call you on your landline.

2

A … So can we discuss the transport arrangements for the Japanese visitors?

B Sorry, but this'll have to be quick, René, I'm about to board a plane!

A So now's not a good time to call?

B Not really, no. I'll be landing in two hours. Can you call me again then?

A Sure, no problem.

3

A Hi, Mike.

B Beatrice? Is that you?

A Yes, I'm calling about…

B … Look, I'm sorry, but I'm just on my way out. Can I call you back tomorrow?

A Yes, I'm around in the morning.

B OK, I'll speak to you first thing.

Unit 11

11.1

Whenever companies and organizations introduce changes, large or small, it can be a slow and sometimes painful process. There will be individuals who oppose the changes and react negatively, but even for the supporters of change, the reality of making it happen can be challenging. The ADKAR model provides the five steps you need to follow in order to achieve lasting change. First of all, 'A' stands for Awareness. This is all about letting everyone know what is changing and how it will affect them. One way to convince people who resist change is to explain the danger of not changing at all; for example, perhaps profits will fall if no action is taken. Step 2 is Desire. In other words, people need to accept that change is necessary and they have to feel motivated to support change. Of course, establishing awareness and desire is one thing, but making it happen is another. That's where Knowledge comes in. Your staff will need to know how to change, what to do – perhaps they will need training in new skills. So knowledge is part of a transitional stage which leads into the second 'A' – that's Ability. After getting the knowledge in stage 3 you still need to know if everyone is able to change and if there are any remaining barriers that will prevent change. Finally, and this is probably after many months or even years of hard work, you can implement your changes, but that isn't the end. Over time people can revert to their old habits and ways of working. Stage 5 is Reinforcement in order to maintain the changes. It means monitoring the processes you have in place and recognizing successes – perhaps giving incentives to staff.

11.2

Rachel … OK. I've spoken about our consultants' findings and we're well aware of your concerns regarding how the changes will affect our staff. As you all know, it is likely there will be some job losses, but we'd like to assure you that we will keep these to an absolute minimum and try to reduce headcount through natural wastage. Decisions will definitely have been made by March as to how big the cutbacks will be. Many of you have asked about a rumoured pay freeze … We aren't counting this out, but this is something we'd like to avoid. Over the next few weeks, we'll be hosting departmental meetings to give more specific information … and we plan to keep you informed about any other changes so you can answer your staff's queries with well-informed answers. Starting from next month, we'll be putting regular updates on our Intranet regarding potential changes … but more about that later. I'd like to pass the next point over to Imran, who has been working closely with the consultants on the subject of bottom-up management.

Imran Thanks, Rachel. Yes, bottom-up management has proven to be very successful in a number of companies and we've been working on a similar concept to implement here at FGR. Hopefully, the new model will be in place by the end of the month. Bottom-up management is quite a simple idea …

… Normally when change takes place, this is decided and implemented by senior management. However, to make the changes work we need the enthusiasm, motivation and energy from everyone who will be affected by those changes. Let's digress for a moment and look at this in more detail. Our idea is to give everyone the opportunity to propose changes which will benefit themselves and the company. We're proposing a Friday afternoon ideas forum where employees can put forward their suggestions for change. Each department nominates someone to present the most popular ideas to senior management, along with a business plan or some sort of proof that benefits can be gained. The first forum will be on Friday the 24th at 3.30. I'll be visiting our suppliers in Bradford on that day, so Rachel will be here to lead the session. You may be wondering if this will work – Friday afternoons are free for most of our employees. We're convinced the opportunities outweigh the disadvantages of staying at work longer. We must see this as a step towards becoming a more effective company. It's crucial to get the employees on our side … and we need to emphasize that there will be money available for remuneration … which could be paid if we see real results after the changes are implemented. This last point is probably going to be difficult to administer at the beginning, but the consultants had an example of remuneration scales for us to consider. I'm sure some of you are sceptical of the consultants' proposals, but we're calling on you to be positive – pass this information on and create enthusiasm … sell the idea of empowerment to our staff and highlight the rewards this could bring us all. Later this year we'll be reassessed to see how effective the changes are …

11.3

1

A I don't like the idea of changing the team meeting to Friday afternoons. People like me who are on flexitime often choose to leave early on Fridays.

B Yes, I have some reservations about it, too. Everyone's concentration probably won't be as good at the end of the week. But I can also see the point of moving it. We can never get everyone together in the same place at the same time during the week because we're all so busy. So at the moment Friday is the only option unless someone has another suggestion.

2

A If you ask me, this new restructuring is just a clever way of getting rid of staff.

B Err, I can see both sides of the argument. On the one hand, management want to streamline the company's operation, but on the other hand employees are naturally worried about possible job cuts.

3

A I can't believe the company is going to make us all learn Spanish.

B It sounds interesting – I like the idea of having a common language for the company – though I also understand that people who aren't confident in their language skills might find it difficult.

4

A Do you think this latest proposal is a good thing?

B Mm. I'm not sure. The main argument for it is that extending our office hours should improve the service. But the argument against it is the added costs. We really need to be certain that it will generate the extra revenue needed.

11.4

1

A Your project is finishing at the end of this week, isn't it?

B In theory, yes, but I might have to spend a bit more time on it – there are bound to be a few loose ends to tie up, there always are. But there probably won't be that much to do, so there's a good chance I'll be free in ten days or so.

2

Newsreader The problems for the government are getting worse, and it is doubtful whether it will be able to hold on to power for much longer. There is certain to be more bad news in the coming week – the latest inflation figures, due out on Tuesday, are likely to show an economic situation that is steadily getting worse.

3

A Cristina, I'm still in Ecuador. I'm just calling to say I definitely won't be able to speak at the conference on Friday.

B Things are still bad, are they?

A Yes, and it'll probably take a few more days at least to sort everything out. Perhaps I'll be able to get back next week sometime, I don't really know.

B OK. Then I'll get Bill to stand in for you – obviously I need someone who will definitely be there. Is that OK with you?

A Yes, that's fine.

Unit 12

12.1

Renata … Could you fill us in on the most relevant information from the seminar?

Caroline Sure. It was extremely informative and, basically, it gave us an overview of figures regarding advertising via blogs and podcasts.

Yari Interesting … What did you find out?

Caroline Well, in general, traditional forms of advertising to our 18 to 30s market are becoming less effective. They're saying that the way ahead is to advertise where our target audience are 'hanging out' – which is on blogs and podcasts.

Renata OK … So what are the facts and figures?

Caroline Apparently, a recent study shows a huge increase in advertising investment via these media just in the last year. In fact, spending went up to $20.4 million.

Yari What's that in terms of growth?

Caroline It's 198.4% … in one year. Which is pretty incredible.

Renata That sounds very promising …

Caroline Yes. One of the presenters, Simon Darby, said companies were investing fast and that we should take this opportunity before our competitors do.

Yari OK. How do these figures compare within the different user-generated media?

Renata 'User-generated media' … meaning …?

Yari Oh, I mean things like blogs, podcasts, RSS feeds …

Renata Ah, OK … thanks.

Caroline Yes. Simon claimed that last year blog advertising accounted for … 81.4% of collective spending on user-generated media, but, roughly speaking, by 2025 it'll only comprise 39.7%.

Renata So how should we interpret this drop?

Caroline Well, supposedly, podcast advertising will be the front runner over the next four years, overtaking spending on blog ads.

Yari Can we look at the figures?

Caroline Yes, I have them here on this graph. According to a recent survey, total projected expenditure on blog advertising will reach $300.4 million in four years, whereas expenditure on podcast advertising will have grown at an annual compound rate of 154.4% to $327 million.

Renata So the bottom line is that user-generated media will be our new advertising platform, whether we like it or not.

Caroline That's right. Simon assured us that this form of advertising more or less guarantees we reach our target audience.

Yari Can you give us the low-down on the types of companies advertising through these media?

Caroline Sure. The overriding trend is for technology, car and media brands to use this form of advertising. I've got examples of some of these companies here …

12.2

So on the whole, there was a noticeable rise in the overall response to this month's campaign. We sent out approximately 5,000 emails and the click rate was 35%. So compared to last month, that figure stayed roughly the same. But what changed was the click through. It went up significantly from 15% to 25%. I think the offer of a 20% discount this month gave the campaign a substantial boost.

Unit 13

13.1

1

If you're working, or doing business, outside your home country, understanding the local culture is essential. You need to be informed about the culture you're working in and be prepared to be tolerant of different customs. And, you know, you can make some very expensive mistakes if you get it wrong. I'll give you an example. My boss, Tony, … he used to sell mainframe computers, and a few years ago he was working in the Middle East. One of the big electricity companies said it was interested in buying a new system. Now, Tony had been there a few years, he was familiar with the country and how things worked … so over a period of two or three months, he had a lot of meetings, making contacts, getting to know the right people … And then a competitor from the US came over – with a better product, and at a better price. Obviously he was used to doing things the American way – so he gave a few presentations, had a few quick meetings – and then he flew back to the States thinking he had a deal. But he didn't. In the end, it was Tony who got the contract, because even though his product wasn't as good, he understood the way business was done. The other guy was very, very good at his job back in the States, in a different context … but in this case, he was actually responsible for losing a multi-million-dollar deal because he'd completely failed to adapt to the culture, to a different way of doing things.

2

We run a training centre for employees of multinational companies who are going to be sent abroad for work … for sometimes up to three years … And they come from many different companies and industries – telecoms, engineering, computers, banking and so on. Our aim is to help people be more aware of the culture they are going to. This involves all kinds of things. First of all, we give them a basic understanding of the country they are going to – its political system, the social structure, basic cultural norms. We talk about any issues that people are sensitive about – it's surprising how many countries have taboo subjects, often political, that you just don't talk about. In the second part of the course, we look at the most significant cultural differences between the person's home country and the host country, and we focus particularly on aspects of the work culture – how meetings are conducted, how agreements are made, attitudes to time, the hierarchy in the workplace and how respectful of authority and seniority employees are, how important personal relationships are – all things which will help them adjust to working in the local culture. And at the end – when they finally arrive at their destination – they will be far more sensitive to important local issues … And their colleagues and the people they meet through work will have much more respect for them.

13.2

1

Dieter There was one situation I remember while I was living in Korea. You know I went out there to help with an engineering project?

Tonya Yeah …

Dieter Well, I was responsible for a team of telecom engineers, great guys. We all got along very well and I was welcomed into the company as if I'd lived over there for years. As time went by, I noticed that things weren't being done that I'd requested them to do.

Tonya Oh?

Dieter Yes. If I asked someone to do something and they said 'yes', nine out of ten times it wasn't done. That was when I was aware we had a problem.

Tonya Go on …

Dieter At first I thought it might be a language problem.

Tonya Well, that's understandable.

Dieter Yeah. But it was actually nothing to do with language. And it wasn't until I talked to a Korean friend that I realized what was wrong.

Tonya What had you done?

Dieter Nothing. I told my friend what had happened and he explained that there were two problems … First, my team didn't want to refuse my request due to respect for my seniority … But also, they didn't want to give an argument why they couldn't do what I wanted. So their answer was 'yes'.

Tonya I see. So, you mean, they didn't want to admit they couldn't do what you'd asked them to do … or to show negativity towards you by saying 'no'?

Dieter Exactly. Luckily, I found this out before I confronted anyone about the jobs that hadn't been done.

Tonya And did you resolve it?

Dieter Yes. After that I was a lot more careful what I asked my team to do and how I phrased the request.

2

Gaby … I was responsible for finalizing the new office building in Warsaw along with my manager in the Netherlands. While I was liaising with both the Polish employees and my manager I discovered our two cultures had quite different approaches.

Nico Go on …

Gaby Well, for example, when we were finalizing the plans for the office space. My manager wanted glass partitions, but the Polish employees hated the idea.

Nico Oh?

Gaby Yeah … but then I realized they hadn't actually told him this – they told me and hoped I'd tell him on their behalf!

Nico So what did you do?

Gaby I told him! It seems that none of them wanted to question an authority figure. So that was the first problem solved.

Nico There were more?

Gaby Oh yes. Another situation occurred when I was mentoring a recent IT graduate, Magda. While we were developing a new database, I gave her the job of asking staff for their views on the database … I even put together a few sample questions.

Nico What happened?

Gaby Well, she came back with very little information. I was extremely disappointed … What's more, the information she had only related to the questions I'd written. She hadn't written any questions of her own to get useful information for us. I didn't know what to do. All in all it was a difficult situation.

Nico So what did you do?

Gaby Well, in the end I asked Anna, a Polish colleague.

Nico What was her view?

Gaby Well, despite Magda's qualifications, she was still the most junior person in the department, so apparently more senior people would be unwilling to answer her questions.

Nico Oh, a hierarchy thing?

Gaby Yes. It came about because of the lack of information about why we were questioning them. It seems that Magda also wasn't comfortable with the task, so she didn't add to the questions I suggested.

Nico So how did you solve the problem?

Gaby Well, I sent out a memo explaining what Magda would be doing and why. I also noted Magda's qualifications and wrote the memo in English. The reason being that Magda needed to be respected by her colleagues and English gave the note neutrality.

Nico And …?

Gaby It really surprised me, but it worked.

13.3

1

A Have you heard the news?

B No … What?

A Apparently, Gabriel is leaving the company and moving to France.

B Surely not!

A Anna says that he bought a house and vineyard when he was on holiday there last month.

B Are you sure?

A Well, rumour has it he's planning to produce wine and he's been doing a winemaking course after work!

2

A You'll never guess what I heard.

B No … What?

A Well … You know that Dimitri went away on business last week and took one of the company's laptops with him?

B Yeah, but that's standard procedure.

A I know, but according to Sam, when Dimitri arrived back in Athens he was in such a hurry to get home, he forgot the laptop and left it in baggage reclaim at the airport!

B Oh, I don't believe it! Did he get it back?

A Not yet, no!

3

A Did you hear the latest about Sandra and Leroy?

B I heard they'd had some sort of argument.

A Yeah, a big one … Apparently, they were both named salesperson of the month and Leroy refused to share the prize.

B No! That's really childish.

A Well, I spoke to Robert and he told me that Leroy thinks he's better than everyone else since he got that award …

B That's nonsense!

A I know … but it's created bad feeling in the whole team!

B I'm not surprised.

13.4

1

Ben and Jerry opened their first ice cream parlour in an old gas station. Everything they knew about ice cream had come from a $5 correspondence course in ice-cream making, but one year later they celebrated their first birthday by giving their customers free ice cream all day. News of the delicious ice cream spread, and soon the two friends were delivering pots of ice cream to stores up and down the state of Vermont from an old Volkswagen car. In the end, the whole of the USA wanted to try the ice cream so they built their first manufacturing plant and with part of the profits, they supported community projects. That tradition of supporting local communities and social projects is one that employees at Ben and Jerry's still continue to this day.

2

Ben and Jerry opened their first shop in 1978. The two men had only taken a correspondence course in ice-cream making and had $8,000 of their own and another $4,000 from investors. Originally the first store sold 12 flavours. Now they produce 40. They employ 446 staff and have 5,812 eating locations. Annual sales for the business are $132 million.

Unit 14

14.1

Interviewer Is it right that you've moved on from top-down staff appraisals to what you call 360-degree appraisals?

Manager No, we still have the more traditional top-down appraisals, but we're introducing 360-degree appraisals as well because they have different functions …

Interviewer In what way?

Manager You have to think of 360 degree as a development tool basically … a trigger for change … rather than a way of deciding if anyone deserves a raise.

Interviewer So how does it work?

Manager Well, in 360 degree, instead of just your boss appraising you, you have several different people giving feedback … So … we hand out a feedback form to everyone you come into contact with – your manager, your colleagues, people on your team, your customers, contractors, suppliers – obviously it depends on the type of job and the organization, but we try to involve as many different people as possible … and with this kind of peer rating, you end up with a more complete picture of how someone is doing in their job.

Interviewer And what do you ask them?

Manager We use a feedback form, with a scoring or value judgement system, asking them to comment on various different assessment criteria – job skills, abilities, attitudes, behaviour. Then you assess yourself using the same form to see how the two compare. … There are two important considerations with 360-degree appraisal. First, it has to be completely confidential … that way you get much more honest answers from people. And secondly, you need to make sure suitable counselling is available when you go through the feedback results.

Interviewer So, at the moment, you don't actually use it for appraising performance?

Manager No, it works better as a development tool. We use it as part of our overall performance management, a way of bringing about change, rather than assessing performance.

Interviewer Right. And does it really help change?

Manager Yes … I had a new member on one of my teams recently … I thought he was very communicative, very open, always said what he thought and I liked that. But when we did a 360-degree appraisal, the staff feedback was all negative, and he came over as domineering and forceful. As a result of this, he did change his behaviour … and became more accepted by the team. And that's what I mean about it being different from top-down appraisals – in that example, a top-down appraisal from me would have told him to carry on speaking his mind … but it was the 360-degree feedback that made us aware of the need for change.

14.2

Angelina … I must say, we're very happy with your overall performance this year. What do you consider were your successes and failures?

Thomas Well … one success certainly was helping to produce the in-house magazine. I thought it was well produced with interesting content. I really enjoyed doing it, particularly interviewing colleagues from other countries for the staff profile column.

Angelina Yes, and I think you demonstrated great prioritizing skills, especially with the tight deadlines you had to meet.

Thomas How can I improve my chances of working more with international colleagues?

Angelina Well, you ought to sign up to one of our language courses. That'll put you in a better position for being selected when international projects come up. It's a pity we didn't think about this when you joined us. If you'd started a language course then, you'd be quite proficient now.

Thomas OK … Can I identify that as a personal goal for the coming year?

Angelina Of course.

Thomas Erm … What I didn't enjoy was when the magazine budget was cut … we had to lose a couple of staff on the editorial team and I ended up doing most of the work myself.

Angelina Hmm … You shouldn't have been expected to take on so much. I noticed your overtime hours were quite high at that time. Look, if this happens again, you need to let us know.

Thomas OK.

Angelina Are there any areas you feel you need to improve on?

Thomas Er, no … not really.

Angelina Hmm, all right. One area I'd like to mention is training. You turned down an office management course we offered you. Why was that?

Thomas I didn't think I really needed it. Besides, we were short-staffed. If Katy hadn't left, I probably would have done the course.

Angelina Mmm … You really should have done that course. I think it would have helped you deal with your workload better.

Thomas Yes … If I'd known that at the time, I might have done it.

Angelina I think you certainly need to focus on gaining some more qualifications. Let's put this course on your list of goals for the coming year, too. Now … were there any constraints that affected your performance?

Thomas Well, I mentioned that we're short-staffed and despite all this extra work, to be honest I've found it difficult to delegate. How should I do this?

Angelina You need to start by … So that brings us on to the office environment and resources. You've managed to create a very positive atmosphere in the new office. The move went very smoothly thanks to your team's organization.

Thomas Thanks.

Angelina On a less positive note … You could have thought a bit more about the call centre rota. Feedback from that department has been poor.

Thomas I know. If we'd taken the old system to our new location, the rota would have been easier to organize … but no one likes the new scheduling program. What's the best way to solve this, do you think?

Angelina I'll need to look into it. Let's arrange a meeting to discuss it next week.

Thomas Thanks. We could do with some training on the new program – there are some functions we don't really understand.

Angelina I'll check the budget.

Thomas If there's enough money, I'd also like another software program. I've already spoken to IT about it.

Angelina OK. Put your request in an email and I'll consider it.

Thomas Thank you. Oh … and while we're talking about money, could we discuss …?

14.3

1

A Hi. Thank you for coming at such short notice. Take a seat.

B No problem. Is everything OK?

A Err, no not really. Look, I'm going to get straight to the point. I've received a complaint about you from someone in your office.

B Who? Was it Rachel who works in …

A Well, before we go any further, I'm not going to say who reported it, but I'd like to tell you what I've been told and then I'd like to hear your side of the story …

2

A Hello, come in.

B Thanks.

A I've asked you here this morning because there's something we need to discuss.

B Sure. Is it about the current restructuring?

A Yes, it is. This is rather delicate, but as you know we've been reviewing the current level of staffing …

B And you want to make me redundant. I guessed this was coming …

A Well, I realise it isn't easy for you to hear this, and it wasn't an easy decision to make, but we don't have much choice …

Unit 15

15.1

Interviewer So you're quite happy with the idea of people in your organization taking a career break?

Employer Yes, although we prefer to use the term 'flexiwork', which is a better description.

Interviewer How did the idea come about? I mean, a lot of employers wouldn't like the idea of their staff disappearing for a year or so …

Employer We introduced flexiwork at a time when our industry was having a bit of a downturn … things were quiet … it meant we could cut the wage bill but also retain staff for when the situation improved again.

Interviewer So it was basically just a cost-cutting measure?

Employer No, it was more of an experiment … one that wouldn't be too expensive … and it's been very successful … in fact, it's now official company policy.

Interviewer Do you think this is something that other companies will take up?

Employer I'm not sure – I think we're lucky because we specialize in consultancy. A lot of our work is project-based, and our consultants do three months here, six months there … so it's quite easy for us to fit this kind of thing in.

Interviewer I think most people would see the advantages for the employee, but are there any other benefits for the company?

Employer Well, yes, apart from the cost savings that I mentioned before, it does a lot for our retention rate, so we don't get nearly so many resignations. If someone wants to broaden their horizons by having a long career break, they can have one, no problem. The other advantage is when we're recruiting, when we're looking for new talent. If we say we don't just allow career breaks, we actively encourage them – as part of your career development – that's very attractive to prospective employees.

Interviewer Presumably there are some people who go off for a few months and don't come back?

Employer For some people, yes, it acts as a catalyst for them to head off in a new direction … but for most people, it gives them a chance to recharge their batteries and they return with renewed enthusiasm. From the point of view of motivation, it's great; it's a win-win situation. And in terms of personal development, people come back having learnt something new – maybe a new language – or they've developed a soft skill like leadership or whatever … but the bottom line is, those new skills are of value to the company as well.

15.2

Manager So what you're saying is you want to take an extended holiday?

Lena No, not really … I'd see it as a sabbatical. A journalist friend has invited me to be her photographer on her next assignment. A team is heading out to the Antarctic to document the impact of global warming.

Manager And you'd like several months off to accompany her?

Lena Yes. It's been a long-term goal of mine to do something like this. I did photography before I moved into IT, but I never saw it as a career. The thing is, I've been inspired by the people I studied with who've become professional photographers.

Manager Hmm. So … you take nine months off and we're left without a technical author and no team leader.

Lena I know, but it's a once-in-a-lifetime opportunity.

Manager But how do *we* benefit from this?

Lena Well, I think it's a win-win situation. I'd enjoy developing my creative side … I'd fulfil a lifelong ambition … so I'd come back to my job feeling more contented and satisfied with what I'd achieved in life …

Manager Yes, and …?

Lena And the experience I'd gain would be invaluable for managing the team.

Manager This isn't common practice, as far as I know. I'm not sure if …

Lena I understand your misgivings – what if I don't come back, and so on – but the plus points are that I'd be working in extreme conditions with a team of strangers, and my leadership skills would be put to the test …

Manager Mmm, I'm not convinced – go on.

Lena But there are also other benefits for you. I intend to put on an exhibition of my work after the trip and I'd like to do this with the support of the company. It would mean we'd get a lot of media exposure as well as great advertising opportunities.

Manager Yes, that sounds interesting; it's certainly worth thinking about.

Lena I really feel that this is a chance I can't afford to miss.

Manager Well, this would set a precedent. I'll have to discuss it with HR … It's not going to be easy to persuade them. I'm afraid your arguments aren't very convincing from a business point of view.

Lena That's hardly fair. I've never refused to take on more work or to do overtime when it's been necessary. I've been extremely loyal when lots of employees went to the new competition and … well …

Manager OK. Fair point. I'll see what I can do.

Lena I'd really appreciate it if you could speak to HR and initiate a meeting for all of us.

Manager OK. I think I can manage that, Lena.

15.3

1

A Hi, Sami. Where were you yesterday? You missed the meeting.

B Didn't anyone tell you? I took the day off. I thought it was about time I used up some of my time off in lieu.

A Oh, I see. So what did you get up to then? Anything nice?

B Nothing much. I caught up on some DIY jobs I started in the summer!

A Not a very exciting way to spend your day off!

B I know, but it needed doing.

2

A Are you back from your holiday already? Did you manage to get away?

B For some of it. I've always wanted to stay up in the mountains, so I had a few days hiking in the Swiss Alps.

A How was it?

B It poured with rain the whole time!

A Oh no.

B It didn't really matter. The hotel had an indoor pool and great spa.

A Nice.

B Yeah, it was a relaxing way to spend a few days.

A Oh, lovely …

3

A How did you spend the weekend?

B We managed to fit in a visit to my partner's family. I was a bit nervous because I hadn't met all of his family before!

A So how was it?

B Actually, it turned out to be a lot of fun. Some of them are keen golfers so I was able to get a game in.

Irregular verb list

Verb	Past simple	Past participle
be	was/were	been
become	became	become
begin	began	begun
break	broke	broken
bring	brought	brought
build	built	built
burn	burnt/burned	burnt/burned
buy	bought	bought
catch	caught	caught
choose	chose	chosen
come	came	come
cost	cost	cost
cut	cut	cut
deal	dealt	dealt
do	did	done
dream	dreamt	dreamt
drink	drank	drunk
drive	drove	driven
eat	ate	eaten
fall	fell	fallen
feed	fed	fed
feel	felt	felt
fight	fought	fought
find	found	found
fly	flew	flown
forget	forgot	forgotten
freeze	froze	frozen
get	got	got
give	gave	given
go	went	gone/been
grow	grew	grown
have	had	had
hear	heard	heard
hide	hid	hidden
hold	held	held
keep	kept	kept
know	knew	known
lead	led	led
learn	learnt/learned	learnt/learned
leave	left	left
lend	lent	lent

Verb	Past simple	Past participle
let	let	let
light	lit	lit
lose	lost	lost
make	made	made
mean	meant	meant
meet	met	met
pay	paid	paid
put	put	put
read	read	read
ride	rode	ridden
ring	rang	rung
rise	rose	risen
run	ran	run
say	said	said
see	saw	seen
sell	sold	sold
send	sent	sent
set	set	set
shine	shone	shone
show	showed	shown
shut	shut	shut
sing	sang	sung
sit	sat	sat
sleep	slept	slept
speak	spoke	spoken
spell	spelt/spelled	spelt/spelled
spend	spent	spent
stand	stood	stood
steal	stole	stolen
swim	swam	swum
take	took	taken
teach	taught	taught
tell	told	told
think	thought	thought
throw	threw	thrown
understand	understood	understood
wake	woke	woken
wear	wore	worn
win	won	won
write	wrote	written

OXFORD
UNIVERSITY PRESS

Great Clarendon Street, Oxford, OX2 6DP, United Kingdom

Oxford University Press is a department of the University of Oxford.
It furthers the University's objective of excellence in research, scholarship,
and education by publishing worldwide. Oxford is a registered trade
mark of Oxford University Press in the UK and in certain other countries

ISBN: 978 0 19 473900 9   Book
ISBN: 978 0 19 473896 5   Pack

Printed in China

This book is printed on paper from certified and well-managed sources

ACKNOWLEDGEMENTS

*The authors and publisher are grateful to those who have given permission to reproduce
the following extracts and adaptations of copyright material:* pp.11, 56 Adapted
extracts and images from 'The Diagrams Book' by Kevin Duncan © Kevin
Duncan 2013 and LID Publishing Ltd 2013. Reproduced by permission. p.32
'Our Reason for Being' from www.patagonia.com. Property of Patagonia,
Inc. Used with permission. p.37 'The Rules of Work: A Definitive Code for
Personal Success' 4th edition by Richard Templar © 2015 Pearson Education.
Reproduced by permission. p.43 Adapted from 'Women Book Business
Travel Earlier, Saving Companies Millions' by Catalin Ciobanu, Javier Donna,
Gheorghe Lungu and Greg Veramendi, 13 April, 2016 from https://hbr.org.
Used by permission of Harvard Business Publishing. p.43 Chart from CWT
Study: 'Gender differences in booking business travel: advance booking
behavior and associated financial impact' from http://www.carlsonwagonlit.
com/content/cwt/ch/en/news/news-releases/20160412-women-book-flights-
earlier-and-pay-less.html. Reproduced by permission of Carlson Wagonlit
Travel. p.57 Adapted text and diagram from 'The Pocket Universal Principles
of Design: 150 Essential Tools for Architects, Artists, Designers, Developers,
Engineers, Inventors, and Makers' by W Lidwell, K Holden & J Butler © 2015
Rockport Publishers, Inc. This edition published in 2015. Reproduced by
permission of Quarto Publishing Group. p.59 Fictitious interview used with
kind permission of James Murray Wells. p.63 Information and diagram
from 'The Long Tail, in a nutshell' by Chris Anderson from http://www.
longtail.com/about.html. This Licensed Material is licensed under a Creative
Commons Licence. p.66 'Technology's Impact on Workers' Pew Research
Center, Washington DC (December 2014) http://www.pewinternet.org/12/30/
technologys-impact-on-workers/. Reproduced by permission. p.72 Adapted
from 'Use the Prosci® ADKAR® Model for individual change to drive
organizational transformation' from https://www.prosci.com/adkar. Prosci
and ADKAR are registered trademarks of Prosci, Inc., used with permission.
p.82 Adapted from 'Music streaming boosts sales of vinyl' by Mark Savage
14 April 2016, and graphic image of 'People who buy vinyl', www.bbc.co.uk.
Reproduced by permission. p.82 'People who buy vinyl' data from ICM
Unlimited. Reproduced by permission. p.97 Adapted from '101 Business Ideas
That Will Change the Way You Work: Turning Clever Thinking into Smart
Advice' by Antonio E. Weiss, © Antonio E. Weiss 2013 Pearson Education Ltd.
Reproduced by permission. p.98 Adapted from 'Career breaks: Been there,
done that' by Charlotte Hindle, http://www.wanderlust.co.uk/magazine.
Reproduced by permission. p.103 'Travel the World While Working Remotely'
from http://www.remoteyear.com. Reproduced by permission.

Sources: pp.12, 46 www.economist.com. p.17 www.verticalresponse.com/blog/
the-30-magic-marketing-words. p.18 www.scribd.com. p.51 http://raconteur.
net. p.58 www.innocentdrinks.co.uk. p.77 www.thefuntheory.com. p.52
www.theguardian.com. p.91 www.benjerry.co.uk

*The publisher would like to thank the following for their permission to reproduce
photographs:* Advertising Archives p.84 (VW advert); Alamy pp.13 (Claudia/
itanistock, Macie/MBI), 14 (LOOK Die Bildagentur der Fotografen GmbH),
24 (amphitheatre/VIEW Pictures Ltd, Saïd at night/Ian Fraser), 27 (Ashley
Cooper), 28 (Sergey Nivens), 52 (Peter Neumark/David Bagnall), 63 (Geoffrey
Robinson), 67 (Frank Kahts), 71 (mediacolors), 76 (Neil McAllister), 77 (stairs/
ZUMA Press, Inc.), 80 (Cultura Creative RF), 84 (woman/ClassicStock, billboard/
Richard Levine), 87 (Dmitriy Shironosov), 92 (Adobe building/Kristoffer
Tripplaar), 97 (Patrick Ward), 98 (turtle/Hemis); Getty pp.6, 12 (sunset),
13 (Peter/Ron Krisel), 18 (rocket/Scott Andrews), 26 (scientist), 30 (car robot/
Jens Schlueter), 32 (Everest), 40 (meeting/Gary Burchell), 46 (call centre/
Rachit Goswami/The India Today Group), 48, 52 (workers/Jon Hicks),
54 (Compassionate Eye Foundation/Hero Images), 58 (seedlings, bottles/
Nicolas Asfouri/AFP), 60, 66 (David Churchill/ArcaidImages), 72, 73, 74,
78 (data/loops7), 86, 88, 91 (Ben and Jerry/Ade Johnson/AFP), 92 (dancers),
94, 100, 103 (lanterns); Oxford University Press pp.18 (rollercoaster),
40 (Stockholm); Shutterstock pp.7, 8, 11, 12 (intern), 17, 20, 23 (jigsaw),
30 (video chat, 3D printer), 31, 32 (kayak), 34, 37, 38 (both), 43, 45, 46 (mill),
51, 57, 68, 77 (balloons), 78 (woman), 83, 84 (radio), 91 (ice cream, cones),
98 (signpost), 103 (boats), 105.

With thanks to: The Ashden Awards p.26 (Rwanda bridge).

Illustrations by: Becky Halls/The Organisation p.89; Liza Whitney p.23.

Cover image: Getty Images/Steve Debenport.

Back cover photograph: Oxford University Press building/David Fisher.

*The authors and publisher would like to thank Saïd Business School for their assistance
in producing the Viewpoint video interviews. In particular, we would like to thank the
following people for their time, assistance and expertise:* Nazia Ali, Ahmed Abu Bakr,
Lydia Darley, Louise Fitzgerald, Kathy Harvey, Thomas Hellmann, Sophie
Kin Seong, Georgia Lewis, Tim Morris, Ana María Ñungo, Thomas Pilsworth,
Andy Poole, Josie Powell, Nancy Puccinelli, Hiram Samel, Andrew Stephen,
Breanne Svehla, Jonathan Trevor, Peter Tufano, John Walugembe.